*Crisis
Management*

CRISIS MANAGEMENT

The Art of Success and Failure
30 Case Studies in Business and Politics

YUNUS D. SALEH

Mill City Press, Minneapolis

Copyright © 2016 by Yunus D. Saleh

Mill City Press, Inc.
322 First Avenue N, 5th floor
Minneapolis, MN 55401
612.455.2293
www.millcitypublishing.com

All rights reserved. No part of this publication may be reproduced, stored in a retrieval system, or transmitted, in any form or by any means, electronic, mechanical, photocopying, recording, or otherwise, without the prior written permission of the author.

ISBN-13: 978-1-63505-151-3
LCCN: 2016907661

Typeset by Mary Ross

Printed in the United States of America

DEDICATION

This book is dedicated to my mother and father, particularly the former, who passed on suddenly in the year prior to its completion. I never had the chance to say goodbye, and this book is one way of honoring their legacy and memory.

PREFACE

This book is generally about success and failure as they pertain to business and politics – and by extension, life itself. However, this book is specifically about the art of crisis management, which, when mastered, can improve one's chances of success as opposed to failure.

Crises are an inevitable aspect of business and politics. The players in these fields are entrusted with a high degree of responsibility, to the extent where when major problems occur, *they* are the first and last place people turn. Accordingly, crises in business and politics are not the exception, but the norm. These realms can be thought of as comparable to major league sports, in that the presence of pressure, high stakes, and large challenges is unavoidable.

The term *crisis* refers to a high consequence, lower probability action known to strike the organization that has the capacity to bring down the entire business[*]. It can be further defined as any accidental, natural, or intentional event that has the capacity to severely impact business, people, the environment or the local community to some degree.

In the global business environment today, there are a number of challenges faced by individuals responsible for the management of businesses, particularly in times of corporate emergency and crisis, which includes threats such

---
[*] Alas, R., Gao, J., & Vanhala, S. (2010). The crisis management in Chinese and Estonian organizations. Chinese Management Studies, 4(1), 18-36.

as: industrial action; supply chain disruption; civil disorder; product contamination; natural disaster; terrorism, and political risk, crisis management plan becomes a potent survival tool.

How, then, does one ensure success by way of effectively navigating crises? There is no better place to turn in this respect than to history. For history offers us bountiful examples of those who have succeeded and those who have failed. Why did some rise why others sank? How can one increase one's chances of rising in an increasingly uncertain and complex world? Such are among the main questions underpinning the examinations and analyses in this book.

The work is based on nearly two decades of practical and theoretical experience in crisis management in both fields of politics and business, since the author has a postgraduate degree in public administration from Utara Malaysia University; spent years working at the National Democratic Institute for International Affairs (NDI), exploring various political conflicts in the Political Party Department, and the last seven years working in financial and banking sectors at the Trade Bank of Iraq (TBI), all of which helped expand his knowledge and involvement into the business and financial realm.

INTRODUCTION

I chose to study and write about the art of success and failure as they relate to crisis management because throughout my life, it has grown increasingly clear to me that such topics are of urgent importance to virtually all human beings. All of us, as we experience our life narratives, wonder on a constant basis how our stories will turn out. How will history judge us? Will our tales be sources of inspiration, or wells of caution for those who study them?

It is my conviction that the substance of this book is indeed relevant to all readers, particularly those who are interested in and/or participate in the realms of business and politics. To be sure, virtually all human beings' lives intersect with business and politics in some way or another. Even the person who shuns materialism and lives in the wilderness has made a decision that can be examined within the context of society's diverse metrics of success and failure.

What, then, constitutes a success? And what, by contrast, makes for a failure? Such questions will drive the substance and subtext of this work, but one distinction I'd like to make in this Introduction is that the successful person differs from the unsuccessful person in that the successful person is less easily surprised...

This is not a psychological trait, per se. This trait stems, simply, from experience. The successful person is accustomed to being in the arena. Accordingly, when surprises come (which they always will), the successful person is better equipped to

CRISIS MANAGEMENT:
THE ART OF SUCCESS AND FAILURE

weather them. Meanwhile, unfortunately, the unsuccessful person is caught off guard.

This distinction is pertinent to the current examination because so much of the forthcoming content relates to crisis management. Indeed, success at the highest levels of society runs congruent with people's ability or inability to navigate crises. Be that as it may, the experienced party, the one who is less prone to being caught off guard, is of higher value than the one bearing less stability and flexibility.

Needless to say, human beings, being only human, will inevitably react to crises in human ways. In other words, we will be emotional. We will at times be impulsive. We will grapple with data that is often complex or incomplete. We will react to constrictions in terms of time and energy. We will be imperfect, always, no matter who we are or how much experience we have.

Such is why human beings with an advanced capacity for managing crises are on a unique tier of value and success. Moreover, such is why I have undertaken the process of writing this book: to foster forms of understanding in the realms of business and politics that can improve upon people's chances for success.

Why business and politics? These spheres are the lifeblood of human activity. The constructs of business and politics drive most of our activities, relationships, and goals, along with other, more banal behaviors that we might not always be consciously aware of. The marketplace shapes our tastes and consumption choices. The offices of government shape our ethics, morals, and basic values. To be sure, we can innovate or rebel in ways that conflict with conventional market or political wisdom, but regardless of our individual behavior, the realms of business and politics will continuously bear a great and urgent influence upon our day-to-day lives. Be that as it may, I have looked into these realms for examples of human conduct within the midst of crises, as they relate to human beings' success and failure.

In the pages ahead, we will conduct an intensive examination of organizational crises from the perspective of what causes them and the symptoms that represent their presence. We will also explore assorted models and theories of crisis management, and then go into examining modes of crisis management planning. Analytically, thereafter, we will take a look at leadership under stress, cultivating an understanding of how leadership and crises intersect, and how one would be wise to proceed accordingly.

When we go on to take a look at the art of decision-making, we'll see with a clear and sober eye how authentic artfulness can underpin decisions. Preparation and predictability, which are the subject of the chapter thereafter, are key elements of carrying out effective and meaningful plans of action ahead of time.

Next, we will examine our core topics in the context of social media, particularly how it plays a role in crisis communications. Needless to say, in the current age, no event of any import exists without leaving its mark on the social media sphere, be it for mass public consumption or within the confines of a given organizational culture (or both). Speaking of the public, we will examine the joint phenomena of pressure groups and public participation, as well, cultivating a deeper understanding of how external forces can have an influence on internal ones.

We will also cast a deep view on the relevance of ethics

in terms of crisis management, namely questioning their general importance. In addition, we shall unearth the aspect of crises that create *opportunities* for us, for within every crisis is indeed the seed of a legitimate opportunity. We will then discuss the sustenance of businesses over the long-term, namely in terms of their overarching continuity and, if relevant, their recoveries.

Though it may come as a surprise to some, organizational culture itself can often be soundly identified as a source of crisis, so we shall study that phenomenon, as well.

Following the discussion of almost each subject included in this book, I have presented case studies in support of the topic at hand. We will explore both successful and unsuccessful examples of management in the midst of crisis. Then, at the book's end, I have included more case studies for further consideration. All such case studies involve notable organizational and political crises from recent years (2008-present).

It is this author's hope that by charting this territory, the reader will cultivate a better understanding of human beings' varied approaches to navigating crises of all different forms...for better or for worse.

Contents

DEDICATION v

PREFACE. vii

INTRODUCTION ix

PART ONE:
Crisis Types, Symptoms, and Causes. 1

Models and Theories Associated with
Crisis Management. 15

Crisis Management Planning 23

Leadership Under Stress 35

Case Study 1: JetBlue Valentine's Day Crisis (2007). .49

Case Study 2: West Africa Ebola Outbreak (2014) . . .55

Case Study 3: Maple Leaf Listeriosis (2008). 61

The Art of Decision-Making 69

Case Study 4: Susan G. Komen for the Cure (2012) . .81

Case Study 5: Lego and Shell vs. Greenpeace 89

Preparation and Predictability. 95

Case Study 6: Tesco Accounting Scandal (2014) . . .117

Case Study 7: How Sweden Survived the 2008
Financial Crisis 123

Case Study 8: How India Survived 2008 131

Social Media and Crisis Communication 137

Case Study 9: The Costa Concordia Disaster (2012) . . 157

Pressure Groups and Public Participation. 163

Case Study 10: Pink Slime Crisis (2012) 175

Do Ethics Matter? 185

Case Study 11: Egyptian Crisis (2013) 195

Case Study 12: BP Oil Spill (2010) 203

Organizational Culture as a Source of Crisis. 209

Case Study 13: J.C. Penney Hiring an Outsider CEO (2012). 221

Case Study 14: The BBC-Jimmy Savile Sexual Abuse Case (2012). 229

Crisis as an Opportunity 235

Case Study 15: The Norway Terrorist Attacks (2011). 247

Business Recovery and Continuity. 257

Case Study 16: How Germany Recovered from the 2008 Financial Crisis 273

PART TWO:
Miscellaneous Crisis Case Studies 281

Case Study 17: Refugees in the EU 2015 Crisis 283

Case Study 18: The Chinese Stock Market Crash (2015). 295

Case Study 19: The Belgian Political Crisis (2007-2011). 305

Case Study 20: Starbucks U.K. Tax (2012) 313

Case Study 21: Sony Pictures Cyberattack (2014) . . .319

Case Study 22: FIFA Corruption Crisis (2014). 325

Case Study 23: Iraqi Failure in Crisis Management .333

Case Study 24: JPMorgan Chase Financial
Crisis (2013) 343

Case Study 25: Southwest Airlines (2013) 349

Case Study 26: Asiana Airlines Crisis (2013) 355

Case Study 27: Tesla Motors Crisis (2013) 363

Case Study 28: The Fall of Lehman Brothers 371

Case Study 29: Siemens China (2012) 379

Case Study 30: Toyota Recall 2010 385

Conclusion: Lessons Learned from
Crisis Management 393

REFERENCES 403

PART ONE:

Crisis Types, Symptoms, and Causes

In most cases, businesses, social, and political groups experience natural calamities, different conflicts, risks, or varying types of industrial unrest. All these constitute crises. Therefore, one can define a crisis as an occurrence that is either natural or human-instigated that affects the normal operation of business and political systems. In this regard, it is important to explore political and business crises with a view toward understanding their symptoms and causes.

In business, the focus is on corporate crises, owing to the complex and dynamic environment within which companies operate. In the context of a company scenario, most scholarly works view a crisis as a temporary, unexpected, insecure, and detrimental situation in a firm, which results from forces within and outside the company's environment. These occurrences affect the company's performance and growth prospects.[1]

The main goal of a crisis management plan is to protect employees, customers, consumers, corporate image, firm assets, and corporate brands. By having a crisis management plan in place, a firm is in a better position to take the necessary actions to minimize disruptions in business, as well as potential liabilities. The plan should have references to the applicable laws and regulations to protect relationships and ensure compliance with regulatory and government agencies. For the effectiveness of the plan to be achieved, it is vital for a firm to educate and train employees and to prepare them and equip them with information on what to do in the event of a crisis. Conducting simulations of crises is a useful way of testing the firm's preparedness to manage a crisis appropriately and for determining the gaps in the crisis process that need to be reviewed.[2]

The first hours of a crisis are the most critical. The crisis management plan assists in preparing the team to react efficiently and rapidly. A firm needs to consider its longevity and reputation when it is determining how to react to a crisis.[3] A crisis can take any form, including the following.

Product or Service Fault

Research reveals that there is a close association between a crisis and a risk that is manifested through risk management. A prudent risk management strategy attempts to trace, forecast, and control individual, business, and ownership risks. It then follows that a crisis is an anomalous condition that results from the occurrence of a risk. If a product puts the firm's customers in harm or is faulty, then the firm ought to take action to deal with the imminent danger. An example of such a crisis was Toyota's recall of millions of cars across the globe in 2010. The recall was done after the company discovered faulty brakes on several of their vehicles. The massive recall rates, followed by fixing the problem, assisted the firm in rebuilding its brand.[4]

Strikes

Strikes can paralyze a firm and impact its profitability. A case in point is British Airways, which was faced by a crisis when its employees took to industrial action. The company settled the dispute with its cabin crew union after several major strikes, which crippled the airline's capabilities in 2010 and 2011.[5] There are many causes of strikes in an organization. The causes can either be employer-centered or staff-instigated. When workers detect any form of discrimination in the workplace, they may resign or seek job transfers. Some companies have experienced strikes associated with poor remuneration, in line with employees look for well-paying firms. Sometimes workers may perceive a workplace to be hazardous or exposing them to health risks. Strikes can also occur when a company suddenly cuts workers' salaries or lays them off altogether.

When strikes occur, the effects are not necessarily far-reaching. A firm may incur legal costs for contravening labor regulations. On the same note, a company risks losing a competent workforce to a rival firm if a strike happens. This reduces the firm's competitive advantage in the market. Employees could also down their tools if they perceive incompetent leadership in the organization. This is because they understand their leaders more than any other stakeholder. Statistics reveal that successful businesses practice transformational leadership. This means that when a firm's management is rigid to change, workers may engage in mass action to express their dissatisfaction.

Natural Disasters

Natural disasters may be due to human activities or natural forces operating within the earth's crust. The occurrence of natural disasters is random and unpredictable. Globally, the most commonly experienced disasters are floods and earthquakes. The massive earthquake that occurred in April 2011 in Japan had a great impact on several firms, as their production capabilities were destroyed. This resulted in a number of car manufacturers running short on supplies, which in turn brought about lengthy waits experienced by new suppliers. This had a major impact on businesses' reputations and profitability. Another example was the April 2010 BP oil spill in the Gulf of Mexico. The oil spill had such adverse effects that top-level managers were terminated.[6]

Heavy sporadic rainfall causes floods, especially in low-lying areas and coastal regions. The effects of floods include the destruction of business premises and crops, the loss of life, and the blockage of roads and railways. This implies that firms will experience losses that accrue from reduced crop production, reconstruction, and the loss of valuable commodities. It is important to note that the occurrence of a disaster creates the need for contingency planning and adequate preparedness based on the nature of the disaster. In fact, buying insurance for a firm's business would be the most appropriate approach to mitigating disaster-related risks.

Pareto's Law

Pareto's law states that, for most businesses, 80% of the firm's business emanates from 20% of its customers. If that is the case, a company should have a strategic plan in the event that half of its clients decide to leave. The firm would, in this instance, be in very high danger of collapsing. It is critical for a firm to shift its reliance on a number of customers contributing to the majority of its turnover and focus on increasing its customer base.[7]

Customers are the greatest asset that a firm can have in the current business world. This group of market participants has needs and expectations that are ever-changing. Hartley[8] affirms that successful businesses accept feedback and respond positively. Multinational corporations have customers with varied cultures, and they constantly seek to produce standardized products to capture an extended customer base. Managing a culturally diverse team is becoming a major challenge to firms seeking to expand their businesses overseas.

Civil Unrest and War

One of the major causes of political crises is war. This can occur within a country or region. Civil unrest in most countries stems from either extremist ideologies or national disagreements. Terror attacks in a country create tension and a sense of insecurity. Citizens feel insecure, and firms close their businesses either temporarily or permanently, depending on the nature of the destruction. The skewed distribution of national resources and representation in government, especially in countries with many ethnic groups, could raise political temperatures. As a result, people risk their lives in the fight for justice and equality.

Any form of war or civil unrest within a country is bound to affect a firm's operations. An example is the crisis currently witnessed in Syria, which commenced in Tunisia and has spread to other neighboring regions and countries over time. Civil unrest and war affect customers based in the affected geographic location and may impact the firm's distribution arrangements, as well as endanger the firm's sites located in the region that is in danger.[9] International sanctions may exist that may complicate trading within the affected country. Taking all factors into consideration, a firm needs to decide whether and when to withdraw from trading in a country that is affected by war or civil unrest. If a firm opts to continue business in a war-affected region, it should make arrangements to protect its assets that pass through or are based in the affected areas.[10]

Takeovers

When a firm is not performing well and this leads to a dramatic fall in its share price, it may be subjected to a takeover. If there is an unwanted bid for a takeover, the firm needs to organize for action in dealing with the threat, which will include but not be limited to persuading its shareholders to withhold from selling their shares to the firm intending to do the takeover.[11]

Generally, a *financial crisis* refers to the collapse of a country or region's financial system. For firms and small enterprises, a financial crisis occurs when firms have huge debts or are not able to pay for many transactions. The 2007–2008 financial crisis is thus a perfect example of a financial downturn.

This financial crisis was associated with the subsequent crumpling of in-mortgage markets and other financial markets, compounded by the collapse of Lehman Brothers in 2008. This caused risk premiums to shoot up across the world. Prior to the crisis, countries like China and the U.S. experienced variations in investments and savings leading to irregular deficits and surpluses levels. This in turn creates variations between the value of imports and exports, thereby causing trade imbalances.

Of importance is the fact that the crisis spread all over the world and to individual businesses. Banks and other financial institutions in many countries reduced borrowing rates, thus impeding expansion plans by many companies. Companies had limited amounts of capital to venture into new businesses. Financial crises within companies resulted from the poor management of funds, unplanned expenditures, and poor financial reporting.

Symptoms of a Crisis

Symptoms are signals pointing to or predicting a crisis. Their detection and timely response by the firm with appropriate activities and actions can abate the repercussions of a present crisis or even prevent one. It is, therefore, critical not to underestimate, disregard, or overlook these signals. However, the signals should not be substituted with the real initiators of a crisis. The symptoms signal a crisis, while simultaneously not being the cause of the crisis.[12] Symptoms occur in different areas and most often seem to be linked and combined. It is very important for a firm to consider that there will be a time gap between the emergence of said signals and the crisis occurrence (appearance, process) toward said signals.

Because of this, it becomes more precarious if the firm disregards or lacks perception of these warning signals. Upon perception of the signals, an analysis should be carried out and interpreted to determine the reasons for the events' emergence and to abate or eliminate the causes by utilizing appropriate approaches and measures. Most often, several unsuccessful attempts are made at solving a crisis because of an inappropriate approach at commencement.[13]

CRISIS MANAGEMENT:
THE ART OF SUCCESS AND FAILURE

A majority of crisis presence assessments and the required measures for solving them are found in accounting report analyses (statements of conditions, balance sheets, statements of financial flows, and resulting derived indicators), while not considering the notion that accounting reports can be recorded solely on the consequences of previous decisions, and it is not obvious that the trustworthiness of accounting reports reflects on the firm's present condition. Accounting reports are necessary for analyzing a firm's present condition; however, they are insufficient for making decisions to solve a potential crisis state.[14]

Roux-Dufort[15] developed the following crisis equation: "crisis = accumulation of ruined equilibriums + ignorance of management," indicating management vigilance insufficiency. Often, direct and continuous communication with employees and organizational representatives, as well as repeated visits to the main corporate process locations (visits to suppliers and consumers, warehouse inspections, manufacturing process inspections, etc.) ought to be sufficient and may impact employees' motivation positively (this is referred to as management by walking-around).[16]

Causes of a Crisis

An accurate interpretation of the emergence of the causes of a crisis and possible means for its removal is a more complex task. When a crisis emerges, a firm's management plays a significant role in terms of the sufficient, timely, and watchful perception of symptoms that indicate a potential crisis. If management fails to react to the symptoms, or if it fails to react correctly, the crisis becomes inevitable.[17]

The causes of crisis emergence may be classified as

external or internal. The causes of an external crisis are those emerging from a firm's outside environment; therefore, external sources are frequently denominated as exogenous or objective. The internal causes are those emerging from within a firm and are therefore denominated as endogenous and subjective.[18]

Therefore, external causes are certain environmental changes that lack timely recognition by the firm and lack a timely and appropriate reaction. The same environmental change may cause a slowdown and unfavorable settings for one firm, while at the same time having an accelerative and favorable indication for another firm.[19] Examples of the emergence of a crisis' internal causes may be observed in the domains listed below[20]:

- Uncompetitive market position
- Problems in the domain of employee management
- Over-expensive production
- A financial function that is neglected
- An informational system that is inefficient, and so on
- Improper management competencies

The success of a business depends to a large extent on the nature of the market in which it operates. Monopoly practices, such as over-pricing, often create barriers to entry for new firms. Besides, monopolistic companies will always produce and sell products for less than they would in a perfect competition environment. Therefore, firms that depend on such practices for critical inputs for their production risk sending some workers home due to high production costs.

CRISIS MANAGEMENT:
THE ART OF SUCCESS AND FAILURE

Product defaults in businesses occur due to changes in market demand and technology. Firms engaged in industrial production encounter challenges related to process innovation and product innovation. These firms have to invest heavily in research and development if they need to acquire a competitive advantage in the market. The cost of acquiring and adopting new production processes is sometimes high, and small enterprises may lose ground to more established companies.

According to Greenspan,[21] incompetent leadership may well put an end to the business if not properly managed. Affective decision-making helps reduce operational risks. The ability of mangers to detect and manage challenges depends on their commitment and cognitive abilities. Poor communication within a firm will affect interpersonal relationships in the workplace. This means that employees will find it extremely difficult to work as a team. This can also reduce their morale and negatively impact their performance.

Despite external causes playing a critical role in corporate crisis emergence in many cases, internal causes are more predominant. In principle, the external environment is representative of uncontrollable aggregate variables that require adjustment by the firm, together with its internal strategies, structures, processes, and the marketing mix, which represent the aggregate of the controllable variables. Potential external crisis causes can be successfully eliminated through internal changes or adjustments within the firm.

In principle, the intertwining of the external and internal causes results in a serious situation (referred to as a crisis multi-causability or "polymorphous phenomenon" by Hensen, Desouza, and Kraft).[22] The formal failure is linked to and impacted by environmental factors, such as economic changes, regulatory changes, and technological uncertainty; ecological factors, such as density, industry lifecycle size, and age; firm-related factors, such as past performance, management tenure, successions, and homogeneity; and psychological factors, such as managerial perceptions. Hamilton and Micklethwait[23] assert that the main factors causing failure can be categorized as poor strategic decisions; ill-judged acquisitions and overexpansion; dominant CEOs; hubris, greed, and the quest for power; internal control failures at all levels; and ineffective or ineffectual boards.

General analysis of a business crisis focuses on the implications of many crisis types on an organization's performance; when a crisis befalls a business, the effects are more or less the same to the individuals. This means that different stakeholders, acting in different capacities, are all vulnerable victims in the wake of a crisis. Besides, the business risks losing customers, let alone the fact that suppliers will be on the necks of the accounting department for unpaid supplies.[24] There is no doubt that there will be commitment issues relating to social corporate responsibility. This is because the effects of a crisis in a firm can spill over to the surrounding environment and the community around it. One can argue that when a crisis strikes a firm, people perceive it individually and it no longer remains the firm's issue alone.

There are many causes of civil unrest in a country. The first one is disagreement over election results. In highly competitive elections, every runner-up and other candidates often dispute results, citing manipulation and massive irregularities. They can convince their followers that the elections might have been compromised. As witnessed in most countries, disputed elections amount to mass action.[25] When people stage demonstrations against election fraud, a given ethnic group may be perceived to be favored. Moreover, land dispute is a major cause of insecurity in many developing countries. Tribal clashes are feasible in situations where people fight each other to defend their land. This presents a crisis, as ownership is not determined.

In conclusion, a crisis can lead to turbulence in normal business transactions, economic status, and the political wellness of a country. It affects firms either directly or indirectly, depending on the cause. The signs of a crisis can be seen through negative changes in returns, reduced job morale, and strike notices. A firm ought to have the appropriate mechanisms to detect and read the symptoms of a crisis in place and come up with the means of mitigating the effects on the business. It is critical for a firm to consider that there is a time gap, as noted earlier, between the emergence and the crisis occurrence (appearance, process) toward said direct signals. A firm should have a crisis management plan that clearly outlines the procedures and resource commitments that will be in place in the event that a crisis occurs.

Endnotes

PART ONE: *Crisis Types, Symptoms, and Causes*

1 Mitroff, I. (2005). *Why some companies emerge stronger and better from a crisis: 7 essential lessons for surviving disaster.* New York: American Management Association.

2 Clark, J., & Harman, M. (2004, May). On crisis management and rehearsing a plan. *Risk Management, 51*(5), 40–44.

3 Kash, T. J., & Darling, J. R. (1998). Crisis management: Prevention, diagnosis and intervention. *Leadership & Organization Development Journal, 19*(4), 179.

4 Kozlowski, C. (2010, January). Crisis management. *Crisis Control Newsletter from RQA, Inc.—A Catlin Preferred Provider to Foodservice, Food Processing and Consumer Products Industries. U0110*(1).

5 BBC. (2011). *Q&A: What's the BA dispute about?* Retrieved from http://www.bbc.com/news/business-11868081

6 Webb, T. (2011). *Japan's economy heads into freefall after earthquake and tsunami.* Retrieved from http://www.theguardian.com/world/2011/mar/13/japan-economy-recession-earthquake-tsunami

7 Dubrovski, D. (2010). Management mistakes as causes of corporate crises: Countries in transition. *Managing Global Transitions, 5*(4).

8 Hartley, R. F. (2005). *Management mistakes and success.* New York: Wiley.

9 BBC.com. (2015). *Syria: The story of the conflict.* Retrieved from http://www.bbc.com/news/world-middle-east26116868

10 Mitroff, I. (2005). *Why some companies emerge stronger and better from a crisis: 7 essential lessons for surviving disaster.* New York: American Management Association.

11 Mitroff, I. (2005). *Why some companies emerge stronger and better from a crisis: 7 essential lessons for surviving disaster.* New York: American Management Association.

12 Augustine, N. R. (2000). Managing the crisis you tried to prevent. *Harvard Business Review, 73*(6), 147.

13 Augustine, N. R. (2000). Managing the crisis you tried to prevent. *Harvard Business Review, 73*(6), 147.

14 Augustine, N. R. (2000). Managing the crisis you tried to prevent. Harvard Business Review, 73(6), 147.

15 Roux-Dufort, C. (2003). *Gérer et décider en situation de crise.* Paris: Dunod.

16 Dubrovski, D. (2010). Management mistakes as causes of corporate crises: Countries in transition. *Managing Global Transitions, 5*(4).

17 Dubrovski, D. (2010). Management mistakes as causes of corporate crises: Countries in transition. *Managing Global Transitions, 5*(4).

18 Dubrovski, D. (2010). Management mistakes as causes of corporate crises: Countries in transition. *Managing Global Transitions, 5*(4).

19 Dubrovski, D. (2010). Management mistakes as causes of corporate crises: Countries in transition. *Managing Global Transitions, 5*(4).

20 Dubrovski, D. (2004). *Crisis management and renovation companies.* Koper: Faculty of Management.

21 Greenspan, A. (2007). *The age of turbulence: Adventures in a new world.* Sydney: Allen Lane.

22 Hensen, T., Desouza, K. C., & Kraft, G. D. (2003). Games, signal detection, and processing in the context of crisis management. *Journal of Contingencies and Crisis Management, 11*(2), 67–72.

23 Hamilton, S., & Micklethwait, A. (2006). *Greed and corporate failure.* New York: Palgrave Macmillan.

24 Moore, S., & Seymour, M. (2005). *Global technology and corporate crisis.* London: Routledge.

25 BBC.com. (2015). *Syria: The story of the conflict.* Retrieved from http://www.bbc.com/news/world-middle-east26116868

Models and Theories Associated with Crisis Management

Introduction

The management of a crisis represents a key component of the success that is likely to be exhibited in an organizational setup. The success that is bound to be made will be dependent largely on the efficiency that is featured when it comes to the management of some of the challenges that may arise in the business mix. In the political setup, there is also likely to be the emergence of crises that call for finesse to achieve a competent resolution. The capacity of the company's success may be tied to its level of preparedness in the hope of mitigating the elements of crisis that come into the fold.[1]

In a business setting, a crisis could manifest itself in the form of the changes made in the course of the day-to-day frameworks in pursuing the operation focus. The slight changes that are made would bear the impact of commissioning a radical revamp of the methods that are used. There is also the chance that a project scope that is developed may have emerging issues with the potential of limiting the viability to achieve a proposed set of objectives. The tweaks that are made could call for a change in personnel or a shift in the primary protocols.

CRISIS MANAGEMENT:
THE ART OF SUCCESS AND FAILURE

In the hope of ascertaining a smooth transition in all the business processes and plans that are made, it is only logical that there is a prior projection that explores the possible reasons crises would emerge. Upon the identification of the causes of the same, relevant plans need to be made to eradicate the looming eventualities.[2] Part of the planning process should entail feasible plans drawn out to manage crisis situations if they emerge.

MODELS AND THEORIES OF CRISIS MANAGEMENT

Unequal Human Capital Theory

More often than not, the cause of a crisis is a failure to consider all aspects that need to be part of a dynamic organization; an example is the discrimination of individuals, especially minorities when the organizational rewards tend to be a preserve of the majority. This effectually alienates minority groups, resulting in a setup where certain duties that are meant to be undertaken unbalance. The opportunities that emerge take the significant processes that the operations are aligned with into account. The elements that are not highlighted in the mega planning modalities tend to be the cause of the observed crises.[3]

There needs to be a review of the factors likely to have an adverse impact on the elements of organizational performance so that they are resolved beforehand to eradicate the potential crises that would limit the realization of the principal goals, mission, and vision. There must be a shift to instill an element of equality in regards to some of the key decisions that are made.

Structural-Functional Systems Theory

Effective crisis management can be feasible when information related to the occurrences of crises is availed. In times of crisis, there is a better chance of solving the emerging issues when all the facts pertaining to the challenges are known. This is only possible when the communication network among the stakeholders and all the individuals taking part in addressing the emerging drawbacks is well developed.[4] It is ideal that the flow of information is identified so that the scope of performance is still on course for realization. In a time of crisis, resolutions are tied to the general efficiency that is inherent in the communication network among the actively involved groups. The performance and the final solution are bound to be robust when there is a clearly defined channel of communication. The channels would keep track of all the trends that yielded the crisis so that a reclamation plan is effected.

Informational flow strategies always have to identify the essence of bureaucracy in the organization so that the designated order of command is upheld. The communication channel is tantamount to nothing less than resolving the primary challenge. The stepwise review of the underlying emerging issues will be resolved better when all the components of authority are taken into consideration.[5] Once the information flow patterns in the organization are established, there will be the inevitable unraveling of the aspects that seem to deviate from the essential focus on all of the entity's objectives.

Diffusion of Innovation Theory

This is another potent theory that can be applied effectively in crisis situations. The core desire is to disseminate and communicate innovation within a designated timeframe. Once the specific innovation is identified, the individual with the knowledge of its applicability conveys the information so that it may be reviewed, pending incorporation. The testing phase is vital in the hope of establishing the relevance that it may have for the given organizational setup. Such testing would be a guarantee of flexibility,[6] It is also the primary determinant of the knowledge base to which all organizational members should have access.

During the assimilation of the innovation, there must be an established communication network that will deliver the relevant alignment to the proposed new methods. Through the established channels of communication lies the essence of the efficient dissemination of the borne ideas. The level of performance that is likely to be realized depends on how swiftly the ideas are communicated. It is of note, therefore, that all the factors that are likely to limit the effectiveness of the communication should be the subject of review so that when the new improvements are conveyed, they yield the desired commitment and the application modules give the expected results.[7]

Crisis Management Model

The successful diffusion of a crisis depends on how well the model used for the same purpose is designed. In the hope of analyzing all the issues attached to the crisis, it is essential that all the factors that may have led to the crisis are reviewed. Comprehending the emerging issues is vital in designing the approach that may be the best fit for use in resolving the noted challenges. Understanding the issue is also imperative for coming up with all the available options that may be explored.[8] Having options yields flexibility.

The model should also feature planning prevention that projects the challenges that are most likely to come into the fold and the corresponding ways of dealing with them when they are in effect. Such preparedness creates a seamless transition when the stopgaps are highlighted, given that there is the chance to consider the available options that have been reviewed. As such, it would be viable to attain a commitment to resolution upon the use of the methods evaluated in the planning phase.

When the crisis itself occurs, the preparedness phase that has already been done becomes handy for navigating through the emerging issues and resolving them amicably. Proper handling of the emerging issues is also the key to navigating through the post-crisis phase.

Crisis Management Planning

In light of the uncertainties that surround an entity during a crisis, it is significant to plan for the best decisions that could be made and also try to antedate possible outcomes that could take place in the aftermath of the derailing issue. Planning presents options, all of which are success-oriented. A comprehensive review of the available options is the best chance to reinstate normalcy in such junctures.

Contingency Planning

There is an important approach to the development of a model that could be used for crisis management. The methods that are chosen for crisis management have a chance to deliver the intended aftermath consequences. A simulated scenario could be staged so that the approaches that are proposed get tested. This also presents an opportunity to establish the most ideal strategy that needs to be considered for incorporation. For effective crisis management, it is crucial that the first decision to be made on the approach to be used for managing the situation is implemented soon after the crisis appears.[9] Working with vigilance is paramount so that the adverse effects of the crisis do not spread into all the elements of the organization. In the contingency plan chosen, it is ideal to have information and guidance to assess the likely implications.

Business Continuity Planning

In light of the inevitable impact of crises on normal business operations, it is crucial that the available options are reviewed so that the one likely to yield continuity for the business practice is used. It is in this capacity that the initial plans to be followed during the objective setting phase are not delayed. The elements of continuity align the normal operations so that the expected chain of activities is upheld.[10] All processes need to be aligned to conform to the performance modalities. In this way, the span designated for the implementation of the focus is not protracted.

Endnotes

Models and Theories Associated with Crisis Management

1 Seeger, M. W., Sellnow, T. L., & Ulmer, R. R. (2012). Communication, organization, and crisis. *Communication Yearbook, 21*, 231.

2 Daft, R. (2012). *Organization theory and design.* Cengage Learning.

3 Chang, C. L., Jiménez-Martín, J. Á., McAleer, M., & Perez Amaral, T. (2011). Risk management of risk under the Basel Accord: Forecasting value-at-risk of VIX futures. Available at *SSRN 1765202*.

4 Cornelissen, J. (2014). *Corporate communication: A guide to theory and practice.* Sage.

5 Hayes, J. (2014). *The theory and practice of change management.* Palgrave Macmillan.

6 Brecher, M. (2013). *Crises in world politics: Theory and reality.* Elsevier.

7 Drennan, L. T., McConnell, A., & Stark, A. (2014). *Risk and crisis management in the public sector.* Routledge.

8 Fischbacher-Smith, D., & Fischbacher-Smith, M. (2014). When good management theory hits the fan: Crisis management and the challenge to the rational-positivistic paradigm of MBA programmes.

9 Coombs, W. T., & Holladay, S. J. (Eds.). (2011). *The handbook of crisis communication* (Vol. 22). John Wiley & Sons.

10 McMains, M. J., & Mullins, W. C. (2014). *Crisis negotiations: Managing critical incidents and hostage situations in law enforcement and corrections.* Routledge.

Crisis Management Planning

Crises have become increasingly commonplace in today's organizations, justifying the need to develop robust crisis management plans to effectively deal with organizational crises. Research shows that no organization is immune to crises, implying that crises are inevitable within organizations. Therefore, to effectively mitigate the problems of organizational crises, management needs to develop a highly detailed plan. Otherwise, an organizational crisis is likely to not only reduce organizational competitiveness in the global market, but also its productivity. A crisis management plan can either make or break organizations during a crisis. This section explores crisis management planning.

Organizational Crisis Management

Crisis management is defined broadly as a firm's pre-established guidelines and activities for preparation and response to critical catastrophic incidents or events (e.g., acts of terrorism, earthquakes, fires, severe storms, kidnappings, workplace violence, bomb threats) in a safe and effective manner. A crisis management plan that is successful incorporates the firm's programs, such as disaster recovery, emergency response, risk management, business continuity, and communications.[1] Additionally, crisis management is concerned with developing a firm's capability to react flexibly and hence enable it to make necessary and prompt decisions during a crisis.

The image of a company is so essential to its success, and managing a crisis is therefore an important part of maintaining a powerful corporate image. An excellent reputation enables an organization to not only satisfy its goals and objectives, but also gain a greater competitive advantage. Business organizations willing to realize success must ensure that they develop a detailed crisis management plan to ensure that crises are effectively managed. Admittedly, excellent crisis management would enable an organization to maintain a potent corporate image.

Through crisis management planning, firms are in a better position to handle unforeseen events that may potentially cause serious or irreparable damage. Human resource (HR) leaders currently have a strategic responsibility and play a role in ensuring that their firms are informed about the human side of a potential crisis and proceeding to plan ahead to assist in minimizing its effects.[2] To increase their effectiveness, HR leaders should work in collaboration, with a top-down commitment, to develop enterprise-wide solutions. Crisis management is based on early issue identification, planning, training, and rapid decision-making in the event of a crisis; it needs a series of steps that involves planning, prevention, evaluation, testing, and implementation to minimize and mitigate the impact and consequences to businesses.

A planned or unplanned crisis can be managed strategically and more effectively if a firm does its crisis management "homework." One of the main aspects of a firm that is proactive is its obligation and ability to take responsibility for its acts.[3] However, while many firms plan for financial success and growth, many do not take steps that are productive to deal with a crisis. The consideration of possible scenarios and the best possible solutions to prepare, prevent, and provide interventions that allow a firm to be better prepared in handling a crisis is necessary.[4] Scenario planning may be utilized as a crisis management strategy; it provides a mechanism for thinking through different ways whereby these scenarios may occur and develop the most suitable business responses.[5]

Steps in the Crisis Management Process

Step 1: Establishing a Strategic Crisis Planning Team

The first step in planning for a strategic crisis is to establish a crisis management team. In an organization, the crisis management team is composed of different directors who play key roles in planning. The HR director is responsible for addressing issues affecting employees and their families and also for having the required succession plans and talent in place to ensure that the work of the firm can proceed. Therefore, the HR directorate helps investigating officers to access affected individuals and their families with a view of resolving human problems created by the crisis under management.

Also included in the team is the finance director, whose primary role is to assess the financial implications of individual disaster types. He or she ensures that adequate funds are allocated for emergencies, in conjunction with the relevant departments; oversees fund disbursements; and records maintenance costs incurred during the crisis. Legal council is there to inform the organization of the feasible legal consequences of the crisis and what ought to be done.

In addition, the media spokesperson is required to communicate important but necessary details without compromising employees' privacy or impeding the investigation process. The security director, in coordination with security experts, will facilitate the development of the plan, train employees, establish a crisis center, and oversee information processing and sharing. The security specialist is an expert in the different contingency planning issues, is often from outside of the firm, assists in educating the team on various options for dealing with different types of crises, gives advice to the team in the event of a crisis, and assists in conducting the debriefing after the crisis. Finally, the team is led by the organization's head, usually a CEO or top director. These leaders are considered the symbol of authority in the organization and will be responsible for making final decisions regarding the crisis.

Step 2: Analysis of Hazards and Capabilities
In this stage, the input of numerous stakeholders is essential for developing the plan. Therefore, they participate in examining the situation at hand and look at the organization's preparedness to tackle it. Here, the security director listens to stakeholders' views regarding the cause of the crisis. In most organizations, some stakeholders have a wealth of experience in crisis management. They can tell whether the unfortunate occurrence in the organization is natural or emanates from managerial loopholes.

Planning for any crisis requires adequate knowledge about the nature and causes of different crises in an organization. Crises relating to employees can be managed through diplomacy and transformational leadership. For instance, an industrial strike requires a more proactive approach than the knee-jerk reaction demonstrated by some managers. Therefore, management will require strategies geared toward maintaining its competent workforce or risk losing employees to emerging competitors.

Moreover, when an organization faces a financial crisis, major operations in the organization may be halted. A financial crisis may result from the embezzlement of funds, the failure to pay for supplies, reduced returns, or uncontrolled expenditures. In this respect, effective planning for financial expenditures would call for accountability, marketing strategies, budgeting by departments in various directorates, and accurate financial reporting.

Nonetheless, organizations should collaborate with workers' unions and government agencies for the purpose of ensuring harmony and conformity with labor requirements. For financial crises, different governments have different financial reporting systems, and organizations are thus obligated to integrate these regulations into their procurement procedures. Some of the regulations salient to organizations are safety and security measures in the workplace, worker remuneration and benefits, taxation requirements, and equity and accountability.

In this planning stage, an organization will estimate the value of its human and non-human resources while evaluating its ability to sustainably manage the crisis at hand. This analysis requires forecasting the magnitude of crisis damage and resource requirements, including how other firms have successfully mitigated crisis-related challenges in the past.

Step 3: Developing the Plan

An organization has to come up with emergency response procedures based on different crises. This will help to avoid firefighting and crisis-based consequences. For instance, in the case of a fire, employees' chances of survival and the magnitude of damage will depend on the effectiveness of sensitization programs undertaken in the past. This could mean establishing fire assembly points, fire alarms, and fire extinguishers within the premises.

During planning, it is important to identify feasible challenges and set priorities. In the case of unrest among employees, an organization will have to decide whether to reinstate all the workers who participated in a mass action or maintain a reasonable number that can be well-paid, promoted, and trained. The global business environment is rather competitive and dynamic. This poses great challenges to firms seeking to expand their operations. As a result, the plan should specify key bottlenecks that affect the organization's financial stability. Some of the challenges include global supply chain management, technological innovations, and changes in human capital requirements. Once the plan is in place, it is necessary to establish a schedule for the different activities that are needed. This includes timelines for training, conducting feasibility studies, engaging stakeholders, decision-making, and effecting change.

Step 4: Implementing the Plan

The final stage of crisis management is implementing the adopted plan. Here, management incorporates various specifications of the plan into the overall strategic plan. This involves evaluating the plan against the objectives of the organization by monitoring progress and conformity with set processes in different departments.

Risk Assessment

Risk assessment is a fundamental aspect of strategic risk management. Companies can examine different risks through the application of a risk reporting process, such as a strengths, weaknesses, opportunities, and threats (SWOT) analysis, and firms can start making better and more informed decisions, enhancing risk communication and building management-based consensus.[6] The following list of questions may aid in risk assessment[7]: 1) What impact will it have on people? 2) How realistic is the probability of the potential crisis identified? 3) Does firm action moderate or halt the crisis? 4) Does the policy implemented meet public scrutiny? 5) Are the resources necessary for taking action available? 6) Is there a willingness to act? 7) What would result from inaction?

Within the crisis management plan, it is important to have a clear chain of command in place. The plan needs to be put in writing to take care of the worst-case scenario, including total inaccessibility of the normal workplace and the inability to use and rely upon the firm's infrastructure and resources for an extended time period. It is also advisable that the crisis management cross-functional team meet every six months to hold discussions on potential crises and the means of responding to them.[8]

A number of small and medium-sized enterprises (SMEs), however, could lack the resources and the staffing necessary for crisis management planning. They may need to consider different options, including access to their respective professional associations and/or chambers of commerce for assistance. They may also consider involving their loss control team in the planning and the addition of commercial insurance professionals for additional support. Outsourcing offers another option. For example, one alternative is to team up with a consultant in crisis management that can steer the process. In essence, teaming up with a vendor is a kind of outsourcing.

Theoretically, outsourcing advantages include savings on finances used on ongoing expenditures, while simultaneously avoiding capital outlay.[9] However, crisis management calls for a firm to plan while considering its needs and culture. Therefore, absolute outsourcing may be impractical, as it would require the vendor to access a significant amount of the firm's information for the development of a comprehensive, effective crisis management plan. Ultimately, it is the responsibility of the firm to manage its own crisis planning.

Communication and Crisis Management Planning

A communication plan is vital in planning for crisis management. HR must always be ready to communicate internally and externally with regard to emergencies on behalf of the employees and the firm. HR may be required to answer queries such as: 1) What resources and information are required for dealing with the immediate emergency? 2) What is the status of the emergency in the different affected locations? 3) How are the employees reacting?[10] In the event of a crisis, internal stakeholders and employees need a convenient way to gain access to communication from the firm. The communication channels that most firms utilize and that provide the broadest access include:

- Daily postings on bulletin boards
- Daily email updates
- Password-protected Internet sites
- An HR help center as part of the firm
- A special firm intranet section on the home page
- Telephone hotline for employee questions

For supervisors and managers, the firm may want to utilize password-protected sections of the Internet, such as information databases or discussion sections that are restricted to managers.[11] In most cases, communication scholars and experts advocate being quick, steadfast, and bold. Based on this proposition, one can contend that a crisis often creates the need for instantaneous and consistent information to fast-track positive responses to the situation. A company may experience adverse effects compounded by rumors, assumptions, and false information, which may ruin its reputation.

Studies have further revealed that it is crucial to ensure that information that reaches the public during a crisis is consistent; there is no doubt that when the public reads from different scripts on the same situation, it creates anxiety and elicits reactions to the detriment of the affected organization. Openness entails disclosing all the necessary information regarding a crisis. Studies have revealed that engaging stakeholders in open communication during a crisis often registers success. On the contrary, organizations that withhold information sometimes find themselves on the verge of collapsing. However, whether or not to disclose information depends on the sensitivity of the crisis under mitigation.

Corporate Apologia in Crisis Management

The term *corporate apologia* is used to mean an act of self-defense. Therefore, in crisis management, it does not imply being apologetic, but rather management's approach to clearing the organization's name in times of crisis. This strategy is essential for managing social legitimacy crises, which refer to the degree to which organizational values and practices contravene social norms and expectations, thereby affecting the organization's social welfare.

In conclusion, a firm needs to have a crisis management plan in place that is enhanced by clear communication lines, run by a competent team, and written down and frequently updated. Stakeholder participation ought to be considered during planning. Organizations must adhere to government regulations and global conventions. Therefore, firms should realize that planning is both a social and corporate obligation and that an organization that fails to plan for a crisis should be prepared for dire consequences and ultimate collapse in the future.

Endnotes

Crisis Management Planning

1 Society for Human Resource Management. (2005). *Glossary of human resource terms*. Retrieved from www.shrm.org/hrresources/hrglossary_published

2 Blythe, B. T. (2004, July). The human side of crisis management. *Occupational Hazards*, Retrieved from www.cmiatl.com

3 Mitroff, I. (2005). *Why some companies emerge stronger and better from a crisis: 7 essential lessons for surviving disaster*. New York: American Management Association.

4 Kash, T. J., & Darling, J. R. (1998). Crisis management: Prevention, diagnosis and intervention. *Leadership & Organization Development Journal, 19*(4), 179.

5 Gunther, R., Seitchik, M., Parayre, R., Schuurmans, F., & Schramm, J. (2005). *2015: Scenarios on the future of human resource management*. Alexandria, VA: Society for Human Resource Management.

6 Gates, S., & Hexter, E. (2005). *From risk management to risk strategy*. New York: The Conference Board.

7 Regester, M., & Larkin, J. (2005). *Risk issues and crisis management: A casebook of best practice*. Sterling, VA: Kogan Page US.

8 Kash, T. J., & Darling, J. R. (1998). Crisis management: Prevention, diagnosis and intervention. *Leadership & Organization Development Journal, 19*(4), 179.

9 Weatherly, L. (2005). HR outsourcing: Reaping strategic value for your organization. *SHRM Research Quarterly, 3*, 29.

10 The Business Roundtable. (2005, February). *Committed to protecting America: CEO guide to security challenges*. Washington, D.C.: Author.

11 Hewitt Associates LLC. (2004, March). *Communicating with employee during times of crisis*. Retrieved September 2, 2005, from www.hewitt.com.

Leadership Under Stress

Each and every organization has gotten to a point where every member of the team has felt overwhelmed, and everyone was simply strained and stressed by the situation at work. It gets even worse when, instead of things progressing and becoming better, they tend to move backward, and the effort that the leaders in the organization and all the work the entire team seems to be putting in regardless of the difficult times becomes futile. During times such as these, the only critical thing in the organization is good leadership, as it may be the only thing with the ability to successfully turn around the end results of the organization.

In the contemporary world, each and every day is faced with its challenges, with the challenges sometimes being sufficiently large that they can be referred to as crises, and sometimes being small enough that they can even be considered negligible, as quick action is not required. Today, more and more crises continue to be witnessed everywhere in the world, and they seem to be targeting businesses, government agencies, and parastatals, as well as the public at large. These crises range from economic disasters, turmoil, and chaos that affect the ways of living of different individuals to terrorism that ends up taking lives and destroying property. It involves all manner of crime that negatively affects the functioning of people, businesses, and the running of countries. With little being done to curb these menaces and crises, the rates of the occurrence of crises can only be expected to grow and become even worse in the coming years, and this poses a very large risk to the leaders of today and those of the future.

The crises experienced each and every day put people in leadership positions in a chaotic world that is full of disasters and catastrophes, regardless of the fact that these leaders might be very good at leadership in normal situations and operational conditions. This is because most leaders are not equipped to handle crises and situations as difficult as the ones the world currently faces, and also because many leaders are prone to making very bad, costly, and disastrous decisions. A decision may make sense at the hour of crisis and during the confusion that comes with the disaster, but once the dust settles, the decision could not only be disastrous, it could also turn out to be costly.[1]

There is, therefore, a great need to train future leaders in the traits and mechanisms that are expected of them in the event of a crisis. Leadership during normalcy in operational conditions and leadership during the emergence of a crisis are quite different and vary considerably. The practices and principles of leadership may not seem like the most practical and easiest to apply in the event of a crisis, although in practice, the principles of leadership are not only useful, but they also create a basis for responding to a crisis available and make it easier to recover from a crisis.

In an organization's operating model, the outline for a smooth-running and hitch-free organization is guaranteed only during normal operating conditions, in the absence of which leadership becomes a quagmire, and chaos, together with uncertainty, becomes the order of the day in leadership, at least until normalcy is regained. Crises can be managed very easily and successfully if their impacts are properly comprehended.[2]

IMPACT OF CRISES ON LEADERSHIP

Crises have an impact on the leadership of any given organization that faces a crisis, and the only way to solve a crisis successfully and maintain leadership under stress is by understanding the impacts of the crisis on the business and the leadership of the organization. The first impact of a crisis on the leadership of any given organization includes the tension, pressure, and stress it puts on the leadership. The leaders are put in a stressful situation and a tense environment such that they undergo physical, mental, and psychological strain and stress. The effect of this is that decision-making becomes very poor, as even the smallest decisions in an organization made under such circumstances could lead to very negative effects. Leaders could also suffer from serious mental and psychological harm as a result of blaming themselves for all the crises the organization is going through, thus leading to health risks and other issues that could result in mental and psychological strain. Remaining calm could have a positive impact on leaders' success even in the face of a crisis.[3]

The speed at which a crisis occurs is very fast, which leaves very little or no time at all to consider different factors in decision-making; there is also very little time to consult other leaders for a more sensible response. Staff and other personnel may also be impacted directly by the occurrence of a crisis, as in the absence of the right people to consult, requiring leaders who lack experience and training to step in when a crisis arises. The absence of the right people in terms of experience and skill could cause the leadership of the organization, and the organization at large, to have a mishap in normal operating conditions, but its effect during a crisis causes an exponential accentuation of the problems. Taking time to consult the right personnel, as well as considering different factors, ahead of time could help in maintaining successful leadership even in the event of a crisis.

Additionally, since most of these organizations are hardly ever prepared to deal with crises, the hierarchy at the specific firm or government institution could pose a challenge to a quick response when there is a crisis and even hinder the recovery process. It is very important for each and every organization to adapt the aspect of flexibility into its structure to ensure its success, both in normal operating conditions and in the event of a crisis.[4]

As the organization grows, stakeholders also tend to increase in number and thus the dynamic expectations of the stakeholders and the channels of communication increase; all of these stakeholders must interact and spend time with the leaders. A crisis may strongly increase the stakeholders' numbers and even their need for the attention of, interaction with, and time of the leaders, and leadership should be prepared to deal with changes in expectations and communication. The occurrence of a crisis tends to either overload the channels of communication or render them completely inoperable, requiring a fast response to create a new protocol or communication channel to keep stakeholders in the loop.[5]

The occurrence of a crisis in a given organization will definitely catch the attention of the media, who will be very eager to report on and point out the mistakes of the company that caused the crisis. The stressful situation and the crisis may be amplified by the spotlight that the media will put on the crisis, and it is important for leadership to comprehend this aspect to come out of the situation successfully. Understanding the importance of simplicity is also key, as complex leadership solutions to any crisis make it unlikely that a solution will produce a successful result.[6]

LESSONS DRAWN FROM LEADERSHIP UNDER STRESS

It is important for the leadership of each and every organization to understand the impacts that a crisis will have on their organizations, regardless of whether the organization is governmental or non-governmental. The impacts aid the leadership of these organizations in responding to the situations with reasonable instructions and from a facilitator's point of view. The lessons drawn from the impacts of crises on leadership can help an organization prepare to deal with a crisis.[7] The five principles of effective leadership under stress are as follows:

> ➢ Leadership may need to exhibit its integrity and character at this time more than ever. The character of the leadership is tested the most during times of chaos and turmoil in an organization. Even when treacherous methods and mannerisms that lack integrity seem to be an easy way out, the leadership of an organization should remain logical and just, maintaining integrity for the sake of the organiza-

tion's personnel, its stakeholders, and the organization at large.

- Regardless of how much strain, tension, and pressure exist during a crisis, the leadership of any given organization ought to lead their personnel and stakeholders by moving forward. Leaders should aim at attaining progress and salvaging the situation, as well as achieving a successful turnover of events through a fast, well-calculated response and progressive recovery process.

- Strategic thinking is another important principle of effective thinking, especially in times of crisis. Decision-making processes are usually difficult to follow, even during normal operating conditions, and they get even harder to follow in the event of a crisis. Thinking strategically involves including and consulting experts in the decision-making process and taking the time to consider all the factors involved, despite the urgency and delicateness of the situation.

- Leaders must also ensure that they remain healthy to continue leading their organizations. The mental, psychological, and physical strain may not only affect their health, but may also have an effect on their decision-making capacity.

- Finally, a leader must also remain calm and reasonable during the course of a crisis. Panic and tension can result in making rash decisions that are often poor, costly decisions. This also enables the leader to have excellent communication skills, maintain a professional disposition, and even apply the experience they have gained in the course of their career in leadership, despite being in the middle of a crisis.[8]

WHAT MAKES A GOOD CRISIS LEADER?

A crisis leader is defined as a highly specialized and skilled manager who has the ability to fully incorporate technical knowhow and collaborative and problem-solving skills in difficult situations, such as during a crisis. A crisis leader is also good at directing the team during difficult situations so that the objectives of the organization are achieved, even during a crisis, and is willing to work in highly stressful and challenging situations while also communicating effectively with his/her personnel and other stakeholders.

First, the most effective crisis leaders have the ability to communicate effectively with their teams. They tend to be articulate and persuasive in their speech and are good listeners who are inquisitive and have the ability to look at a situation from different perspectives. They also adapt easily to others and are incorporative and collaborative. Second, they are good at applying the experience they have gained through years of practice, even in times of crises. The recovery operations and contingency plans of different organizations can only be understood through experience, and this is an effective tool in recovery and successful crisis leadership. Good crisis leaders are also able to maintain a positive attitude, and thus are good at effective crisis leadership. This means that they are able to function and maintain good management skills when there are time limitations, high levels of tension and stress, and in decision frames that are considered inadequate, to carry out the duties that go beyond everyday work tasks. The right attitude helps crisis leaders maintain positive dispositions, even in difficult times. This means that they should be seen as stable, calm, and focused on successfully meeting the objectives of the organization, regardless of the circumstances.[9]

A good leader should also have collaborative skills for dealing with the entire team. He or she should be able to interact cohesively with and coordinate the rest of the team. This ensures that the solution to the problem will be found from the collaboration of the leadership, stakeholders, and personnel, who all bring in their different areas of expertise and experience. The collaborative nature of these leaders also helps them understand the fact that as leaders, they cannot solve the problem alone or even feel solely responsible for the emergence of the problems.

Good leaders should also have the capability to make good decisions in the event of a crisis, as hesitation and reluctance will compromise their effectiveness. They also ought to have the skill to categorize the objectives of the organization into long-term and short-term goals, making their achievement of the goals and the ability to follow and complete all the steps easier.

An effective crisis leader also has the capability to facilitate suggestions and advice from other people and to involve all members of the team, especially the experts, in decision-making. They should also be liable people that take responsibility for resolving the crisis and appreciate the efforts of all team members. They can prioritize the tasks that could resolve the crisis and those that can wait a little longer. Their critical thinking skills should be top-notch because they need to be able to understand, define, and assess the uniqueness of each crisis, with a clear picture of all the possible consequences of the solution to the crisis.[10]

Besides these character traits, effective crisis leaders need to recognize their role in the problems that exist and their role in finding solutions to the problems. This simply means that the leaders ought to accept the existence of the problem and not ignore the small problems that make up the crisis. This will help to ensure that the root cause of the crisis is recognized to start solving it, as the roles of every member of the team have been established, especially that of main leadership. Short-term solutions to the crisis will be identified, and the symptoms that led to the crisis situation will be well-understood; thus, an avoidance of the same crisis situation is possible. For this to happen, all members of the team that form the leadership must be willing to be honest about the causes of the crisis.

Seeing things for what they are and considering the reality of a given crisis situation allows leaders to not shy away from the reality of the consequences of being faced with a crisis. These crisis leaders ought to have enough integrity to see a crisis as an opportunity to help the organization, and not see the situation as simply something that is only beneficial to them as individuals.[11]

Effective crisis leaders understand that things might get worse than they already are, and this can support them in preparing for even worse times if the crisis gets worse. This consideration is essential for them to take actions seriously that can be performed to correct and rescue the organization in a crisis. The understanding that things may get even worse if the leaders do not take action in the right direction to salvage the situation will arouse the need for a fast response and recovery, meaning that they ought to restructure their organization to be cushioned against bad times.

Regardless of the fact that a crisis is a difficult time for any organization, an effective crisis leader has to see the importance of strategic thinking in terms of establishing the causes and effects of each and every action taken to try to remove the organization from the crisis. They are also very good at digging out detailed information about what led to the occurrence of the crisis. The fact that they are capable of these things helps them to be able to look at the problem or crisis in a more realistic manner and to develop practicable solutions, regardless of the external pressures that the leadership may face.[12]

Due to the ability to look at a crisis strategically and even plan for how to deal with it, a good crisis leader should be able to consider different alternatives to resolve the crisis. This can involve asking a specialist to brainstorm and find solutions for the crisis situation, regardless of what the leader thinks is the most applicable solution. They are also willing to use another solution when their solution is not the best. They are willing to make a decision based on experts' advice, which is usually the best alternative in a crisis. Listening to their intuition, along with the advice they get from the experts in their companies, is usually the best solution. This intuition comes from their many years of experience in leadership. They also need to explain the decisions made during this crisis to the stakeholders to ensure that the effectiveness of the decision is not affected by resistance from the stakeholders and personnel.

In a crisis, leaders hardly ever worry about the growth of revenue, but they do worry about whether the company has enough money to survive the crisis. Good crisis leaders understand the importance of putting money aside for a rainy day. They also understand that the problem can only be solved by the collaboration of the team.[13]

In situations in which people need to make sacrifices, the leader in a crisis ought to be the one volunteering to make a sacrifice first. This will only encourage other people to go ahead and sacrifice as well. This gesture is usually a depiction of leadership values in the event of a crisis. The leader ought to lead the team in making near-term sacrifices so that they guarantee the long-term resolution of problems.

During normal operating conditions, changes and adaptations are things that are often ignored and pushed to the side. Every effective crisis leader understands that a crisis brings an urgency to carry out the changes that are needed for the organization to solve the crisis. Understanding this concept allows the leader to know exactly what ought to be done to turn around a crisis.

Also, since even after a crisis, the organization may never return to commanding the same market share as it did before the crisis, an effective crisis leader sees an opportunity in the crisis and is usually planning marketing strategies that will move the market share in favor of the organization. Crises have been known to place leaders in situations that they have not experienced before. This means that leaders do not necessarily have all the answers. The reason they ask experts for their input in a crisis is because they have not dealt with the crisis before, and they have to take the risk of believing that the decision they choose to implement is going to be successful. That decision does not necessarily have to be perfect, as an imperfect decision can always be fine-tuned so that eventually it resolves the crisis. Finally, it is important for an effective leader to admit his/her mistakes, especially to stakeholders, if the decision does not turn out to be effective, even after being fine-tuned.[14]

Endnotes

Leadership Under Stress

1 Driskell, J. E., & Salas, E. (1991). Group decision making under stress. *Journal of Applied Psychology*, 76(3), 473.

2 Larsson, G., Johansson, A., Jansson, T., & Grönlund, G. (2001). Leadership under severe stress: A grounded theory study. *Concepts for Air Force Leadership*, 441–447.

3 Boin, A. (2005). *The politics of crisis management: Public leadership under pressure.* Cambridge University Press.

4 Yukl, G. A. (2002). Leadership in organizations. *National College for School Leadership.*

5 Mitroff, I. I. (2004). *Crisis leadership: Planning for the unthinkable.* John Wiley & Sons Inc.

6 Pillai, R. & Meindl, J. R. (1998). Context and charisma: A "meso" level examination of the relationship of organic structure, collectivism, and crisis to charismatic leadership. *Journal of Management*, 24(5), 643–671.

7 Clinton, J. R. (2012). *The making of a leader: Recognizing the lessons and stages of leadership development.* NavPress.

8 Adair, J. E. (2005). *How to grow leaders: The seven key principles of effective leadership development.* Kogan Page Publishers.

9 Boin, A. (2005). *The politics of crisis management: Public leadership under pressure.* Cambridge University Press.

10 Goleman, D., Boyatzis, R., & McKee, A. (2013). *Primal leadership: Unleashing the power of emotional intelligence.* Harvard Business Press.

11 Snowden, D. J., & Boone, M. E. (2007). A leader's framework for decision making. *Harvard Business Review*, 85(11), 68.

12 Ackerman, R. H. & Maslin-Ostrowski, P. (2002). *The wounded leader: How real leadership emerges in times of crisis. The Jossey-Bass Education Series.* San Francisco, CA: Jossey-Bass, Inc.

13 Russell, R. F. & Gregory Stone, A. (2002). A review of servant leadership attributes: Developing a practical model. *Leadership & Organization Development Journal*, 23(3), 145–157.

14 Mishra, A. K. (1996). Organizational responses to crisis. *Trust in Organizations. Frontiers of Theory and Research*, 261–287.

Case Study 1: JetBlue Valentine's Day Crisis (2007)

The provision of airline services is a line of business that requires the utmost finesse to attain consistent and reliable daily schedules. In the case of JetBlue, serious delays in normal operations emerged that had been occasioned by changes in weather conditions. In the events preceding the actual challenges, a winter ice storm was observed, with the thought that it was bound to clear out and turn to rain. Therefore, no proper plans were made for the contingency as was first projected.[1] Most of the normal operations that were allowed to continue were the loading of flights and their entry into the runway.

The passengers in planes that had moved out onto the runways had to bear the brunt of the bad weather that never got better. They waited for over six hours before they could return to the open gates. This was an obvious breach of the regulations stipulated by the Federal Aviation Administration (FAA) to oversee the overall safety of flight services. A rule directs that there should be no flights when weather conditions are icy.[2] There were widespread delays and an enormous amount of losses because of the failure to have genuine preparedness to manage crises that are likely to emerge in the course of dispensing with such services.

CRISIS MANAGEMENT:
THE ART OF SUCCESS AND FAILURE

During normal operations, JetBlue has up to 156 departures scheduled, but on this day, only 17 actually left. There were more concerns that came into the fold, with massive adverse effects running deep into the system. The worst of the effects was the displacement of aircraft and their crews; these trends continued for an unprecedented five days starting on the fourteenth day of February. During this period, management made the decision to cancel the scheduled flights, seriously inconveniencing the passengers.

In light of the mounting losses and severe damage to its reputation due to the delays caused to its customers, it was only logical that JetBlue management came up with a lasting solution that would reinstate normalcy. Dealing with customers is a sensitive task that needs to take into account the long-lasting effects that will be felt in the event of anything going wrong.[3] There had to be assurances given to clients about the steps that had been taken to reinstate normal operations and end the stand down.

The CEO, David Neelam, designed a simple but effective message that would be ideal in getting through to the affected customers and even the prospective ones that were still hoping to use JetBlue services. In his message, Neelam made the move to tender a public apology for the over 131,000 customers that had been directly affected by the challenge, the apology implied that most of them had to reschedule their journeys. After the apology, there was a review of the overall situation and the decision was made to offer compensation for the damages that had been caused by the delays.[4] A full refund, a ticket, and a free round trip fare were offered to the passengers who were stuck on a plane for more than three hours.

Case Study 1: JetBlue Valentine's Day Crisis (2007)

On the second day after the situation had been resolved and most services reinstated, the company issued a Customer Bill of Rights. This was the key to the documentation of the compensation packages that would be offered in the case of delays that occurred during normal operations. As a leading capacity, the strategy that was employed by David Neelam was on point in the hope of reestablishing customer trust after the inconvenience that had already happened and reclaiming the image of the organization.[5]

The key to resolving the public relations challenge does not require taking hardline stances, but rather letting the public and the affected people know that the company regretted what happened. This is a way of letting people know that the shortfalls had been identified and acknowledged that would take center stage in preventing a repeat of similar challenges in the future.

In the JetBlue case, the approach that was taken was the most suitable, given that any slight, wrong move would have resulted in a diminished customer base. It was a small airline company that was only a decade old. The key to its success had been the goodwill of its passengers and the efficiency of its service delivery. Any negativity, like that observed in 2007, could have had the effect of losing loyal customers to immediate competitors.[6] There would have been further losses going forward that surpassed the ones already seen when the weather beat all expectations.

For the leader of an organization, it is essential to develop the ability to identify market niches, as well as the possibilities that could impede the expected developments. This is part of the desire to be objective in the workplace and in the plans that are made, given the potency the leaders have in creating workable plans to yield the desired success levels. David Neelam was seen as a strong communicator who knew the context he faced and thus chose the proper perspective to match the environment. The positive results that were in the offing can thus be tied to the ability to pin down the actual issues at hand to develop a suitable resolution.[7]

As a leader, it is also crucial to observe the essence of flexibility, especially in the decisions that could be made during a time of crisis. It is ideal to not hold on to the primary methods of overseeing operations when there are noted shortfalls. Flexibility comes to light when proposals should be made for new approaches that could be resorted to in the quest to boost results and general performance.[8]

The excellence that takes effect would thus be a direct result of the flexibility that allows for better approaches to be incorporated into operational strategies.

Endnotes

Case Study 1: JetBlue Valentine's Day Crisis (2007)

1 Hanna, J. (2008, March). *JetBlue's Valentine's Day crisis*. Harvard Business School. Retrieved from http://hbswk.hbs.edu/item/jetblues-valentines-day-crisis

2 Hanna, J. (2008, March). *JetBlue's Valentine's Day crisis*. Harvard Business School. Retrieved from http://hbswk.hbs.edu/item/jetblues-valentines-day-crisis

3 Hanna, J. (2008, March). *JetBlue's Valentine's Day crisis*. Harvard Business School. Retrieved from http://hbswk.hbs.edu/item/jetblues-valentines-day-crisis

4 Maital, S., & Seshadri, D. V. R. (2012). *Innovation management*. Sage.

5 Easterby-Smith, M., & Lyles, M. A. (Eds.). (2011). *Handbook of organizational learning and knowledge management*. John Wiley & Sons.

6 Easterby-Smith, M., & Lyles, M. A. (Eds.). (2011). *Handbook of organizational learning and knowledge management*. John Wiley & Sons.

7 Turner, J. R. (2014). *The handbook of project-based management* (Vol. 92). McGraw-Hill.

8 Avolio, B. J., & Yammarino, F. J. (Eds.). (2013). *Transformational and charismatic leadership: The road ahead* (Vol. 5). Emerald Group Publishing.

Case Study 2: West Africa Ebola Outbreak (2014)

The West Africa Ebola outbreak in 2014 was one of the deadliest occurrences of the disease since it was discovered in 1976. Researchers traced the beginning of the 2014 outbreak to a toddler who died in a village called Meliandou in southeastern Guinea. In March 2014, hospital staff alerted the Ministry of Health, revealing that the mysterious disease had affected the southeastern region of Guinea. The disease then crossed the border and started killing people in Liberia. Other cases were reported in Sierra Leone. At this point, the medical charity known as Medecins Sans Frontieres (MSF) declared that the disease was out of control. In August 2014, the United Nations (UN) health agency revealed that Ebola was an international public health emergency that required a coordinated response to stop the disease from spreading.[1]

CRISIS MANAGEMENT

Disease outbreaks, such as Ebola, not only cause human suffering and deaths, but can also lead to economic losses in affected countries. Such a crisis may require responses by governments and external health partners. In this Ebola outbreak, national preparedness plans played a vital role in responding to the emergency. The plans involved establishing some of the key components vital to an emergency response, such as financing, coordination, incident management systems, community engagement, and public awareness. The efforts involved strong government commitment and initiative, extensive interagency collaboration, significant amounts of resources, and stakeholder involvement.[2] Despite the existing challenges in some of the West African countries, some of the governments tried to commit resources and efforts to manage the health crisis. Countries such as the Democratic Republic of Congo (DRC) and Senegal implemented Ebola preparedness plans, which enabled them to contain the disease. There was a detailed response plan in Senegal. A national crisis committee was created in March 2014 in Senegal, even before a single case of the disease was identified in the country. This move played a vital role in crisis management because it enabled the country to contain any future cases of infection and even prevent outbreaks. The DRC had also implemented robust response plans, which were developed following experiences with the disease.[3] Although countries like Mali and Nigeria had also affected by the outbreak, they benefitted from the disastrous experiences of other countries; these nations were on alert, and they were better prepared for the outbreaks. Some of the countries that reported thousands of deaths, such as Sierra Leone, Liberia, and Guinea, did not have national preparedness plans. In Guinea, there was an outbreak in one of the villages in December 2013. The disease was confirmed in March 2014 after laboratory tests. Despite reports that there was an outbreak of the disease across the borders of Guinea, Sierra Leone, and Liberia, those nations did not develop emergency preparedness protocols until deaths started being reported. At this point, the disease was getting out of control, causing many deaths.

To prevent the disease from spreading, the World Health Organization (WHO) scaled up its preparedness efforts in countries that were at high risk for the disease. The countries at risk were evaluated based on their closeness to the affected countries. Other factors that were examined were the strengths of the health systems in the region and trade and migration patterns. The preparedness efforts involved visits by the preparedness-strengthening teams from the WHO.[2] The WHO also provided tools and technical guidance to the countries that were at risk.

HOW POLITICAL LEADERSHIP SHOWED GREAT COURAGE IN MANAGING THE DISEASE

The political leadership of President Ellen Johnson Sirleaf is an example of good leadership character under pressure. With the country struggling and many Liberians dying, President Sirleaf met with representatives and leaders of the registered political parties so that they could discuss how to address the Ebola outbreak in the country. The Liberian president did not just call the leaders to update them on the Ebola outbreak; she wanted to solicit their input to come up with strategies that would help contain the disease.[4]

The other move by President Sirleaf that depicts great courage in addressing the crisis was her decision to seek help from other countries. President Sirleaf urged countries like Canada to do more about the outbreak that was ravaging her country. Some of the things she asked for were testing centers, skilled health workers, and training for the people who were helping to contain the disease. She admitted that her country did not have an adequate health system to deal with the outbreak. She also acknowledged that other factors, such as the mobility of the population and cultural practices, contributed to the spread of the disease.[5] However, international support and improved knowledge would help address the crisis. Her move helped Liberia receive international aid from multiple sources, such as UN agencies.

President Bai Koroma of Sierra Leone also demonstrated good leadership character in addressing the crisis. Despite the national disaster, the president even went to affected villages to remind citizens to remain vigilant in fighting the disease. His government launched a post-Ebola recovery program in Sierra Leone, and he reminded people of the importance of monitoring the implementation to enhance mutual accountability and transparency. He also launched the Zero Ebola National Campaign, which required citizens to stay at home so that social mobilizers and health workers could visit them in their homes and inform them about the activities that can help eradicate the disease. The president also launched Operation Northern Push, which involved ensuring a significant security presence in the communities to enhance security and safety. This operation also aimed at enforcing quarantine measures by isolating and tracking individuals who tried to leave,[6]. The moves taken by President Koroma depicted him as a good example of a leader under stress because they helped prevent the transmission of the virus.

The leadership of President Conde of Guinea also provides an example of good leadership character in addressing such a crisis. One of the moves made by the president was to replace the minister in charge of territorial administration with the army general. He said that the decision would help fight the outbreak in the country. The government faced violent resistance to campaigns geared toward fighting the disease, which undermined plans to develop the health sector. Despite the challenges, the president worked toward mobilizing local authorities to increase awareness in local communities.[7]

In summary, the outbreak of Ebola in West Africa had a huge impact on the countries that were affected, as evidenced by the number of deaths that were caused by the outbreak. Although countries like Sierra Leone, Liberia, and Guinea did not have national preparedness plans, the implementation of such plans in other countries played a vital role in managing the crisis. Other governments tried to commit resources and efforts to manage the health crisis. Countries like the DRC and Senegal implemented Ebola preparedness plans to enable them to contain the disease. The political leadership of some of the presidents in West Africa also played a huge role in managing the crisis. President Sirleaf sought help from other countries to address the outbreak that was ravaging her country. President Koroma launched campaigns and operations aimed at enhancing security and safety in the communities. President Conde also demonstrated good leadership character, despite the pressure his government was facing, by mobilizing local authorities to increase awareness in local communities.

Endnotes

Case Study 2: West Africa Ebola Outbreak (2014)

1 Smout, E. (2015, April). *Communicating in a crisis like Ebola: Facts and figures.* Retrieved from http://www.scidev.net/global/ebola/feature/communicating-crisis-ebola-facts-figures.html

2 Kieny, M., Evans, D. B., Schmets, G., & Kadandale, S. (2014). Health-system resilience: Reflections on the Ebola crisis in western Africa. *Bulletin of the World Health Organization, 92*(12), 849–924.

3 Okunogbe, A. (2015). *What the Ebola crisis taught us about emergency preparedness in Africa.* Retrieved from http://www.rand.org/blog/2015/06/what-the-ebola-crisis-taught-us-about-emergency-preparedness.html

4 Cooper, H. (2014, October). *Liberia's Ebola crisis puts president in harsh light.* Retrieved from http://www.nytimes.com/2014/10/31/world/africa/liberias-ebola-crisis-puts-president-in-harsh-light.html

5 Arsenault, A. (2014, October). *Liberia's Ellen Johnson Sirleaf says Ebola was like "unknown enemy."* Retrieved from http://www.cbc.ca/news/world/liberia-s-ellen-johnson-sirleaf-says-ebola-was-like-unknown-enemy-1.2785503

6 Zee Media Corporation. (2015, June). *Sierra Leone launches new operation to eradicate Ebola.* Retrieved from http://zeenews.india.com/news/health/health-news/sierra-leone-launches-new-operation-to-eradicate-ebola_1615242.html

7 Jalabi, R. (2015, July). *Guinea's president on global aid push: "Ebola forced us to change completely".* Retrieved from http://www.theguardian.com/world/2015/jul/12/guinea-president-alpha-conde-ebola-aid

Case Study 3: Maple Leaf Listeriosis (2008)

Many organizations that provide services or products used on a daily basis by humans try their best to meet consumer expectations. However, there are times when they make mistakes that can be detrimental to both the consumers and the company. Maple Leaf Foods is among the leading food processing companies in Canada; it processes meat brands that are popular in the country and also supplies products to hotels and restaurants. On August 12, 2008, the management of the company noticed a possible listeriosis contamination at one of its plants close to Toronto.[1] Maple Leaf Foods and the Canadian Food Inspection Agency confirmed food contamination and issued a health hazard alert on August 17, 2008.[2] The Canadian Food Inspection Agency warned the public to avoid consuming the Sure Slice brand of corned beef and roast beef due to possible contamination with Listeria monocytogenes.[3]

Several economic and health effects of the contamination affected both consumers and the company. The contamination became the largest listeriosis epidemic in the world, and Maple Leaf Foods recalled more than 200 products that were processed at the Bartor Road facility in Toronto. At the end of September, more than twenty people had died from ailments associated with the contamination, and there were

CRISIS MANAGEMENT:
THE ART OF SUCCESS AND FAILURE

several sick people undergoing medical care.[4] The Company had economic losses from the recalled products and lawsuits from consumers. Lawsuits were brought by about 5,000 complainants and exceeded C$50 million.[5] Consumers always care about their safety, and any product or service that jeopardizes that is unlikely to record sales. Consumers started avoiding the company's products and resorted to competing products. Restaurants and hotels started getting their supplies from other suppliers. The media also started portraying a bad image of the company and questioning the credibility of its processes. The bad public image, lawsuits from affected consumers, and economic problems greatly affected Maple Leaf Foods' operations.

Companies have different methods of responding to crises. Some shift blame to other people, keep silent, or maintain a low profile. Today, most companies have a department that deals with public relations in a bid to portray a good image to existing and potential consumers and investors. Some organizations also hire public relations consultants, who help in guiding the staff and everyone associated with the company on the best ways to be ambassadors of the company. The way that a company reacts in times of crisis determines the confidence that consumers will have in the company and its products. Maple Leaf decided to be highly visible throughout the crisis. Just after the news hit that a consumer had died from the contamination, the president of the company held a press briefing in his office that aired on all common broadcast media and was also watched on video sites such as YouTube.[6] He confirmed that some of the products were contaminated with Listeria, explained what the contaminant was, expressed deep concerns, and apologized to all the affected consumers.[7] He explained that the company assumed responsibility for the contamination.[8] By assuming responsibility, the company exonerated the government from any blame that might be placed on policies and regulations. It takes courage for an organization to accept responsibility for problems, and the company earned respect for the bold move. The mainstream media termed the move as honorable and bold, and it earned the president of the company, Michael McCain, recognition as a business newsmaker for 2008.

Maple Leaf Foods took several steps to deal with the crisis and help in the recovery. The first step that it took was restoring public relations. The leaders of the company held several news conferences, and their website also contained information concerning the procedures the company was taking to eliminate any more contamination.[9] Keeping the public informed ensured that they could follow the company's progress in containing the contamination. It made consumers believe that Maple Leaf Foods was genuinely concerned about the problem and did not have anything to hide or any bad intentions. The company also used television commercials to further apologize to the affected people, and this portrayed the company's sincerity. It depicted that, inasmuch as they had apologized the first time, they understood that the affected people were still nursing either physical pain or psychological pain from the loss of loved ones.[10]

The company also used a recovery strategy and restructuring to recover from the crisis. The management of Maple Leaf Foods redirected the energies and resources of the company toward improving food safety. This allowed the department of food safety to hire new staff and use a policy of hiring the best recruits, even if it was expensive.[11] This would ensure that the employees in the food safety department did their best to avoid future contamination and help to restore the faith of consumers in the company's products. The company overhauled its technical systems and developed marketing campaigns to highlight the technical measures to convince trade consumers and customers that they could trust Maple Leaf Foods' products and brands.[1] Gaining the trust of consumers was a step toward ensuring purchases of the company's products. The restructuring of the company enabled it to cut operating costs, and it also sought more equity capital to maintain its balance sheet.[12] The measures that Maple Leaf Foods took to help in the recovery helped it to become profitable after the crisis and get back into business. In October 2009, it announced a profit of C$22.5 million in the third quarter.[13] In 2008, revenue dipped from C$1.34 billion to C$1.29 billion, and in 2007, it recorded a loss of C$12.9 million.[14] The profits in the third quarter of 2009 indicated the effectiveness of the measures it incorporated to ensure profitability.

Most companies encounter a crisis at one point or another, and leadership plays a key role in determining the management of the crisis. Appropriate measures by managers, like in the case of Maple Leaf Foods, help in the efficient management of crises and bring an organization back to profitability. Crises are a result of events that have concrete and immediate impacts that relate to emotions and are visible, and the organization can use generalized and localized ways to communicate corrective actions. Crisis communication is an attempt at controlling information and limiting any negative public reactions that can compromise a company's operations and reputation. Crisis communication is a strategy that helps to manage the problems faced by powerful institutions and corporations in periods of risk and uncertainty.[15] Jaques[16] explained that the involvement of an organization's management in conflict management is important for developing a systematic strategy and convincing others within the company to cooperate. A leader should lead both in the good times and in the bad. There are different forms of leadership, but the most important aspect is efficient communication both within the organization and with customers and other stakeholders. Effective communication is the most important tool that every leader should have for effective leadership.[17]

Open communication promotes the sharing of information between employees and management. It helps to eliminate the barriers that may exist in other forms of communication. This open communication should also be applied when dealing with consumers. It keeps them updated on the processes within the organization and improves the trust that they have in the company. It makes customers feel that they are an important part of the organization and that the company recognizes their contribution to its success. Open communication increases loyalty and commitment to an organization, and the manager at Maple Leaf Foods used this to restore consumer confidence in their products. DuBrin[18] explained that open communication helps organizations to overcome problems and become successful. The leader of Maple Leaf Foods utilized this concept to overcome the crisis and get back to profitability. His open communication renewed the confidence consumers had in the organization and assured its trade partners of better quality products and

CRISIS MANAGEMENT:
THE ART OF SUCCESS AND FAILURE

services. The crisis at Maple Leaf Foods provides a lesson to other organizations about the importance of maintaining open communication within the organization and with consumers at all times.

Endnotes

Case Study 3: Maple Leaf Listeriosis (2008)

1 Witzel, M. (2013, April). Maple Leaf Food's response to a crisis. *Financial Times*. Retrieved from http://www.ft.com/intl/cms/s/0/8c8d3668-adb5-11e2-82b8-00144feabdc0.html#axzz3u8RDU1Xh

2 Greenberg, J., & Elliott, C. (2009). A cold cut crisis: Listeriosis, Maple Leaf Foods, and the politics of apology. *Canadian Journal of Communication, 34*(2), 189–204.

3 Greenberg, J., & Elliott, C. (2009). A cold cut crisis: Listeriosis, Maple Leaf Foods, and the politics of apology. *Canadian Journal of Communication, 34*(2), 189–204.

4 Witzel, M. (2013, April). Maple Leaf Food's response to a crisis. *Financial Times*. Retrieved from http://www.ft.com/intl/cms/s/0/8c8d3668-adb5-11e2-82b8-00144feabdc0.html#axzz3u8RDU1Xh

5 Greenberg, J., & Elliott, C. (2009). A cold cut crisis: Listeriosis, Maple Leaf Foods, and the politics of apology. *Canadian Journal of Communication, 34*(2), 189–204.

6 Greenberg, J., & Elliott, C. (2009). A cold cut crisis: Listeriosis, Maple Leaf Foods, and the politics of apology. *Canadian Journal of Communication, 34*(2), 189–204.

7 Greenberg, J., & Elliott, C. (2009). A cold cut crisis: Listeriosis, Maple Leaf Foods, and the politics of apology. *Canadian Journal of Communication, 34*(2), 189–204.

8 Greenberg, J., & Elliott, C. (2009). A cold cut crisis: Listeriosis, Maple Leaf Foods, and the politics of apology. *Canadian Journal of Communication, 34*(2), 189–204.

9 Witzel, M. (2013, April). Maple Leaf Food's response to a crisis. *Financial Times*. Retrieved from http://www.ft.com/intl/cms/s/0/8c8d3668-adb5-11e2-82b8-00144feabdc0.html#axzz3u8RDU1Xh

10 Witzel, M. (2013, April). Maple Leaf Food's response to a crisis. *Financial Times*. Retrieved from http://www.ft.com/intl/cms/s/0/8c8d3668-adb5-11e2-82b8-00144feabdc0.html#axzz3u8RDU1Xh

11 Witzel, M. (2013, April). Maple Leaf Food's response to a crisis. *Financial Times*. Retrieved from http://www.ft.com/intl/cms/s/0/8c8d3668-adb5-11e2-82b8-00144feabdc0.html#axzz3u8RDU1Xh

CRISIS MANAGEMENT:
THE ART OF SUCCESS AND FAILURE

12 Witzel, M. (2013, April). Maple Leaf Food's response to a crisis. *Financial Times*. Retrieved from http://www.ft.com/intl/cms/s/0/8c8d3668-adb5-11e2-82b8-00144feabdc0.html#axzz3u8RDU1Xh

13 Owram, K. (2009, October). Maple Leaf Foods recovers from listeria crisis. *The Star*. Retrieved from http://www.thestar.com/business/2009/10/28/maple_leaf_foods_recovers_from_listeria_crisis.html

14 Owram, K. (2009, October). Maple Leaf Foods recovers from listeria crisis. *The Star*. Retrieved from http://www.thestar.com/business/2009/10/28/maple_leaf_foods_recovers_from_listeria_crisis.html

15 Greenberg, J., & Elliott, C. (2009). A cold cut crisis: Listeriosis, Maple Leaf Foods, and the politics of apology. *Canadian Journal of Communication, 34*(2), 189–204.

16 Jaques, T. (2012). Crisis leadership: A view from the executive suite. *Journal of Public Affairs, 12*(4), 366–372.

17 DuBrin, A. (2015). *Leadership: Research findings, practice, and skills*. Boston, MA: Cengage Learning.

18 DuBrin, A. (2015). *Leadership: Research findings, practice, and skills*. Boston, MA: Cengage Learning.

The Art of Decision-Making

Decision-making is a common phenomenon in every organizational setting, as well as in politics. It is a process that pools together the efforts of all decision-making units in the organization. Usually, it is the responsibility of the top leadership or management to come up with strategies to move the organization forward. To achieve long-term objectives, decisions have to be made with a great deal of accuracy to ensure that the outcomes are in line with the set goals. Decision-making takes place for many reasons. First, it may be done when developing new strategies. The process entails giving direction when management or political leadership comes up with a new idea that may be beneficial to the team.[1] Second, decision-making may take place after assessing progress during a particular period. If it is discovered that the existing strategies are not yielding the desired results, the situation necessitates the formulation of new strategies.

A crisis refers to a difficult situation with great intensity that has a high degree of uncertainty. Usually, such a period is marked by instability because the existing strategies failed to yield the expected results. A crisis calls for immediate intervention by the top decision-making units to return the situation to normal. The decision-making

CRISIS MANAGEMENT:
THE ART OF SUCCESS AND FAILURE

should be swift and accurate to avoid further aggravating the already bad situation. It is during such periods that the qualities of good managers must manifest themselves. Junior employees usually look up to their seniors, expecting to receive guidance and direction on the way forward.

Management has to take several things into consideration. First, they have to assess the level of the crisis to determine its impact on the organization's operations and profitability. Second, they have to assess the available resources to determine whether they are sufficient to return the situation to normalcy. Resources in this context refer to both financial and human resources. A crisis situation may require the injection of extra funds to finance the recovery process. Additionally, the decision-making process in times of crisis may require the formation of a select committee comprised of individuals with the technical knowhow to solve the situation at hand. Such a committee may be constituted on the basis of work experience, education, or training.[2]

During a crisis situation in an organization or in politics, stress is a common phenomenon. Stress comes about due to pressure from different corners. It is important to note that a crisis situation in business is different from a crisis in politics in several aspects. In a business scenario, a crisis may occur when the organization takes a loss within a particular fiscal period. The crisis situation may be worse if the organization continues to take losses in more than one trading period. Such a situation is an indication that things are definitely not working out as they should. Another instance of a crisis situation in business is when there is a labor dispute. Such a situation may occur when employees are dissatisfied with their pay or the working conditions in which they operate. Such a dispute may result in a slowdown or a strike by workers if they feel that management is not doing enough to address their grievances.

In politics, a crisis usually occurs due to different opinions. The situation may be aggravated by a lack of political commitment by rival groups to drop their hardline stances and open up a dialogue with their counterparts.[3] A good example may be when the delegates of a particular political party are dissatisfied with the party's top management. Another perfect example of a crisis in politics is when the ruling party in a country faces criticism from the opposition parties. Usually, such disagreements are common when the opposition is dissatisfied with the policy decisions undertaken by the government. Failure to handle such situations with care and diligence may end up polarizing the country.

Despite the differences in the nature of crisis situations in business and politics, the approach to problem-solving in both situations is quite similar. The main objective of problem-solving in crisis management is to return the situation to normal.[4] Therefore, the decision-making groups must be aware of several things. First, they should have an idea of what the normal situation is supposed to look like. This means that they must be able to recognize that something is amiss. Problem identification helps them to be aware of what needs to be solved. Logically, it is impossible to find the solution to a problem if the problem itself is unknown. Second, the decision-making groups must have an idea of how to return the situation to normalcy. This step is usually the most important process in problem-solving, and it involves the exchange of ideas between different individuals in an effort to come up with the most viable solution. The idea that appears to be the most feasible is the one that is selected and worked on to solve the problem.

Having discussed the nature of crisis situations in business and politics, the focus now shifts to the numerous methods and tools that decision-making groups can apply in problem-solving processes. It is important to highlight that such situations have a high degree of pressure or stress. Therefore, the decisions arrived upon must be sufficient to relieve the pressure that usually builds up during a period of crisis. The first tool that is recommended to arrive at a feasible solution is brainstorming. Brainstorming is a concept that refers to the coming together of different minds. Each individual within the decision-making framework is expected to think of a way in which the problem at hand can be treated. This highlights the importance of selecting only the best minds to join the decision-making team.

After a thorough thought process, the next step is to analyze all the proposed options critically. It is important to assess what every team member has come up with. This enables an objective comparison of all ideas brought forward. The team analyzes the merits of each proposal, assessing its strengths and weaknesses. The feasibility of the suggested steps is also analyzed, with great emphasis on the probability of achieving long-term success. The cost implications of the various proposals are also put into perspective. The management team is usually keen on the most cost-effective course of action to avoid aggravating the situation further.[5] After the analysis of all the suggestions, the team picks the one that appears to meet all the desired criteria in terms of cost-effectiveness, practicability, and the probability of success in solving the crisis.

Another method for arriving at a feasible solution is by applying the divide-and-conquer technique. This technique is most applicable for very complex problems in the organization or political structure. For instance, if a business incurs a huge financial loss, it may be important to break the chain of procedures and business priorities down into separate categories, such as purchases, supplies, debtors, payments, and so on. The decision-making units then undertake a comprehensive audit trail of each line of operation in a bid to identify the loopholes that may have contributed to the heavy loss.

This technique saves a great deal of time and allows a detailed investigation to take place. It becomes easier to identify existing problems when different elements are analyzed separately. In most cases, it is difficult to find problems in all sections or lines of operation. Usually, it is the small issues in specific lines of operations that cause inefficiencies in the entire system. The divide-and-conquer technique allows the dissection of the entire system, thus making it easier to identify the underlying problems. For instance, in the case of a business taking losses, the problem may be caused by inefficiency in recording transactions. However, such a problem may be difficult to identify unless a proper breakdown of the business operations is undertaken.

During a crisis, the decision-making team can also use a means-end analysis to come up with a viable solution. However, this method requires that the team have knowledge about the desired end result. The means-end analysis entails working in steps. Those steps should either be close to the desired end result or geared toward the end result. This method has one main advantage: the decision-making department can choose to continue with a particular solution or drop it altogether, depending on how well it suits the problem-solving process.

Abstraction is another common decision-making tool used in organizational settings. Abstraction entails resolving a specific problem by relying on a theoretical model. What the decision-makers need to do is identify a suitable model that fits the problem in question. The team in charge of the problem-solving process must have the capacity to analyze a theoretical model and understand its specifications. In doing so, they will have an easier time applying the model in a real-life situation. A particular theory may appear simple and suitable on paper; however, the application process may prove to be a big headache; thus, it is important to relate the model to the problem before its application.

Decision-makers can also use an analogy tool to arrive at a viable solution. An analogy, in this case, refers to a solution that has been used previously to resolve a similar problem. For instance, if a particular solution has been used to solve an issue in the sales department, it may be logical to try to utilize the same tool for a similar problem in the purchasing department. Just like in abstraction, the only requirement is to ensure that the proposed solution is compatible with the problem at hand. Failure to do this may aggravate the problem as a result of blind duplication.

It is often said that necessity is the mother of invention. The occurrence of a particular problem may mark the advent of an entirely new solution to that kind of problem. In this regard, decision-makers are advised to try out as many possible solutions as possible. This process is called hypothesis testing. It begins by making an assumption about a particular issue. It is closely related to brainstorming because both entail thinking about random solutions in the hope of coming up with one that is most favorable. In the case of hypothesis testing, the endgame is to prove whether a proposed solution can work.

This process has several advantages over other methods. First of all, it stretches the creativity of the decision-making team. It also helps to prove why some solutions cannot work. Therefore, at the end of the process, the team will have identified the hypotheses that can work and those that cannot.[6] In the process of trying out different hypotheses, the team also gets the opportunity to identify other areas in which the rejected proposals might be applicable.

Finally, a problem can be solved using the root cause analysis method. This method entails working backward to identify the genesis of the problem. Logically, it is impossible to solve a problem that one does not understand. In this regard, the root cause analysis method provides the decision-making group with the raw facts on the cause of a particular problem. It requires an elaborate audit trail of the events that took place before the problem arose.

Once this step is complete and the genesis of the problem identified, it becomes easy to make corrections. For instance, if it is established that a problem came about due to human error, the right course of action is taken. If it was caused by a technical error, the team is able to find the right person or tool to fix it. The main advantage with the root cause analysis method is that it helps to prevent the same problem from recurring in the future.[7] Once the cause has been identified, the solution tends to seal the loopholes. Therefore, the problem becomes less likely to arise again.

In crisis situations in both business and politics, the main agenda is to restore normalcy, as a crisis normally represents a state of disequilibrium. The solutions discussed above, if applied appropriately, can go a long way in problem-solving. However, there are several qualities that crisis leaders must possess to pull their organizations out of difficult situations successfully. The first quality is critical thinking. Such individuals must possess the ability to engage their minds in top gear to come up with good solutions. For instance, brainstorming was mentioned as an important problem-solving method. It requires critical thinking to come up with workable solutions.

A crisis leader must also possess coordination. Usually, the decision-making process is handled by a team. The leader of such a team must understand the importance of team cohesion. It enables him or her to cooperate with fellow team members toward attaining the overall goal. The individual must also be goal-oriented. Being goal-oriented ensures that all activities are geared toward arriving at a feasible solution to the problem at hand. When the individual is in charge of a team, being goal-oriented enables him or her to coordinate the activities of each team member. Such a situation means that different individuals undertake different tasks. A goal-oriented leader is able to monitor everyone's activities to ensure that no one goes astray or is left behind.

Crisis managers and leaders must possess effective communication skills. In business and politics, the sharing of information is a common phenomenon, as people need to discuss various issues. However, poor communication skills can hinder the effective exchange of information. A good communicator is open, eloquent, and audible. He or she is able to articulate ideas in a precise way that his or her colleagues can understand. The irony is that one may have the best ideas and suggestions, but still fail to express them adequately due to poor communication.[8] It becomes even worse if the individual is the one in charge of the entire team. It gets difficult to give directions and coordinate the activities of the entire team because of the imminent breakdown in the chain of communication. The worst-case scenario is when the correct information is conveyed but misunderstood or misinterpreted due to poor communication skills.

As mentioned earlier, stress is a common phenomenon during a crisis. The pressure that comes along may hinder effective decision-making. In this regard, a good crisis manager must have the capacity to work under pressure. He or she should handle stress adequately. This requires that the individual be emotionally strong. Being too emotional may inhibit one's ability to remain calm and composed. The leader must have the ability to hold his or her head high and be an excellent example rather than panic during times of crisis. This is where experience comes into play. Experience is a good thing for a crisis leader because he or she may have handled similar situations in the past. Experience helps the individual to maintain his or her composure and work effectively under stress.

In conclusion, it is safe to say that crises cannot be totally avoided in either business or politics. Instead, the

CRISIS MANAGEMENT:
THE ART OF SUCCESS AND FAILURE

relevant stakeholders should be adequately prepared to handle them whenever they occur. Crisis leaders should be able to identify the viable options that can solve their problems. They should also possess the qualities of good crisis leadership to apply problem-solving successfully during the decision-making process.

Endnotes

The Art of Decision-Making

1 Witzel, M. (2013, April). Maple Leaf Food's response to a crisis. *Financial Times*. Retrieved from http://www.ft.com/intl/cms/s/0/8c8d3668-adb5-11e2-82b8-00144feabdc0.html#axzz3u8RDU1Xh

2 Greenberg, J., & Elliott, C. (2009). A cold cut crisis: Listeriosis, Maple Leaf Foods, and the politics of apology. *Canadian Journal of Communication, 34*(2), 189–204.

3 Greenberg, J., & Elliott, C. (2009). A cold cut crisis: Listeriosis, Maple Leaf Foods, and the politics of apology. *Canadian Journal of Communication, 34*(2), 189–204.

4 Witzel, M. (2013, April). Maple Leaf Food's response to a crisis. *Financial Times*. Retrieved from http://www.ft.com/intl/cms/s/0/8c8d3668-adb5-11e2-82b8-00144feabdc0.html#axzz3u8RDU1Xh

5 Greenberg, J., & Elliott, C. (2009). A cold cut crisis: Listeriosis, Maple Leaf Foods, and the politics of apology. *Canadian Journal of Communication, 34*(2), 189–204.

6 Greenberg, J., & Elliott, C. (2009). A cold cut crisis: Listeriosis, Maple Leaf Foods, and the politics of apology. *Canadian Journal of Communication, 34*(2), 189–204.

7 Greenberg, J., & Elliott, C. (2009). A cold cut crisis: Listeriosis, Maple Leaf Foods, and the politics of apology. *Canadian Journal of Communication, 34*(2), 189–204.

8 Greenberg, J., & Elliott, C. (2009). A cold cut crisis: Listeriosis, Maple Leaf Foods, and the politics of apology. *Canadian Journal of Communication, 34*(2), 189–204.

9 Witzel, M. (2013, April). Maple Leaf Food's response to a crisis. *Financial Times*. Retrieved from http://www.ft.com/intl/cms/s/0/8c8d3668-adb5-11e2-82b8-00144feabdc0.html#axzz3u8RDU1Xh

10 Witzel, M. (2013, April). Maple Leaf Food's response to a crisis. *Financial Times*. Retrieved from http://www.ft.com/intl/cms/s/0/8c8d3668-adb5-11e2-82b8-00144feabdc0.html#axzz3u8RDU1Xh

11 Witzel, M. (2013, April). Maple Leaf Food's response to a crisis. *Financial Times*. Retrieved from http://www.ft.com/intl/cms/s/0/8c8d3668-adb5-11e2-82b8-00144feabdc0.html#axzz3u8RDU1Xh

12 Witzel, M. (2013, April). Maple Leaf Food's response to a crisis. *Financial Times*. Retrieved from http://www.ft.com/intl/cms/s/0/8c8d3668-adb5-11e2-82b8-00144feabdc0.html#axzz3u8RDU1Xh

13 Owram, K. (2009, October). Maple Leaf Foods recovers from listeria crisis. *The Star*. Retrieved from http://www.thestar.com/business/2009/10/28/maple_leaf_foods_recovers_from_listeria_crisis.html

14 Owram, K. (2009, October). Maple Leaf Foods recovers from listeria crisis. *The Star*. Retrieved from http://www.thestar.com/business/2009/10/28/maple_leaf_foods_recovers_from_listeria_crisis.html

15 Greenberg, J., & Elliott, C. (2009). A cold cut crisis: Listeriosis, Maple Leaf Foods, and the politics of apology. *Canadian Journal of Communication, 34*(2), 189–204.

16 Jaques, T. (2012). Crisis leadership: A view from the executive suite. *Journal of Public Affairs, 12*(4), 366–372.

17 DuBrin, A. (2015). *Leadership: Research findings, practice, and skills*. Boston, MA: Cengage Learning.

18 DuBrin, A. (2015). *Leadership: Research findings, practice, and skills*. Boston, MA: Cengage Learning.

Case Study 4: Susan G. Komen for the Cure (2012)

Crisis Timeline

On January 31, 2012, Planned Parenthood announced that the Susan G. Komen for the Cure Foundation had withdrawn funding to the organization, worth $680,000, for breast screenings and educational programs.[1] The decision was seen by many as an attempt by the charity group to make a statement against legal abortion, as Planned Parenthood is known as the nation's largest abortion services provider, among other sexual health-related services. Therefore, the decision created a lot of controversy and caused reactions from stakeholders and the public. Many were infuriated by this decision, leading to demonstrations, boycotts from partners, and criticism from all corners. This announcement also came at the height of the political season, when one of the hotly debated issues was abortion, which contributed to the full-blown nature of the crisis. The decision looked like a politically inspired decision, which was not appropriate for an organization such as this. The reason for the decision, they claimed, was Congressional scrutiny into whether Planned Parenthood used federal funds to pay for abortions.[2]

A day after the announcement by Planned Parenthood, Susan G. Komen issued a statement in response that contained vague comments and did not address the issue.

Social media posts in reference to the matter were also unclear and asked the public to help the company "move past the issue," which most people were not willing to do. Four days after the announcement by Planned Parenthood, Susan G. Komen reversed its decision to cut funding. However, the masses did not buy into this change of mind, and the crisis escalated, hurting the organization even more.

What Fueled the Crisis

The crisis was caused primarily by the way Susan G. Komen handled the matter, in addition to the timing of the announcement. The first mistake the organization made was letting Planned Parenthood break the news to the public. This was not only reckless and endangered its reputation, but it was also an error in their communication strategy. This act portrayed the organization in a negative light, sparking speculation that the decision was fueled by political interests.[3] In addition, it would have been aware that the arguments surrounding Planned Parenthood, both positive and negative, would blow the controversy out of proportion. If the organization had made the announcement itself and provided valid, factual, and substantial reasons to the public, Susan G. Komen could have shaped the media storyline and the public's perception. This, many experts believe, would have caused a minor controversy and eliminated the risk of a crisis.

The lack of communication also added fire to the crisis. Susan G. Komen did not respond immediately to the statement issued by Planned Parenthood to make matters clear to the public or defend their decision. It waited for a day, and the response was vague and failed to acknowledge and address the fundamental concerns of all the parties and audiences involved.[4] This left the public and the stakeholders with more questions and made them feel as if the organization was out of touch with them. The responses from the company took on a defensive tone, as opposed to an explanation of their reasons for their decision. Also, the company lacked remorse in its communications. Further, there was no constructive communication with its major affiliates, which revealed that the organization was not prepared to handle the situation well.[5] The social media posts and responses also added more fire to the crisis, and it was best for Susan G. Komen to keep quiet about certain issues and let the fire die down. Claims that the organization sought a quiet settlement with Planned Parenthood further revealed that the group could have found a better communication strategy for letting the public know.

The way the two organizations handled the media coverage of the events also determined the course of the crisis. Planned Parenthood seemed more mature and consistent in their mass and social media posts before, during, and after the crisis. Susan G. Komen, on the other hand, made a mistake in taking the war to social media and responding to social media posts in defense of their positions at the height of the crisis. The media perception of Susan G. Komen was negative due to the way it handled things. It would have been more appropriate for its representatives to keep their social media posts consistent while defending themselves online.[6]

Furthermore, the institution provided conflicting reasons for their decision. This can be attributed directly to the lack of communication between the stakeholders. For instance, board member John D. Raffaelli issued a statement to a popular newspaper stating that the changes to the Komen policy were meant to end their relationship with Planned Parenthood, while the founder and spokeswoman of Komen, Nancy G. Brinker, offered a contradictory statement.[7]

The Timing

The timing was inappropriate, as it was during the political season, and abortion was a main issue of debate. The decision was interpreted as political.[8] Komen could have waited for a politically neutral period to make this decision. In addition, it could have been ready with a response to the announcement to be made as quickly as possible. The company's responses revealed unpreparedness, especially given that the decision was made a month prior to the announcement. The statement could have been more comprehensive, including an explanation of where the money allocated to Planned Parenthood was being redirected to cover the same services.[9]

The Aftermath

In the aftermath of this crisis, senior vice president Karen Handel resigned seven days after the announcement. On the same day, Nancy G. Brinker issued a statement to the public taking responsibility for mishandling the situation with Planned Parenthood. She and the president stepped down a few days later. The reputation of the organization was damaged severely. The organization also lost staff members, volunteers, and financial support.[10]

Recovery from the Crisis

The primary task Komen faced was rebuilding their reputation and having the public and major stakeholders trust them again. The first step was reversing the decision to fund

Planned Parenthood. This proved to the public that the decision was indeed not politically motivated. The organization also used personal stories to revive support by reminding people that it is saving lives. Komen shifted their communication strategies, adopting a new open conversation approach and more interaction with the public through social media.[11] Moreover, it depoliticized its actions and the organization in general by issuing a statement to clear things up, focusing on the mission, and even eliminating stakeholders directly involved in the decision, such as the founder and then-CEO Nancy G. Brinker.[12] This was an effective rebuilding strategy.

Endnotes

Case Study 4: Susan G. Komen for the Cure (2012)

1 Associated Press. (2012, January). *Cancer charity halts grants to Planned Parenthood*. Retrieved December 14, 2015, from http://www.foxnews.com/us/2012/01/31/cancer-charity-halts-grants-to-planned-parenthood-1227146736/

2 Wallis, D. (2012, November). *Komen Foundation struggles to regain wide support*. Retrieved December 14, 2015, from http://www.nytimes.com/2012/11/09/giving/komen-foundation-works-to-regain-support-after-planned-parenthood-controversy.html?_r=0

3 Ruse, A. (2013, June). *What really happened at the Komen Foundation*. Retrieved December 14, 2015, from http://www.crisismagazine.com/2013/what-really-happened-at-the-komen-foundation

4 Sun, L. K. (2012, February). *Susan G. Komen foundation takes steps to rebuild trust after PR fiasco*. Retrieved December 14, 2015, from https://www.washingtonpost.com/national/health-science/2012/02/04/gIQAdljRqQ_story.html

5 Ponder, M. (2013). *Susan G. Komen and the national women's healthcare debate: A crisis communication case study*. Atlanta, GA: National Conference on Health Communication, Marketing and Media.

6 Ponder, M. (2013). *Susan G. Komen and the national women's healthcare debate: A crisis communication case study*. Atlanta, GA: National Conference on Health Communication, Marketing and Media.

7 Sun, L. K. (2012, February). *Susan G. Komen foundation takes steps to rebuild trust after PR fiasco*. Retrieved December 14, 2015, from https://www.washingtonpost.com/national/health-science/2012/02/04/gIQAdljRqQ_story.html

8 Wallis, D. (2012, November). *Komen Foundation struggles to regain wide support*. Retrieved December 14, 2015, from http://www.nytimes.com/2012/11/09/giving/komen-foundation-works-to-regain-support-after-planned-parenthood-controversy.html?_r=0

9 Waters, R. (2014). *Public relations in the nonprofit sector: Theory and practice*. New York, NY: Routledge.

10 Watt, S. (2012). A postfeminist apologia: Susan G. Komen for the Cure's evolving response to the Planned Parenthood controversy. *Journal of Contemporary Rhetoric, 2(3)*, 65–79.

11 Watt, S. (2012). A postfeminist apologia: Susan G. Komen for the Cure's evolving response to the Planned Parenthood controversy. *Journal of Contemporary Rhetoric, 2(3),* 65–79.

12 Wallis, D. (2012, November). *Komen Foundation struggles to regain wide support.* Retrieved December 14, 2015, from http://www.nytimes.com/2012/11/09/giving/komen-foundation-works-to-regain-support-after-planned-parenthood-controversy.html?_r=0

Case Study 5: Lego and Shell vs. Greenpeace

Dating back to the 1960s, Lego and Shell were involved in a chain of co-branding marketing partnerships. Children across the globe enjoyed playing with Shell-branded Lego toys. However, after tremendous pressure from the Greenpeace campaign over Lego's long-standing advertising contract with Shell, Lego succumbed and ended the partnership, which dated back more than 50 years. Initially, the toy-producing company repelled the pressure and negative publicity from Greenpeace, implying that the Greenpeace campaign used the Lego brand and trademark to target the oil-producing Shell directly. Even after indicating that Lego would not be renewing the promotional contract, Lego CEO Jorgen Vig Knudstorp insisted that he did not appreciate Greenpeace's methods. Instead, he felt that Greenpeace should have made direct contact with Shell and that every stakeholder, customer, and anyone who enjoys Lego's products should not have been forced to be a part of Greenpeace's disagreement with Shell.[1]

Greenpeace is a globally recognized activist group that emerged to develop activities, strategies, and mechanisms to prevent climate change and ensure that the Arctic is in good health. Since its inception, it has garnered massive support and has great social resources that aid its causes.

CRISIS MANAGEMENT:
THE ART OF SUCCESS AND FAILURE

Given its massive support, when it targets a company, the company's management has to decide how much time to spend fighting it or to give in to the demands. In this case, it is not logical to criticize Lego for its surrender. After all, the Greenpeace campaign caught Lego off guard in that they had no time to develop strategies to counter or handle the situation. The intense media attention, the sheer immensity of the numbers of people supporting the campaign, and the increasing pressure forced Lego to surrender and disengage from the partnership. Even though there were no indications of decreased profits, sales, or share prices due to the negative attention, the campaign influenced many people, leading them to express dissatisfaction with Lego. Thus, Lego had no option other than to surrender.

Greenpeace applied a form of ambush marketing. Ambush marketing is a strategy that polarizes people with the aim of developing critical reasoning and thinking in determining which side to support. In one way, it is a humorous and clever method of creating awareness, but it often uses nontraditional media channels. In another way, it is destructive and can be described as akin to theft. Like that applied by Greenpeace, an ambush marketing campaign is enacted by a rival toward the official sponsor in an attempt to create divided attention and recognition of the other brand and to seek profit or money, Greenpeace's campaign was meant to achieve recognition of what they felt were Shell's destructive strategies and trading mechanisms in the Arctic. The direct assault on Shell's business marketing operations was a calculated move to inflict maximum damage and embarrassment.[2]

According to Pritchard,[3] Greenpeace developed a

campaign aimed at countering Shell's drilling activities by following the essence of Jay Conrad Levinson's[4] seminal work on "guerrilla marketing," which applies military-like tactics, such as sabotage, ambushes, elements of surprise, and raids, to launch imaginative, high-energy ambushes that have the ability to spread virally across traditional and social media. In fact, Greenpeace's video, *LEGO: Everything is NOT Awesome*, which was used to criticize Lego's collaboration with Shell, is the most viral in the organization's history. As of December 20, 2015, the video had 7,563,626 views on YouTube, and on Facebook, it had more than 24,215 likes and had been shared more than 99,947 times. On YouTube, the video is accompanied by text that acknowledges a love for Lego, encouraging people to act in a manner that will stop the collaboration between the company and Shell. According to Greenpeace,

> We love LEGO. You love LEGO. Everyone loves LEGO. But when LEGO's halo effect is being used to sell propaganda to children, especially by an unethical corporation who is busy destroying the natural world our children will inherit, we have to do something. Children's imaginations are an unspoilt wilderness. Help us stop Shell from polluting them by telling LEGO to stop selling Shell-branded bricks and kits today.

With the video, Greenpeace quickly mobilized multitudes through online activism. The Internet has changed numerous aspects of life, including our ways of conducting business and public awareness activities. The Internet has been used to create a network of supporters and followers.

CRISIS MANAGEMENT:
THE ART OF SUCCESS AND FAILURE

It is easy to accumulate support and force the breakdown of relationships and partnerships between companies and organizations, as happened between Shell and Lego. Given the support that Greenpeace received from the world population, Lego probably acted to dismiss its partnership with the oil company to protect its public image, while ensuring that it did not lose its customers and esteemed followers.

It is easy to demonize oil-producing companies, but demanding disengagement is simplistic. Arguably, the move that Greenpeace made was hypocritical because it is not easy to live in current times without the supply of energy that is provided by Shell and other oil-producing companies. Perhaps, the best method of ensuring that climate change and ruining the Arctic are prevented would be in having an intelligent and balanced debate with Shell with the aim of critiquing the bad things that they are involved in and embracing the good. Shell managers and other oil-producing companies' executives are aware that climate change is real, that it is facilitated by people, and that it is has the potential to cause numerous disastrous events. Unlike activists, engineers and scientists have the potential to develop substitutes for fossil fuels and change Shell from an oil company into a green energy-producing company.

Endnotes

Case Study 5: Lego and Shell vs. Greenpeace

1 Reestorff, C. M. (2015). "LEGO: Everything is not awesome!" A conversation about mediatized activism, Greenpeace, Lego, and Shell. *Conjunctions. Transdisciplinary Journal of Cultural Participation*, 2(1), 21–43.

2 Pritchard, C. (2015). Can the ambush of Greenpeace be seen as a method of ambush marketing, and if so, what (if any) effect did it have? *Laws of the Game*, 1(1), 5.

3 Pritchard, C. (2015). Can the ambush of Greenpeace be seen as a method of ambush marketing, and if so, what (if any) effect did it have? *Laws of the Game*, 1(1), 5.

4 Greenpeace. (2014). *LEGO: Everything is NOT awesome*. Retrieved from https://www.youtube.com/watch?v=qhbliUq0_r4

Preparation and Predictability

Crisis preparedness is a crucial phase of crisis management. In this stage, organizations, governments, and individuals develop plans for saving lives, as well as for minimizing damage. According to Barton,[1] crisis preparedness is a progressive cycle dealing with planning, organizing, equipping, training, exercising, improving, and assessing activities. The primary role of preparedness is to guarantee the efficacious coordination and improvement of organizational capabilities to effectually respond to and recover from the impacts of a crisis or a disaster. Generally, preparedness measures are geared toward soliciting ways to improve crisis response operations, not only through positioning, but also through provisioning inventories to be used purposefully for emergency use, as well as training a number of organizational personnel on how to deal with a crisis. A well-developed crisis management plan created to guide crisis response during the preparedness phase facilitates efficient coordination.

As opined by Hagar,[2] preparedness actions play a crucial role in crisis management because they regularly serve to develop response capabilities required in the event that a crisis emerges. Crisis preparedness is significant in reducing the crisis damages. There are three critical dangers that crises are likely to bring and which justify the need to come up with a robust crisis preparedness plan: loss of reputation and financial costs. Many economists believe that since economic crises can cause temporal or permanent unemployment, there is a need to come up with a comprehensive crisis management plan to reverse any adverse social consequences.[3]

Crises can also have a tremendous impact on the profitability and productivity of business organizations. When a crisis strikes, it can have a relentless impact on the physical, financial, and emotional structures of the company. For example, environmental pollution, industrial accidents, occupational diseases, and product defects visit somber damage on employees, the community, and consumers. For an organization, crises can significantly dent its corporate image among the public, leading to a loss of customer loyalty, which indirectly impacts profitability.[4]

Paraskevas[5] contended that the damage a business experiences during a severe crisis is largely dependent on the nature of the crisis preparation phase, as well as the efficiency of the organization's response to the crisis. It is imperative to make use of a highly proactive strategy during crisis management to come up with a robust method of crisis management, further justifying the need for a crisis management plan. Zaremba[6] asserted that crises in organizations are inevitable. This implies that they must develop a potent crisis preparedness plan for overcoming crises. In this regard, crisis preparation is critical when it comes to building a system that ensures an effectual crisis management plan.

CRISIS PREPAREDNESS CONTINUED

According to Tanase,[7] a crisis results from environmental threats, augmented by organizational weaknesses. Seeger,[8] on the other hand, described a crisis as an unexpected, specific, and non-routine event creating a higher level of uncertainty in the organization, hence threatening the realization of organizational goals and objectives. An organizational crisis is very ambiguous, further necessitating a judgment or decision that culminates in a change for better or for worse. In the context of business, a crisis encompasses negative and positive results, hence the need to deal with it effectively to enable the organization to realize its set business objectives.

Crisis preparedness is made up of activities used by a company for the purposes of avoiding or preventing a crisis, as well as its respective results. A company can best overcome or prevent a crisis through proactive determination of the factors that might cause a crisis, as well as installing protective warning systems to avoid the adverse effects normally associated with a crisis.[9] The study conducted by Weick and Sutcliffe[10] ascertained that the companies that embrace crisis management systems are always more prestigious, financially better, and more likely to survive for longer than those that do not embrace crisis management systems. Researchers have also stressed the significance of learning in crisis management. Companies that have experienced a crisis become excellent at enhancing the crisis preparation phase, besides creating competitive power in the long run.

COMPREHENSIVE PREPAREDNESS PLANNING

Crisis preparedness planning is a crucial part of the crisis management planning that organizations are expected to follow to the letter. The fundamental role of crisis planning preparation is to strengthen the ability of the community or a business organization to curb incidents where it is deemed possible, as well as manage crises where necessary. In a nutshell, preparedness planning is all about developing programs or mechanisms that make an organization highly resilient to crisis. There are pertinent areas of crisis management planning that must be effectively addressed if this phase is to be effectual. These areas include program management, prevention, planning assumptions, training, exercises, crisis evaluations, and crisis management plans. These components of crisis preparedness planning are shown in the figure below.[11]

Figure 1: Crisis preparedness planning

Source: *Stein and Rawles (2011)*[1]

PROGRAM MANAGEMENT

Program management is an extremely critical element of crisis preparedness because it ensures that the organization is capable of performing vital functions under normal circumstances by developing techniques for crisis management. Program management stresses the significance of management, ensuring that any uncertain event that can thwart the operation of the company is dealt with effectively. Therefore, management must ensure that the management process is robust and that flexible systems are developed that can be used to deal with the crisis effectively. The principles guiding the active engagement of management in disaster preparedness planning are similar to the other areas of responsibility, where managers are expected to implement techniques to ensure that the objectives of the organizations are fully realized. Therefore, just like in the other management duties, the organizational manager has the prime responsibility of ensuring that the overall priorities are set, objectives are determined, resources are allotted, and follow-up planning takes place to effectively deal with a crisis.[13]

There are two documents that the manager, together with preparedness planners, ought to produce to lay down the rules of dealing with a crisis whenever it happens. These documents include a detailed preparedness program and an overall preparedness policy. Before developing the two documents, it is imperative that the organization explores the status of the existing planning to ensure that efforts are specifically concentrated on important areas.[14] The primary aim of the policy is to ascertain the framework to be used by the organization for the purposes of crisis preparedness. Some of the aspects addressed in the policy document include a summary of the preparedness responsibility to be conducted by the organization, the formal requirements, the objectives of emergency preparedness, and an overall disaster prioritization, among others. The fundamental purpose of a disaster preparedness program is to widen the preparedness policy to translate management's priorities into concrete activities.[15]

Resource Prioritization

Resource prioritization is an essential part of an organization's management; it ensures apposite allocation and the use of resources that have been devoted to disaster preparedness and response.[16] Admittedly, preparedness planning is an activity that calls for resources if it is to be efficacious. Ritchie[17] highlighted that requirements for personnel, equipment, systems, and facilities are inevitable. In respect to this, it is indispensable that managers make decisions about aspects like development, procurement, composition, maintenance, and geographical distribution.

Follow-Up

Follow-up is another crucial element of crisis management that managers must conduct. Follow-up ensures that the objectives of the preparedness planning live up to the requirements, set objectives, and agreements determined in the organization's preparedness program and policy. To ensure that apposite disaster preparedness follow-up is properly instituted, management must ensure the availability of the individuals that will be involved in the follow-up activities, identify the activities that ought to be supervised closely, and determine how the varied forms of follow-up ought to be conducted.[18]

Planning Assumptions

Just like management programs, planning assumptions are highly imperative in crisis preparedness. Making planning assumptions about crises helps different organizations to arrive at a resonant knowledge base that can eventually be used in the development of elaborate preparedness planning. Some of the factors to consider in making planning assumptions include determining organizational functions that are deemed highly important, ascertaining the types of threats that constitute the biggest risks, and specifying which threats are relevant to the organization. The following are some of the areas worth addressing while making planning assumptions.

Mapping Critical Functions

Mapping critical functions enables organizations to prioritize pertinent areas in their attempt to implement preparedness activities. Mapping these functions ensures that an organization acknowledges the types of goods, activities, and services that it must maintain to avoid massive losses in the event that a crisis strikes the organization. It is important that the organization map its insecure areas to protect them and avoid experiencing losses.[19]

Threat Identification and Monitoring

Jennex[20] posited that threat identification and monitoring is an important area of crisis management and preparedness. It is imperative that the organization keep up-to-date regarding the spectrum of threats that can impact its vital functions; the identification of new threats, coupled with laying down efficacious mechanisms for monitoring threats, is very useful in crisis preparedness. In particular, identification and monitoring threats call for the organization to gather reliable and valid information relating to threat prevention.

Vulnerability and Risk Analysis

Vulnerability and risk analysis is likewise significant in crises preparedness. Organizations that are serious about protecting themselves against threats must be able to effectively conduct risk and vulnerability analyses to ascertain the threats that pose a risk to the organization in question. The primary purpose of this type of analysis, according to Ayyub,[21] is to develop an overview about those threats that are riskier to the organization's success. Excellent risk and vulnerability analysis forms the foundation for suggesting measures and countermeasures for threat mitigation. When vulnerability and risk analysis is done on a regular basis, it will help in the mitigation of risks before they become harmful to the organization. There are different methods that an organization may employ while conducting risk and vulnerability analysis. For instance, the Danish Emergency Management Agency's model is an effectual framework that an organization may employ while conducting risk and vulnerability analysis. This model consists of four implements that an organization can adopt in the management of crises. The model can be used in either individual or sector-specific organizations.

PREVENTION

No one can deny the role played by prevention in promoting crisis preparedness. Regester and Larkin[22] highlighted the significance of the effectual implementation of preventive initiatives in protecting an organization from crises. The fundamental objective of crisis prevention is to absolutely avoid or reduce the occurrence of a crisis in the organization. Additionally, crisis prevention may be geared toward reducing consequences to manageable levels, where they can be handled effectively using normal operating procedures. Crisis prevention is extremely pertinent to all facets of society and plays a crucial role in crisis prevention.

Therefore, crisis prevention is pertinent to areas such as construction work, town planning, information security, handling hazardous substances, traffic safety, and fostering health and safety in workplaces. Preparedness planning in the context of crisis prevention ought to be conducted through what is known as the risk-based approach, in which the tolerance of the organization to varied incidents sheds light on the initiatives it employs in crisis management. While making decisions in regards to disaster prevention, the organization should consider the incidents that it intends to prevent, how prevention can be incorporated into its planning process, and how such incidences can be prevented.

Before making decisions on which risks to prevent, it is critical to determine the degree of risk severity, as well as to develop a risk matrix showing the degree of the severity of such risks, as shown in Figure 2. The risk matrix determines the types of threats that are unacceptable, as determined by the risk probability, as well as the possible risk consequences based on the risk incident. While choosing risks that are unacceptable for the organization, the focus must be fundamentally directed to those that are potentially dangerous or serious. A significant number of organizations live with many risks, yet they are able to reduce them easily. Figure 2 represents a risk matrix that an organization may use.[23]

Figure 2: Organizational risk matrix

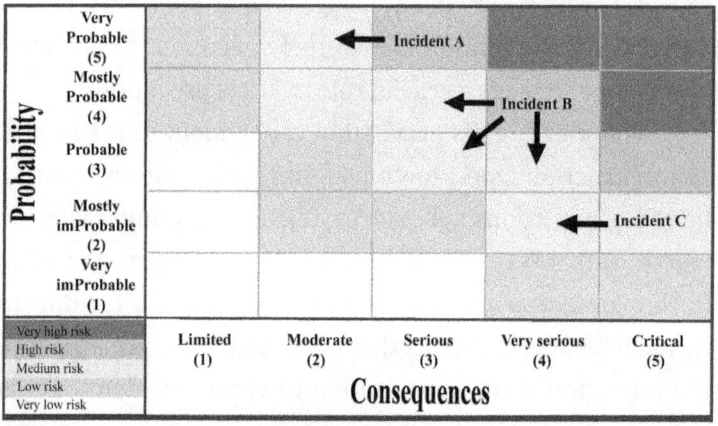

Probability		Limited (1)	Moderate (2)	Serious (3)	Very serious (4)	Critical (5)
Very Probable (5)					Incident A ←	
Mostly Probable (4)					Incident B ←	
Probable (3)					↓	
Mostly imProbable (2)						
Very imProbable (1)						Incident C ←
				Consequences		

Legend: Very high risk / High risk / Medium risk / Low risk / Very low risk

Source: *Regester and Larkin (2005)*[24]

Methods of Preventing Crisis Incidents

Some of the methods that can be used in risk prevention can be divided into physical measures and measures that influence individual behaviors. The physical measures are directed toward making physical components, such as systems, facilities, and equipment, more resilient. Physical prevention measures are solely directed toward the prevention of certain types of incidents, such as fire doors and smoke detectors. Risk prevention by physical measures is regulated by directives, legislation, and technical codes. To ensure lucid crisis management between different organizational units, there is a need to ensure that the organizational departments and the government work collaboratively.[25]

Besides the physical measures that are regularly put in place, crisis management and preparedness can also be done through influencing behavior. Behavior prevention is directed toward building, maintaining, and altering individual attitudes and behaviors. The major aim of influencing individual behavior is to strengthen the individual's ability to react appositely or prevent undesired incidents. In this case, the targeted group may include external partners, employees, customers, clients, and the general public. In circumstances where organizational employees are the targeted group, training becomes imperative. Through training, employees are equipped with the required skills and knowledge for disaster prevention.

There are a number of issues that the organization ought to consider before deciding on the type of crisis management technique to be used; organizations must ensure that they only implement programs that are highly efficacious when it comes to crisis management. Another important factor is the cost. Admittedly, installing physical techniques is more costly than influencing behavior. Therefore, in situations where cost is the overriding factor, organizations should consider influencing employee behavior toward crisis management because it is considered more cost-effective than the other methods.[26]

Integration of Prevention in the Planning Process

Prevention is extremely critical since it can drastically lessen the cost involved in the operational response to a crisis. In this regard, it is important that crisis prevention be made part and parcel of the disaster management and preparedness planning process. A mobile power generator may be used to prevent risks that might result from a power outage. In some organizations, power disruptions can lead to significant losses in terms of organizational productivity. The following procedure may be used in disaster prevention.

Figure 3: Disaster Anticipation and Prevention Process.

TRAINING

The success of an organization's disaster preparedness planning is highly dependent on the expertise and skills of the individuals tasked with implementing the crisis preparedness programs. Before deciding on how to train employees, it is important that the organization's management explores the competencies required to facilitate crisis preparedness planning, as well as crisis management. This encompasses considerations regarding whether the individuals with such competencies ought to be employed directly by the organization of if they can come from outside. To equip organizational employees with the skills and knowledge necessary to effectively respond to an organizational crisis, there is a need for management to come up with a highly efficacious training program containing a catalog of training activities. Devlin[27] emphasized the significance of equipping all employees involved with solid knowledge concerning organizational preparedness programs, preparedness policies, and the general organizational crisis management plan. In this regard, emphasis should be placed on employees' awareness in respect to their unit's crisis management plan.

While making decisions on the types of people to offer training to, it is imperative to consider the following classes of people: the operative employees who are always tasked with providing solutions to certain operational tasks during crises; the crisis managers who hold the overall responsibility of ensuring efficacious organizational crisis management; the staff participants; and the chiefs of staff at the company's regional, local, and national levels. Other people include employees in support functions, including secretarial staff, IT support, and cafeteria staff, as well as communication specialists who must communicate with the general public and the media during a crisis. These people play pivotal roles in crisis management and, therefore, ought to be equipped with the relevant knowledge and skills on how to deal with a crisis whenever it strikes.

In a nutshell, training employees on how to respond to a crisis is important for both the employees and the organization at large. By training employees on how to deal with a crisis, an organization nurtures a pool of employees with the relevant knowledge and skills on how to deal with a crisis in the best way possible, reducing the likely impacts of a crisis. The organization may be able to expand the number of employees with competencies in preparedness by engaging many people in the work to help in making the crisis management plans up-to-date by fostering apprenticeships among novice workers and the veterans who are able to replace one another in the event of an incident.

EXERCISES

This is another important step in crisis management preparedness planning. During emergency preparedness, many questions are raised regarding what an organization ought to do. Devlin[28] opined that the content of exercises ought to be arranged in a manner that relates to the organization's objectives, emergency preparedness responsibilities, and the particular threat scenario that the organization expects to come across. An exercise may focus on the organization's handling of certain activities.

An exercise may be conducted to unearth what works well in the management of a crisis and hence ought to be maintained, as well as what does not work well and therefore ought to be changed. Basically, an exercise is specially designed to reinforce the organization's aptitude to deal with a crisis. The organization can also make use of exercises to enhance preparedness by testing new procedures and techniques in a controlled environment. In circumstances in which an organization conducts training in areas where it is performing extremely well, the probability that the exercise will become a showcase is relatively high. This exercise might also be characterized by limited benefits in favor of new knowledge gained.[29]

Just like training, exercises should encompass individuals and organizational units that regularly conduct crisis management, as well as operational responses during real crisis incidents. The people who participate in crisis management may be members of different departments within the organization, including IT departments, communication departments, and selected staff members, together with other support positions. Participating in a crisis preparedness planning exercise is solely geared toward strengthening their ability to deal with a crisis in the best way possible. Therefore, exercises are an important component of a crisis preparedness plan, which all organizations willing to remain competitive and achieve long-term success must implement.[30]

EVALUATION

The term *emergency preparedness evaluation* refers to a systematic assessment of the conduct of an organization during a crisis with precise targeted data collection, a formulated purpose, independent assessment, and finally, a focused analysis regarding how said organization responded to the crisis. Evaluating performance during crisis management enables an organization or a community to determine their areas of strengths and weaknesses as far as crisis management and preparedness are concerned.[31]

Evaluation is fundamentally aimed at determining what worked well during crisis management and therefore ought to be maintained and what did not work well and therefore requires improvement. According to Coombs,[32] the assessment of organizational behavior during an extraordinary crisis can be very useful because it provides knowledge and experience that can be used to modify the existing crisis preparedness mechanisms, which will boost the organization's resiliency against crisis or disaster even further.

CRISIS MANAGEMENT PLAN

The 21st century has been characterized by many uncertainties. Hence, organizations willing to survive and gain a greater competitive advantage must be able to develop a comprehensive crisis management plan. Developing a comprehensive crisis management plan helps the organization deal with any form of crisis so that the goals and objectives of the organization are not affected, even in the event of a crisis. According to Reid,[33] the fundamental purpose of a crisis management plan is to provide a protocol or system of dealing with a crisis whenever an organization is bombarded with crises. Therefore, the crisis management plan describes how crisis management ought to be conducted, as well as how emergency preparedness capabilities ought to be prioritized in circumstances where ordinary routines and resources are not adequate.

For the organization's crisis management plan to be effectual, it is prudent that it satisfy the following criterion: the action-oriented plan must have or demonstrate precise guidelines showing how the organization anticipates managing extraordinary crises. It clearly sets out the roles and responsibilities of each individual during crisis management. For instance, it stresses who does what and when and how it is to be done. Another crucial feature of a good crisis management plan is comprehensibility.

Reid[34] opined that crisis management plans ought to be as comprehensible as possible, and that the content of the plan ought to be arranged logically and systematically, as well as written in plain language for ease of understanding. Other critical features of a crisis management plan include being up-to-date, accessible, mandated by legislation, understandable, and realistic. In respect to what has been documented in this section, it is clear that an organization willing to achieve its goals and objectives must be ready to develop a comprehensive crisis management plan to protect itself against uncertainties that regularly affect business organizations.

THE ROLE OF TECHNOLOGY IN DISASTER PREPAREDNESS AND RESPONSE

The role of technology in disaster preparedness and response is increasingly gaining prominence. According to Palen and Liu,[35] information and communication technology are increasingly revolutionizing the world of crisis preparedness and response. Social media technologies have not been left behind; many studies have shown that social media tools have progressively become integral tools for managing a crisis, Palen and Liu have asserted that social media platforms have significantly altered the sphere of crisis management. With the software tools currently available, including news aggregators, online discussion platforms, and other forms of social media, organizations are now able to disseminate, acquire, and analyze information in the most effective and comprehensive manner more than ever before.

Despite the significance of social media in helping organizations to keep crises from spiraling out of control, organizations have been warned that they should not take these technologies for granted since they are also able to intensify crises with equal measure. Therefore, even as organizations employ these technologies as tools for preventing the spread of a crisis, they should use caution, as such tools can also intensify crises.

OTHER TECHNOLOGICAL TOOLS CURRENTLY USED IN DISASTER PREPAREDNESS

Remote sensing is another technological tool that is presently used in disaster preparedness. The sensors create networks, which are used in a number of ways during disaster preparedness, including providing data used in weather prediction and mitigating the likely impact of a disaster or crisis based on weather predictions as well as on earthquake detection. Earthquakes are not only known for damaging property, but can also lead to the loss of a productive employer. Therefore, the use of sensors enables an organization to mitigate the likely impact of natural disasters. Sensors are also widely used in the control or prevention of human-made crises. Doppler radar is an effective technological tool currently used by different organizations to guide the identification of tornados, hurricanes, and other weather phenomena that are capable of causing damage. Structural motion detectors provide pertinent information regarding the nature and severity of earthquakes. Satellite imagery is another significant technological tool used in disaster management and planning. Satellite imagery facilitates the mapping and planning of operations in critical wildland fires. Tsunami detectors, which are another tool used in disaster prevention and planning, provide an advanced warning system that warns people about the location and the nature of a predicted tsunami. These are some of the warning systems that are widely used in organizations as preparedness tools for managing a crisis.

Endnotes

Preparation and Predictability

1 Barton, M. J. (2013). *Crisis preparedness for professionals.* U.S.A.: Independent Publisher.

2 Hagar, C. (2012). *Crisis information management: Communication and technologies.* Oxford, UK: Chandos Pub.

3 Kumpikaite, V., Grybauskas, A., Juodelis, M., & Strumyla, D. (2011). Companies' management during economic crisis. *Economics and Management, 16,* 789–795.

4 Kuzgun, I. A. (2010). The temporary lay-off as an instrument in crisis management: Case of Turkey. *International Journal of Emerging and Transition Economies, 3*(2), 195–207.

5 Paraskevas, A. (2006), Crisis management or crisis response system? A complexity science approach to organizational crises. *Management Decision, 44*(7), 892–907.

6 Zaremba, A. J. (2014). *Crisis Communication: Theory and Practice.* Hoboken: Taylor and Francis.

7 Tanase, D. (2012). Procedural and systematic crisis approach and crisis management. *Theoretical and Applied Economics, 5*(5), 177.

8 Seeger, M. W., & Ulmer, R.R. (2001). Virtuous responses to organizational responses to organizational crisis: Aaron Feuestein and Milt Cole. *Journal of Business Ethics, 31,* 369–376.

9 Kovoor-Mısra, S., Zammuta, Raymond F., & Mitroff, Ian I. (2000). Crisis preparation in organizations: Prescription versus reality. *Technological Forecasting and Social Change, 63,* 43–62.

10 Zaremba, A. J. (2014). *Crisis Communication: Theory and Practice.* Hoboken: Taylor and Francis.

11 Stein, M. R., & Rawles, J. W. (2011). *When disaster strikes: A comprehensive guide for emergency planning and crisis survival.* U.S.A.: Chelsea Green Publishing.

12 Stein, M. R., & Rawles, J. W. (2011). *When disaster strikes: A comprehensive guide for emergency planning and crisis survival.* U.S.A.: Chelsea Green Publishing.

CRISIS MANAGEMENT:
THE ART OF SUCCESS AND FAILURE

13 Fagel, M. J. (2013). *Crisis management and emergency planning: Preparing for today's challenges.* U.S.A.: CRC Press.

14 Fagel, M. J. (2013). *Crisis management and emergency planning: Preparing for today's challenges.* U.S.A.: CRC Press.

15 Fagel, M. J. (2013). *Crisis management and emergency planning: Preparing for today's challenges.* U.S.A.: CRC Press.

16 Ritchie, B. W. (2009). *Crisis and disaster management for tourism.* Bristol, UK: Channel View Publications.

17 Ritchie, B. W. (2009). *Crisis and disaster management for tourism.* Bristol, UK: Channel View Publications.

18 Ritchie, B. W. (2009). *Crisis and disaster management for tourism.* Bristol, UK: Channel View Publications.

19 Jennex, M. E. (2012). *Managing crises and disasters with emerging technologies: Advancements.* Hershey, PA: Information Science Reference.

20 Jennex, M. E. (2012). *Managing crises and disasters with emerging technologies: Advancements.* Hershey, PA: Information Science Reference.

21 Ayyub, B. M. (2011). *Vulnerability, uncertainty, and risk: Analysis, modeling, and management.* Reston, VA: American Society of Civil Engineers.

22 Regester, M., & Larkin, J. (2005). *Risk issues and crisis management: A casebook of best practice.* London: Kogan Page.

23 Regester, M., & Larkin, J. (2005). *Risk issues and crisis management: A casebook of best practice.* London: Kogan Page.

24 Regester, M., & Larkin, J. (2005). *Risk issues and crisis management: A casebook of best practice.* London: Kogan Page.

25 Doherty, G. W. (2007). *Crisis intervention training for disaster workers: An introduction.* Ann Arbor, MI: Loving Healing Press.

26 Doherty, G. W. (2007). *Crisis intervention training for disaster workers: An introduction.* Ann Arbor, MI: Loving Healing Press.

27 Devlin, E. S. (2007). *Crisis management planning and execution.* Boca Raton, FL: Auerbach.

28 Devlin, E. S. (2007). *Crisis management planning and execution.* Boca Raton, FL: Auerbach.

29 Devlin, E. S. (2007). *Crisis management planning and execution.* Boca Raton, FL: Auerbach.

30 Devlin, E. S. (2007). *Crisis management planning and execution.* Boca Raton, FL: Auerbach.

31 Coombs, W. T. (2012). *Ongoing crisis communication: Planning, managing, and responding.* Thousand Oaks, CA: Sage.

32 Coombs, W. T. (2012). *Ongoing crisis communication: Planning, managing, and responding.* Thousand Oaks, CA: Sage.

33 Reid, J. (2000). *Crisis management planning and media relations for construction and engineering firms.* New York: Wiley.

34 Reid, J. (2000). *Crisis management planning and media relations for construction and engineering firms.* New York: Wiley.

35 Palen, L., & Liu, Sophia B. (2007). Citizen communications in crisis: Anticipating a future of ICT-supported participation. *Proceedings of the ACM Conference on Human Factors in Computing Systems,* CHI 2007, 727–736.

Case Study 6: Tesco Accounting Scandal (2014)

Tesco is among the leading retailers in the U.K. and among the largest food retailers worldwide. The company also sells non-food products, like clothing and electrical goods. Jack Cohen founded it in 1919 when he started selling extra groceries in a stall in Brixton's East End market. The Tesco brand continued to rise in the 1930s. Cohen decided to construct a headquarters warehouse in north London, and the company became a private limited company in 1932. It floated to the top of the stock market with a share price of 25p in 1947. Today, it has 326,000 employees who operate 2,318 stores worldwide. In 2007, the company recorded income of £42.641 million, making a profit of £2.648 million.

Apart from its retail business, the company also started a grocery store and expanded the market with an extensive variety of retail products. It has also extended the store with a variety of services, such as insurance, a travel agency, and telecom and financial products. Tesco also has a manipulative petrol retailing business. Nevertheless, it exists predominantly within the supermarket and hypermarkets with different diversifications. The company has also consistently continued operations that comprise various other services, such as banking and Internet services.[1]

Tesco's focus is its customers and employees. Additionally, it focuses on understanding its customers and offering them better products and services. Tesco's mission is to formulate value for customers to gain their loyalty. It aims at growing profit and becoming the largest retailer worldwide to benefit its customers and shareholders. Tesco's core values are to construct value for customers and gain their loyalty.

Many of the largest global consumers have flown in audit teams to run a ruler over their U.K. action after the 2014 accounting scandal at Tesco.[2] Companies such as Unilever, Coca-Cola, and Proctor & Gamble supplied audit teams with information about their operations with Tesco on the back of Tesco uncovering a £263 million profit shortfall. In 2014, Tesco faced the biggest crisis in its history following the employment of Dave Lewis as the CEO, who found a black hole in its profits. The shortfall was related to the payment timing from company suppliers.[3] Industrial sources stipulated that the Tesco crisis set off alarm bells around its competitors, prompting them to do their own due diligence.

The crisis led to the suspension of eight executives; Chris Bush, the U.K. managing director was among them. The investigation went on after the suspension of the officials, and a payment worth £2 million was withheld from Tesco's former CEO and CFO. The scandal investigation was done by the Deloitte accounting firm, who declined to comment on its results. The only thing that was confirmed was the £263 million shortfall and the fact that the scandalous operations went on for longer than six months. The results of the investigation were issued to the financial conduct authority to perform further research. Because of the scandal, the

Case Study 6: Tesco Accounting Scandal (2014)

company's shares lost their value in 2014, with major investors like Warren Buffett and David Herro selling their stakes.

The crisis was the result of a lack of good governance; changes in management and past issues led to Tesco's failure in preparations and predictability. This lack of good governance was a major threat to the company; this was portrayed during the investigation, as eight executives were suspended. Additionally, management changes were another facilitating factor in the company crisis that led to the profit shortfall. The lack of good governance put people such as Richard Broadbent under pressure and caused the former CEO to face questions about his responsibility. Critics of Broadbent said that he did not have any retail experience. Moreover, the company operated with no dedicated finance director following the resignation of Laurie McIlwee.

The company faced some challenges that also resulted in the financial crisis. For instance, there was an intense competitive rivalry that forced retailers to look at cost savings and approaches that could make them different from their competitors. Hence, this made Tesco report more profits than they had to make them appealing to the public. Their marketing campaigns were stating increasing efficiency and effectiveness that made them overvalue their profits so that they would not lose their market share.

Tesco is an example of how people respond to serious news in an unpredictable manner. However, Tesco was profitable even after the changes in its reported profits, making the market response disproportionate. Nevertheless, the news shook public confidence in the company, worsening its issues. There was a high probability that the market was factoring in an inevitable situation, thus engendering other cheap and engrossing consequences. Such consequences were a freshly instigated regulatory investigation and possible class rumblings.[4]

The Tesco scandal has brought many companies issues to light. For example, Tesco's lack of good governance has taught public companies to have a strong corporate governance culture. The management changing issues boosted the company en route for creating a robust system structured to prevent any possible accounting schemes in the future. Another important factor is the top management that acts as a key factor adding to the integrity of the financial reporting process. Additionally, companies have been advised by the government to look at the adequacy of their internal controls on a regular basis to prevent the crisis that Tesco faced in 2014. Further, it is preferable to control and minimize risk in responding to a crisis. Hence, the Tesco crisis case shows that a company cannot hide once irregular news has come out; Tesco scrambled to respond to the growing crisis.[5]

In conclusion, it can be said that the lack of good governance, impulsive changes in management, and maladministration caused the Tesco crisis in 2014. The Tesco scandal has brought many companies to light. For example, Tesco's lack of good governance has taught public companies to have a strong corporate governance culture. Hence, the company cannot hide once irregular news has come out; thus Tesco scrambled to respond to the growing crisis so that it would be able to continue its operations.

Another important aspect that companies have learned is that top management acts as a key factor in adding to financial reporting processes; integrity is paramount. Another lesson learned is that the circumstances unfolding around

Tesco were an example of how people respond to serious news in an unpredictable manner. Companies should avoid scandals because they have severe impacts on their reputations and other major consequences. Such consequences include companies' shares losing their value. For instance, major Tesco investors like Warren Buffett and David Herro sold their stakes in 2014. The scandal also led the public to lose confidence in the company. The crisis caused some executives to lose their jobs and forced them to undergo investigation procedures, humiliating them in front of the public.[6]

Endnotes

Case Study 6: Tesco Accounting Scandal (2014)

1 Graham, R. (2014). *Accounting scandal made Tesco suppliers call in audit teams*: The Telegram story on Tesco shares losing half their value in 2014.

2 Graham, R. (2014). Tesco crisis: Everything you need to know. *The Telegram.*

3 Graham, R., & Ben, M. (2014). The investigation into Tesco's £250m profit shortfall unearths corruption of culture. *The Telegram News.*

4 Graham, R. (2014). Tesco crisis: Everything you need to know. *The Telegram.*

5 Jenny, A. (2014). The accounting scandal in Tesco draws scrutiny of serious fraud office in Britain. *International Business.*

6 Lawrence, E., Alexander, C., & Geoffrey, G. (2014). *Risk management and crisis response*: Tesco's accounting scandal a lesson for all public companies.

Case Study 7: How Sweden Survived the 2008 Financial Crisis

The 2008 financial crisis saw nearly the whole world undergo an economic meltdown with dire consequences. For instance, many citizens and corporations alike were unable to repay their loans and mortgages, resulting in bankruptcy. Similarly, the financial crisis resulted in massive layoffs, as firms could not cope with the wage bills amid reductions in sales owing to low purchasing power. Many countries took three to four years before the effects of the 2008 global recession could be fully eliminated. The U.S., for instance, struggled with tough economic conditions until 2014. In contrast, certain countries took relatively little time to recover. Countries like Sweden took only a year before their economy was deemed to have fully recovered. This case looks at the role of a good response and preparation in alleviating the economic problems that face a country. The economic meltdown that Sweden underwent in the 1990s prepared them well, and their reaction to the 2008 financial crisis can be used as a case in point to illustrate how a well-prepared response can be helpful.

SWEDEN'S RESPONSE AND WHAT OTHER COUNTRIES CAN LEARN

Sweden underwent one of the most catastrophic economic

meltdowns in the 1990s. It was characterized by the collapse of the banking sector and commercial real estate. Inflation rates soared to unmanageable levels as the unemployment rates in the country hit double figures.[1] The country had trouble borrowing owing to the collapse of its currency as well as a huge budget deficit. The country opted to make structural changes in their fiscal policy as well as other important changes that have aided in ensuring that the country is cushioned from another economic meltdown. Sweden's quick recovery in 2008 highlights the effects of the changes that it made.

The first change made by the country pertains to its fiscal policy. Sweden has highlighted how it is imperative for a country to keep its fiscal house to ensure that it can maneuver when the economy stagnates owing to difficulties. Just before the economic meltdown in 2007, Sweden managed to have a budget surplus of 3.6%. This was in line with its target of having at least of 1% surplus in the yearly budget and performance.[2] In contrast, the U.S. had a budget deficit of close to 3%. The budget surplus enabled Sweden's government to have a cushion it could use without having to put the country into more debt. While Sweden's debt is closing in on 45% of its national economy, that of the U.S. is nearing 100% of its economy.

The lack of fiscal problems provided the country with some freedom in how it could react to the economic downtime. The country could therefore come up with a range of reactions that could not hurt its fiscal situation further and result in a deeper or future financial crisis. It is evident that the financial depression that the country underwent in the 1990s enabled them to come up with measures that helped

Case Study 7: How Sweden Survived the 2008 Financial Crisis

it to weather the 2008 recession. In contrast, countries such as the U.S., which had undergone a recession in the 1930s, failed to learn from their situations to avert future financial meltdowns.

Another important lesson that Sweden learned from their financial meltdown in the 1990s was the use of fiscal stimulus in helping a recovering economy. It is evident that fiscal stimulus is best employed in a natural way to blend into the economy as opposed to offering one-time stimulus packages that are meant to bail out sectors of the economy.[3] As opposed to the U.S. and many other European countries, Sweden did not come up with special one-time offers or a stimulus package that was meant to ensure that the economy recovered.

Although Sweden had to inject a certain amount into infrastructure spending, as well as providing tax breaks and reducing the income tax, it largely avoided huge special stimulus packages that were meant to jump-start the economy. The country provided the most basic response that can be undertaken by any country. They provided healthcare and the most important services, as well as income opportunities, to its citizens.[4] In contrast, countries such as the U.S. were engaged in lengthy debates on the best ways through which the government could help to end the economic depression that the country was facing. The question became whether it was the government's role to increase its spending with the aim of ensuring that the economic meltdown was fought as quickly as possible. In the end, an $800 million stimulus package was approved, targeted at various sectors of the economy that were facing the threat of massive collapsing under the watch of the government. Given that the package was a one-time occurrence, its effects took months or even years before they could be felt in the economy.

Sweden demonstrated how spending when the economy is doing well is important in managing future economic crises rather than coming up with sudden plans to spend to save the economy, ensuring that a well-organized monetary policy is ready to cushion the economy when hard times set in.

The aggressive use of monetary policies by the Swedish central bank is another highlight that marked the importance of responding well to an economic crisis. In the wake of the 1990s economic crisis, citizens and corporations alike had little trust in Sweden's central bank. The rate of inflation had soared too high, and the central bank set the interest rates well over 500% to help save the dwindling value of their currency. However, after the economy started recovering, the central bank set an inflation rate of lower than 2% annually. The country also worked on expanding its balance sheet to accommodate more borrowing. At the start of the economic meltdown, the central bank used monetary policies in the form of interest rates aggressively to tackle the lack of borrowing or funds available to borrowers. Interest rates were lowered to zero to ensure that more households could receive funds and expand their disposable income. This enabled many to be able to make purchases that stimulated the economy to recovery.

Although the U.S. Federal Reserve (the Fed) also managed to reduce interest rates, it was not as aggressive as the Swedish central bank. The Fed managed to expand its balance sheet to 15% more than the value of the gross domestic product. However, this was still a lower value

Case Study 7: How Sweden Survived the 2008 Financial Crisis

than the 25% greater value that the Swedish central bank managed to achieve during the 2009 financial crisis. Such are the mechanisms that enabled the country to be able to pull out of the financial crisis more quickly than other countries, such as the U.S.

Managing a flexible currency is also a way through which the Swedish authorities were able to ensure that the financial crisis was not as biting as that witnessed during the 1990s. The Swedish authorities refused to adopt the euro as their currency. This turned out to be a wise decision during the global recession.[5] During the 2009 global recession, many individuals opted to store their cash in the universally used dollar, while some opted to store their money in the form of the euro. The Swedish krona quickly lost its value against world currencies.[6] However, this boosted exports, as products from Sweden became relatively cheaper than those from countries that used the euro and the dollar. A boom in exportation served to cushion the economy against the tough conditions.

In contrast, the dollar and the euro, the currencies considered to be the global currencies, gained substantially, owing to the fact that many people trusted them. As a result, exporters in countries such as the U.S. endured tough times owing to reduced sales. Many importers shunned products from the U.S., owing to the high prices attributed to an improving dollar. This served to hurt the economy further during the ongoing recession. It highlighted the disadvantages of a powerful currency during an economic meltdown.

The last lesson from this example that other nations can learn in a bid to manage future economic problems is how the Swedish government was able to handle its bankers.

CRISIS MANAGEMENT:
THE ART OF SUCCESS AND FAILURE

Banks contributed immensely to the financial crisis, especially in the U.S.[7] The reckless borrowing that was taking place in the U.S. led to unsecured loans that contributed to mortgage repayment difficulties that were a big contributor to the financial crisis. However, measures put in place by the Swedish authorities ensured that banks were cautious with the loans they gave out. In addition, the Swedish banks developed self-restraining measures that were aimed at cushioning themselves against losses in the case of a meltdown owing to risky loans. This was after they incurred heavy losses during the 1990s financial crisis.

In contrast, the U.S. banks were largely unconcerned about the risks that they could face and those in which they put their customers. Without many regulations, the banks in the U.S. and other financial institutions had the power to lend funds that were unsecured. This resulted in huge losses, as most of the loans went unpaid.

Evidently, the measures that the Swedish government put in place after the financial meltdown in the 1990s led to fewer problems and a quick recovery after the 2008 financial crisis. Had other countries put the same measures in place that the Swedish government did, the financial meltdown that was witnessed in 2008 could have been avoided, or at least more easily managed.

Endnotes

Case Study 7: How Sweden Survived the 2008 Financial Crisis

1 Dougherty, C. (2008). Stopping a financial crisis, the Swedish way. *New York Times*, 22.

2 Dougherty, C. (2008). Stopping a financial crisis, the Swedish way. *New York Times*, 22.

3 Scancomark. (2013, June). *More evidence that Sweden survived the economic crisis best.* Retrieved January 2016, from http://scancomark.com/Market/More-evidence-that-Sweden-survived-the-economic-crisis-best-105013062013

4 Scancomark. (2013, June). *More evidence that Sweden survived the economic crisis best.* Retrieved January 2016, from http://scancomark.com/Market/More-evidence-that-Sweden-survived-the-economic-crisis-best-105013062013

5 Fouche, G. (2011, August). *Why Scandinavia can teach us a thing or two about surviving a recession.* Retrieved from http://www.guardian.co.uk/society/joepublic/2009/aug/05/scandinavia-recession-welfare-state

6 Jones, E. (2009). The euro and the financial crisis. *Survival, 51*(2), 41-54.

7 Fratianni, M. U., & Marchionne, F. (2009). The role of banks in the subprime financial crisis. *Review of Economic Conditions in Italy, 1.*

Case Study 8: How India Survived 2008

As most countries' economies began to recover, many nations started looking back at how India coped with the 2008 crisis. Regardless of the extraordinary global downturn, India continued to be the world's second-fastest-growing economy. While most nations grieved negative growth, India's gross domestic product (GDP) grew by more than 6% during this period, and by 7.9% in 2009. India's survival was a huge achievement given that they were hit by the Pakistani terrorists in Mumbai, India's economic nerve center and commercial capital, in November 2008, in the middle of the crisis. The extremists dented India's international image as an evolving economic giant, an accomplishment story of the epoch of globalization, and an attraction for investors and tourists. India survived the crisis simply because of a disconnection between their global financial markets and their internal economy.[1]

To start with, the financial markets in India are not very developed. The very conservative state-owned banks control over 70% of all banking assets. Additionally, they are the primary supporters of the substructure and building projects that employ a vast number of citizens. This distinction between money-related markets and the "real" economy guaranteed that the withdrawal of assets from the

CRISIS MANAGEMENT:
THE ART OF SUCCESS AND FAILURE

business sectors did not overflow onto whatever was left of the economy. Framework and lodging activities were not wrecked by the emergency that forestalled the widespread non-rural unemployment seen in cutting-edge economics. India has a decent national reserve bank, the RBI, which was administered and maintained by Subbarao during the recession in 2008. Both Subbarao and his predecessor Yaga Venugopal were and are extremely judicious brokers. They applied the brakes to banking money advances even before the emergency.

India was and still is an exceptionally poor country with a great deal of low-hanging products and possibilities for development; the foundation was similar to a pad, absorbing the weight of the emergency and helping the economy to recuperate quickly.

During the same period, China also tried to act quickly to protect its developing economy amid the emergency. In 2008, Chinese chief Wen Jiabao reported the need for a RMB 4 trillion financial boost to diminish the effect of the crisis on the Chinese economy. This boost was a balancing-out element then and a key driver of Chinese interest from that point forward. The mining blast in Odisha, the 35% expansion in India's petroleum send-outs, and a corresponding increment in iron mineral prices that helped in India's fast recuperation were all immediate consequences of China's boost.[2]

The most critical thing to note about Indian development post-2008 is that the states that were the most open in terms of exchange endured a decrease in growth, while those that were less open were stronger. These states drove full Indian development in the fallout of the emergency.

Case Study 8: How India Survived 2008

Farmer's representatives present nearly half of the workforce in India, and have regularly seen development rates between 2 and 3.5% for individual five-year plans. The minimum support prices (MSP) was expanded at unprecedented rates, and the provincial and rural development rate expanded to above 4%. Despite the fact that the commitment of agribusiness to the GDP was around 16%, development in the division and the related increments in homestead wages and local wages pushed the undivided interest in the economy up, and along these lines, the general development rates increased. This is one of the less-discussed explanations for India's efficient performance in the post-emergency years. Likewise, the cost of horticultural items was high in the world markets, which increased wages as well. The disease from the worldwide money-related emergency required proper financial and monetary strategy reactions to guarantee enough liquidity in the economy, the efficient operation of business sectors, and financial security.

To counter the negative influence of the worldwide stoppage on the Indian economy, the national government reacted by giving local monetary institutes jolt bundles to expand the use of public activities to create jobs and open resources. India's national bank took many money-related facilitating and liquidity upgrade measures to encourage a stream of assets from the fiscal framework. The government of India reacted to the test unequivocally through its financial and money-related approaches. The three monetary jolt bundles went into large-scale well-being projects for the provincial poor, the advance ranch waiver, and a payout after the Sixth Pay Commission report to motivate and enhance the economy.[3]

CRISIS MANAGEMENT:
THE ART OF SUCCESS AND FAILURE

This financial convenience prompted an increment in monetary deficiency from 2.7% of the GDP in 2007-08 to 6.2% in 2008-09. The distinction between the exact figures of 2007-08 and 2008-09 constitute the aggregate financial boost. This advance given to business sector costs added up to 3.5% of the GDP for 2008-09. These measures were robust in capturing the fall in the GDP development rate in 2008-09, and India achieved a development rate of 6.7%.

The arrangement position of the RBI in the first half of the year was situated toward controlling financial extensions, given the clear connection between money-related development and inflationary desires, mostly because of the apparent liquidity overhang. In the initial six months of 2008-09, the year-on-year development was lower than the development of store cash. The government took diverse monetary and lawful measures in the midst of the initial half of 2008-09 to control swelling. The key RBI technique rates along these lines moved to signal a cash-related pressure position.[4] The repo rate (RR) was extended from 7.75% toward the beginning of April 2008 to 9.0% by August 30, 2008. The converse repo rate (R-RR) was left unaltered at 6.0%. The money holds proportion (CRR) was expanded in six tranches from 7.50% toward the start of April 2008 to 9.0% by August 30, 2008.

Lately, the scale conversion approach has been guided by the universal standards of checking and the administration of trade rates with adaptability, without a settled or preannounced target or band, while permitting the main request and supply conditions to decide the swapping scale developments of the Indian rupee over a period in an organized way. Subject to this transcendent goal, the RBI's mediation in the foreign trade business sector has been driven by the goal of lessening overabundance instability, keeping up a sufficient level of stores, and building up an organized outside trade market. The stream in the measure of outside cash in the private business segment drove an increase in the expense of the Indian rupee. The overall cash-related crisis, on the other hand, exchanged the rupee credit, and after the end of a good shock around January 2008, the rupee began a moderate reduction.[5]

In the midst of the monetary emergency, India was less impacted than others solely because of the national division and due to private solicitations, strict keeping money rules, and the mentality of the all-inclusive community.[6]

Endnotes

Case Study 8: How India Survived 2008

1 Scientific research. (2010, November). Retrieved from http://www.SciRP.org/journal/me

2 Sheel, A. (2015, October). *How India's central bank has survived a global crisis of confidence.* Retrieved from Afrweekend: http://www.afr.com/opinion/how-indias-central-bank-has-survived-a-global-crisis-of-confidence-20151011-gk676b

3 Tharoor, S. (2010, August). *How India survived the financial crisis.* Retrieved from Project syndicate: https://www.quora.com/What-are-the-main-reasons-India-survived-the-global-economic-recession-of-2008

4 Viswanathan, B. (2013, February). *What are the main reasons India survived the global economic recession of 2008.* Retrieved from http://www.project-syndicate.org/commentary/how-india-survived-the-financial-crisis

5 Tharoor, S. (2010, August). *How India survived the financial crisis.* Retrieved from Project syndicate: https://www.quora.com/What-are-the-main-reasons-India-survived-the-global-economic-recession-of-2008

6 Quora. (2013, February). *What are the main reasons India survived the global economic recession of 2008.* Retrieved from https://www.quora.com/What-are-the-main-reasons-India-survived-the-global-economic-recession-of-2008

Social Media and Crisis Communication

CRISIS COMMUNICATION

Coombs[1] defined crisis communication as the process of preventing or minimizing the damage that a crisis causes within an organization and its outside stakeholders. Therefore, crisis communication is a proactive approach to crisis management. The crisis management process occurs in three phases: pre-crisis, response phase, and post-crisis activities.[2]

There are two types of crisis communication: form crisis communication and content crisis communication.[3] Form crisis communication involves disseminating the right information in a consistent manner. The information from a company regarding a crisis should show as little variation as possible. Content communication, on the other hand, is associated with corporate apologia.[4] An organization can publicly deny having had a hand in a crisis. It may blame the situation on external forces while clearing its name.

In the pre-crisis phase, the organization's media relations personnel scan and monitor social media conversations to detect crisis symptoms. A number of crises have symptoms, and the organization needs to identify them as quickly as possible, with a view to avoiding the crisis.[5] An organization needs to prepare for crises adequately by developing a communication plan. The plan should entail coming up with feasible crises in the organization, training a crisis management team and media relations officers, and establishing appropriate communication strategies.[6]

The effectiveness of the crisis communication plan depends on its flexibility since crises vary in nature. As a result, the plan should be tested and rehearsed on a regular basis to improve and remove any feasible incompetency during implementation. The main purpose of listening to social media platform conversations is to identify a problem at an early stage, including stakeholders' understandings.[7] In some situations, it enables firms to consider social media messages in the crisis management plan.

In the response phase, the organization needs to recognize the occurrence of a crisis and gather the information necessary for effective decision-making. In effect, the relations personnel streamline communication within the organization and with outside stakeholders. Coombs[8] emphasized the need to decide on a response mechanism that is quick, accurate, and consistent. The primary goal of this response is to restore the organization's reputation while building trust with stakeholders.

The response stage requires an organization to identify the platform where the crisis conversation is prevalent. Qualman[9] reiterated that an organization that is present and actively participates in these platforms would not only win the trust of its stakeholders and members of the public, but also escape reputation damage. The shared information needs to be as accurate as possible.

In addition, this is the stage where the organization is required to discourse a crisis internally while management should be mindful of others externally by offering satisfactory explanations and accepting responsibility where necessary.[10]

Post-crisis analysis is very significant in crisis management. The obligation here is to examine the progress of the crisis management and incorporate the outcomes in the communication plan for better management of future crises. Notably, most organizations communicate the crisis management progress to stakeholders, highlighting possible causes and mitigation strategies employed.[11]

Success after a crisis is all about refurbishing an organization's image in the public arena. The stakeholders would see the organization's practical efforts and gain confidence in the company. The result is a successful recovery from the crisis. Crisis communication is essential for enhancing public relations. Therefore, it is important to understand public relations theory when dealing with a crisis.

According to public relations theory, organizations seek to maintain rather intimate relationships with important members of the public for the purposes of reducing financial stress, psychological trauma, detrimental perceptions, and critiques.[12] Research has shown that this relationship prudently creates common understanding and benefits.[13] One can argue that establishing strong relationships with the public restores the organization's reputation following a crisis and prevents adverse consequences. Thus, achieving positive relationships requires openness, consultation, devotion, and active participation. In effect, different stakeholders, including the community, will assess alternatives and present their suggestions to the organization for decision-making.

More often than not, stakeholders and the general public blame the organization when a crisis occurs. However, maintaining a positive relationship with these groups relieves the organization of responsibility, and everyone works toward finding an amicable solution.[14] Park and Reber[15] established that people's perceptions of the cause of a potential crisis greatly influence the attribution of responsibility, the degree of the relationship notwithstanding. It follows that, when an organization enjoys a strong relationship with the public, resolving crisis-related conflicts becomes rather easy due to mutual understanding.[16]

Situational crisis communication theory (SCCT) is another important scholarly contribution to understanding crisis management. According to Coombs,[17] SCCT advocates for examining the potential effects of a crisis on an organization's reputation and choosing an appropriate response during and after the crisis that is aimed at protecting the organization's reputation.

According to SCCT, stakeholders need to know the history of the company in terms of crisis occurrence. The necessity here is to establish whether the crisis has repeated itself or has resulted from a continuous mistake that should be handled once and for all. The theory also touches on prior reputation, which provides a picture of how the firm has handled its stakeholders in the past.

An organization's preparedness to deal with a crisis can be studied from the stakeholder's perception of the firm. There is a multidimensional approach to the position of stakeholders in an organization. First, the descriptive perspective pictures stakeholders as competing and having cooperating groups of interests whose presence and participation are fundamental to the progress of the organization. Second, the instrumental approach offers a structure for assessing a feasible relationship between effective stakeholder management and achieving organizational success. Finally, the normative system views stakeholders as people or groups of people who are interested in a company, regardless of whether the company has an interest in them or not.

THE BASICS OF SOCIAL MEDIA CRISIS COMMUNICATION

When creating communications regarding a crisis within an organization, there are some basics that must be complied with for effectiveness. First, the communication basics must be upheld and remembered; while passing information through social media, it is important that the communication be done with utmost honesty, openness, and candor while acknowledging the risk itself and collaborating and coordinating with the most reliable sources of information. Without the social media platform, there would be no reasonable crisis management actions; thus, the communication process is termed as being an accelerant of management and an extinguisher of the crisis itself. Second, there is a need to keep monitoring social media and the Internet as a whole; with the understanding of the partnership between the organization and the public, there is a need to have a monitoring structure set in place. In larger organizations, there is the possibility that they tend to employ large-scale social media monitors for the usual updates of the mentions of their brands within the Internet platform.

THE EFFECTS OF SOCIAL MEDIA DURING A CRISIS

Communication is an essential aspect of crisis management. Effective crisis communication within an organization depends on social media. According to Birgfeld,[18] social media plays an important role in spreading a crisis, giving it new dimensions, and changing the crisis communication situation throughout the crisis management process.

Social media encompasses a distributed network of communities, open conversations, participation, and increased connectivity. Coombs[19] emphasized that these networks promote chats and social contact among users. Consequently, people are able to establish, give their views on, and share content with various groups.

Social media can either build or destroy an organization when a crisis strikes. Successful organizations counteract the threats and opportunities that social media presents in the business arena. Arguably, social media can spark a new crisis or promote an existing one because it provides information to organizational stakeholders.[20]

Social media is the channel through which the mainstream media obtains information about a crisis. Through direct commentaries and analysis, social media has the potential to disclose confidential information about a crisis, and this could elicit reactions from stakeholders and the general public. Gonzalez and Smith[21] recognized some sense in the fact that social media content tends to be provocative and involve rumor-mongering that could plunge an organization into further crisis.

Apparently, social media is the most common challenge that organizations face in crisis communication. The news of an occurrence of a crisis can reach stakeholders faster than an organization imagines. Therefore, stakeholders are a happy lot in the wake of a crisis because they can influence people's perspectives online before the organization do.

Moreover, social media is a stage on which stakeholders can express their feelings and become actively involved when a crisis takes place. In this respect, workers, consumers, and lobby groups share their concerns on social media and can influence interested individuals to campaign against a company.[22] Statistics show that over 70% of world lobby groups are active users of Facebook, Twitter, and YouTube.[23] This implies that social, economic, and professional groups are becoming increasingly powerful in the advent of social media, and organizations have to involve them when facing a crisis or risk losing ground to competitors.

Furthermore, social media spreads word of mouth. People can easily share comments regarding a crisis in an organization.[24] It is imperative to realize that consumers will actively participate on social media platforms if they are not satisfied with the explanations provided. Successful organizations engage their stakeholders and supervise the crisis management progress. In doing so, they ensure rapid, precise, and trustworthy responses so that perceptions and concerns do not amount to another crisis.[25]

In some cases, social media can result in a communication crisis, which in turn creates a double crisis.[26] A double crisis occurs in an organization mainly due to poor communication methods, and particularly the failure to either respond to social media conversations or participate in social media. There is no doubt that an organization that fails to share a crisis situation on social media is doomed to fail, as Taylor and Perry concluded.[27]

CRISIS MANAGEMENT:
THE ART OF SUCCESS AND FAILURE

When a crisis occurs, the public needs to be informed; failure to provide this information is a sign of ignorance on the part of the company. Going forward, organizations should reveal the occurrence of a crisis to the public as early as possible and engage them with the measures in place, not forgetting the progress made. It is important to understand the effects of social media on crisis communication and give emphasis to how companies can exploit social media in response to a crisis.

THE EFFECTIVE USE OF SOCIAL MEDIA IN CRISIS COMMUNICATION

Many scholars believe that, despite the many challenges, social media presents a myriad of opportunities that companies can exploit to manage probable crises.[28] Thus, social media needs to be an integral part of a company's crisis response plan. Social media platforms connect an organization with various stakeholders and the public in general. Solis[29] established that firms can avoid crises by seeking the opinions of and taking feedback from customers and stakeholders via social media.

Studies have revealed that most of the social media platforms that threaten the success of organizations can equally facilitate effective crisis communication if properly harnessed.[30] The authors argued that social media offers platforms for one-on-one interaction with different stakeholders, and this enables the organization to present its position and get their perspectives on the situation at hand.

Nonetheless, as noted earlier, the public requires immediate information on a crisis situation. They need to know about the events as they unfold in the organization and the organization's response.[31] The initial response should focus on alerting people about the crisis dangers and safety measures. Coombs[32] emphasized the mere fact that a swift response following a crisis is more than essential.

In a more critical analysis of crisis situations, Donnelly[33] found that a faster response shows an organization's control of a crisis. The organization can give its interpretation of the situation; this could minimize the ruin of its reputation. Today, reliable updates and timely message content can be pumped through social media.[34] Additionally, social media platforms have programs that enable the correction and removal of inaccurate or unintentional posts. They therefore offer an opportunity to withdraw provocative statements against an organization; thus, organizations need to utilize social media platforms to pass on a quick response to a distributed network of individuals.

Through social media, stakeholders can support a company during a crisis, depending on the existing relationship. When the company communicates effectively with its employees and loyal customers, they may convince other people that the situation is not as bad as presented in the mainstream media. Consequently, the public might rise up in support of the organization and pledge resource commitments to salvage the crisis.[35]

Hanna[36] observed that social media platforms promote bilateral talks. Crisis communication is essential in crisis management. Social media can facilitate constructive communication between a company and its stakeholders. The development of positive relationships is embedded in effective communication, and companies that engage in conversations often experience very few cases of crisis.

These cases are temporary and have a minimal effect on the productivity and reputation of the organization. Companies can also improve on their language in social media platforms by identifying the responses that inflict anger.

Effective crisis communication also requires companies to separate business and crises. According to Donnelly,[37] organizations should create a dark site or a social media hub for a crisis. The site forms an inactive part of their website that only becomes active when there is a crisis. During a crisis, the organization shifts to the dark site so that that it is present throughout the crisis. However, the presence of the organization on this site should not affect the normal running of usual business.

On the separate site, the company can add crisis information faster. The social media hub would ensure that all the information is available on one platform. Consequently, an organization that seeks to adequately prepare for a crisis should create business social media accounts.

Apart from the dark site or social media hub, Donnelly[38] emphasized the need to create different Facebook or Twitter accounts for a given crisis. One of the subjects of these accounts should be the name of the crisis. This design will enable stakeholders to comment on the right page without attacking the business side of the organization.

In the corporate world, business partners have a keen interest in an organization's success. The partners will hold the company accountable for any losses in their investment portfolio. A company then needs to separate business from the crisis, allowing the company to constructively engage these associates through the social media hub or other separate accounts.

SOCIAL MEDIA AS A TWO-WAY COMMUNICATION CHANNEL

This is another significant feature of social media, and it entails the ability to enable two-way communication between stakeholders and organizations; social media platforms will always provide the opportunity of inviting consumers to respond, while expecting their responses to the different types of crises, after which the organizations are left to handle the crises at different levels. As this continues, potential opportunities will also promote higher expectations on behalf of all the stakeholders, who will then be quite expectant of immediate communication processes that have been adequately planned and provide answers to their raised concerns.[39] Such kinds of expectations will also act as potential disadvantages; other organizations have still stuck to the concept that social media has been connected to some forms of threats that usually outweigh the potential advantages.[40] According to Coombs, the "newer media" has allowed individuals and stakeholders within organizations to have virtual meetings to share information that might be investigated and analyzed more effectively when discussing urgent issues. However, it may also create a negative impression in the event that the company stakeholders decide to expose the company as being a villain while spreading their perceptions. Ultimately, it can be said that social media is an electronic meeting place where individuals converge to share ideas, as well as navigate and spread communication about diverse forms of crises.

SOCIAL MEDIA AS A TOOL

The most significant key to the handling of crisis control as well as the ultimate flow of information through the media to the public is dependent on the aspects of social media.[41] The various aspects of social media have had a large impact on handling a crisis due to the dissolution of geographical fences. Wigley and Zhang[42] discussed the concept that social media has enabled news to be broken immediately once it has hit the conduits of online communication, such as Twitter, Facebook, and WhatsApp; it only takes a few minutes before exploding and spreading to over a thousand virtual participants. Therefore, the old methods of crisis communication with regards to the control and regulation of distributing information have become a matter of history in the current world and are quite unserviceable for major companies and organizations.[43]

In modern times, public relations (PR) professionals have lost the time they would utilize to do their planning long before the news hit social media and spread uncontrollably to the public; therefore, crisis communicators now possess the reactive position and role of establishing damage control strategies whenever the crisis has been fed to the public, and they have already evaluated the impacts of such. It is thus clear that social media has to be employed by organizations in times of crisis, though it has both positive and negative impacts when used.[44] One of the major advantages accompanying the use of social media in crisis management is the fact that it brings about a higher degree of transparency in interactions between consumers and correspondent organizations. Coombs[45] asserted that, prior to the advent of social media, people had difficulty in accessing some organizations that were considered as being at the center of a crisis. Currently, organizations have set up different methods of communication, and even more significant is the fact that they have established communication tools responsible for the delivery of communication without delays. The use of social media is advantageous in the sense that it has rendered useless the middlemen who have long served as the filters of communication through which messages had to pass before hitting the public; during the transfer processes, messages had been distorted, changing their meaning and intended purpose when they reached the public arena; for instance, editors, interpreters, and censors would interfere with information that was to be transferred. In using social media, the message is sent directly to the recipient without passing through a middleman or agent of transfer, thus reducing delays and modifications and accelerating the concept of communication to an improved level.[46]

THE ROLE OF SOCIAL MEDIA PLATFORMS IN CRISIS RESPONSE

In recent years, there have been numerous innovations in social media platforms. Organizational managers need to understand and embrace the most popular platforms in crisis communication. As Schultz[47] noted, social media can either save an organization from a crisis or plunge it into a further crisis, depending on its use of crisis communication. Therefore, it is salient to discuss some of the most commonly used social media platforms, which are classified based on their content dissemination and targeted users.

Microblogs

Twitter is the most common platform under this category. The platform provides messages in the form of tweets, which followers (stakeholders) of a company can share and give their views on. Twitter content is easily accessible via quick-search tools, and an organization's conversations can be available to millions of users within a short time.[48] Most people who use Twitter are influential in society, and they can share tweets with their respective groups of influence on other platforms or the mainstream media. Therefore, companies should not only be present on Twitter, but should also study crisis signs visible on Twitter because of its ability to spread information quickly and to many people.

Social Networks

Facebook has become the most popular social network ever used. Corporations can create Facebook pages in which they engage stakeholders. On these pages, organizations can also share information and important links. The advantage of using Facebook is that only individuals interested in an organization can access their information.[49]

Content Communities

Organizations have found YouTube to be the most convenient platform on which to apologize and issue a statement during and after a crisis. Viewers can easily follow the speeches of organizational heads on this platform and respond accordingly.[50] When stakeholders can watch videos of top managers addressing the public about a crisis, they view such leaders as competent and honest.

As opposed to social networks, YouTube membership requirements are slightly stringent, especially based on age. However, the danger is that someone can upload a video of a crisis as it happens. In this regard, the organization can do very little to convince the public that it is not in a crisis. Such videos can create panic and elicit public reactions to the detriment of the organization.[51]

Blogs

Crisis managers in the contemporary economy have recognized the importance of bloggers in their companies.[52] A company manager or a leader who has a blog can express a crisis situation in a rather more autonomous and personal statement than via the general website. Leader blogs often provide a feeling of management's control and inculcate sensible comments on the situation. The managers need to establish the blogs early enough to accommodate a reasonable number of necessary participants before a crisis happens.[53]

CRISIS MANAGEMENT

The manner in which an organization communicates about a crisis will always be the determinant of whether the crisis becomes escalated and out of control, causing a setback, or controlling the situation and protecting the company's reputation. Therefore, the major impacts of successful communication from organizations will always be based on the factors that the organization will continue with its operations, manage the crisis successfully, and keep the support and trust of major stakeholders. While working on managing a crisis, there is a need to agree on whether to keep the information locked up or go public with it; in cases where the information still lies within the confines of the organization, there would be no need to go public, but when the information is already in the public domain, there is an urgent need to react to the matter with a statement that is in accordance with the media information.

Social media may explode with information relating to an organization, and this could, to some extent, attract negative comments regarding the organization. Therefore, it is the work of the communications team within the company to ensure that such information on social media such as Twitter, Facebook, and other social sites is monitored and that suitable responses are given without fail to avert the crisis and threats to normal operations.

In summary, crisis communication entails the dissemination of information. Effective crisis communication requires stakeholders' participation. Active participation occurs through social media platforms. However, the same platforms can threaten an organization's reputation through criticism and the rapid spread of false information. Companies can achieve successful crisis management through the effective exploitation of social media platforms as tools for effective communication.

Endnotes

Social Media and Crisis Communication

1 Coombs, W. T. (2010). Parameters for crisis communication. *The handbook of Crisis Communication*, 17–53.

2 Coombs, W. T. (2010). Parameters for crisis communication. *The handbook of Crisis Communication*, 17–53.

3 Fearn-Banks, K. (2007). *Crisis communications: A casebook approach.* 3rd edition. Mahwah, N.J.: Lawrence Erlbaum Associates.

4 Coombs, W. T. (2010). Parameters for crisis communication. *The handbook of Crisis Communication*, 17–53.

5 González-Herrero, A., & Smith, S. (2008). Crisis communications management on the web: How internal-based technologies are changing the way public relations professionals handle business crises. *Journal of Contingencies and Crisis Management, 16*(3), 143–153.

6 Coombs, W. T. (2011). *Ongoing crisis communication: Planning, managing and responding.* Sage Publications.

7 Parent M., Plangger, K. & Bal, A. (2011). The New WTP: Willingness to Participate. *Business Horizons*, [online] *54*(3), 219–229.

8 Coombs, W. T. (2010). Parameters for crisis communication. *The handbook of Crisis Communication*, 17–53.

9 Qualman, E. (2009). *Socialnomics: How social media transforms the way we live and do business.* NJ: Wiley.

10 Veil, S. R., Buehner, T., & Palenchar, M. J. (2011). A work-in-process literature review: Incorporating social media in risk and crisis communication. *Journal of Contingencies and Crisis Management, 19*(2), 110–122.

11 Coombs, W. T. (2011). *Ongoing crisis communication: Planning, managing and responding.* Sage Publications.

12 Park, H., & Reber, B. H. (2012). The organization-public relationship and crisis communication: The effect of the organization-public relationship on public's perceptions of crisis and attitudes toward the organization. *International Journal of Strategic Communication, 5*, 240–260.

13 Lee, S., & Kim, D. (2012). The impact of using social media with political purposes on the intention of political participation of social media users. *Journal of PR Research, 16*(1), 78–111.

CRISIS MANAGEMENT:
THE ART OF SUCCESS AND FAILURE

14 Brown, R. (2009). *Public relations and the social web: How to use social media and Web 2.0 in communications*, [e-book]. London: Kogan Page Limited.

15 Park, H., & Reber, B. H. (2012). The organization-public relationship and crisis communication: The effect of the organization-public relationship on public's perceptions of crisis and attitudes toward the organization. *International Journal of Strategic Communication, 5*, 240–260.

16 Choi, H., & Kim, H. (2011). The influence of OPR (organization-public relationships) formed by the usage of Twitter on publics' conflict resolution will. *Journal of PR Research, 15*(3), 5–40.

17 Coombs, W. T. (2010). Parameters for crisis communication. *The handbook of Crisis Communication*, 17–53.

18 Birgfeld, R. (2010). Focus:Why crisis management and social media must co-exist. *SmartBlog-on Social Media*.

19 Coombs, W. T. (2011). *Ongoing crisis communication: Planning, managing and responding.* Sage Publications.

20 Mei, J. S. A., Bansal, N., and Pang, A. (2010). New media: A new medium in escalating crises? *Corporate Communications*, [online] *15*(2), 143–155.

21 González-Herrero, A., & Smith, S. (2008). Crisis communications management on the web: How internal-based technologies are changing the way public relations professionals handle business crises. *Journal of Contingencies and Crisis Management, 16*(3), 143–153.

22 González-Herrero, A., & Smith, S. (2008). Crisis communications management on the web: How internal-based technologies are changing the way public relations professionals handle business crises. *Journal of Contingencies and Crisis Management, 16*(3), 143–153.

23 Lawrence, D. (2011). A digital crisis is coming your way. Are you ready? *Forbes*.

24 Lawrence, D. (2011). A digital crisis is coming your way. Are you ready? *Forbes*.

25 González-Herrero, A., & Smith, S. (2008). Crisis communications management on the web: How internal-based technologies are changing the way public relations professionals handle business crises. *Journal of Contingencies and Crisis Management, 16*(3), 143–153.

26 Johansen, W., & Frandsen, F. (2007). *Krisekommunikation: Når virksomhedens image og omdømme er truet.* Samfundslitteratur.

27 Taylor, M., & Perry, D. (2005). Diffusion of traditional and new media tactics in crisis communication. *Public Relations Review, 31*(2), 209–217.

28 Solis, B., & Breakenridge, D. (2009). *Putting the public back in public relations. How social media is reinventing the aging business of PR.* FT Press.

29 Solis, B., & Breakenridge, D. (2009). *Putting the public back in public relations. How social media is reinventing the aging business of PR.* FT Press.

30 González-Herrero, A., & Smith, S. (2008). Crisis communications management on the web: How internal-based technologies are changing the way public relations professionals handle business crises. *Journal of Contingencies and Crisis Management, 16*(3), 143–153.

31 Fearn-Banks, K. (2007). *Crisis communications: A casebook approach.* 3rd edition. Mahwah, N.J.: Lawrence Erlbaum Associates.

32 Choi, H., & Kim, H. (2011). The influence of OPR (organization-public relationships) formed by the usage of Twitter on publics' conflict resolution will. *Journal of PR Research, 15*(3), 5–40.

33 Donnelly, J. (2010). Sudden impact: An analysis of five commonly held beliefs about managing crises that erupt online. *The Public Relations Strategist*, Winter 2010, 30–32.

34 Veil, S. R., Buehner, T., & Palenchar, M. J. (2011). A work-in-process literature review: Incorporating social media in risk and crisis communication. *Journal of Contingencies and Crisis Management, 19*(2), 110–122.

35 Lawrence, D. (2011). A digital crisis is coming your way. Are you ready? *Forbes.*

36 Hanna, R., Rohn, A., and Crittenden, V.L. (2011). We're all connected: The power of the social media ecosystem. *Business Horizons*, [online] *54*(3), 265–273.

37 Donnelly, J. (2010). Sudden impact: An analysis of five commonly held beliefs about managing crises that erupt online. *The Public Relations Strategist*, Winter 2010, 30–32.

38 Donnelly, J. (2010). Sudden impact: An analysis of five commonly held beliefs about managing crises that erupt online. *The Public Relations Strategist*, Winter 2010, 30–32.

39 Coombs, W. T. (2010). Parameters for crisis communication. *The handbook of Crisis Communication*, 17–53.

40 Wigley, S., & Zhang, W. (2011), A study of PR practitioners' use of social media in crisis planning. *Public Relations Journal, 5*(3), 1–16.

41 Wigley, S., & Zhang, W. (2011), A study of PR practitioners' use of social media in crisis planning. *Public Relations Journal, 5*(3), 1–16.

42 Wigley, S., & Zhang, W. (2011), A study of PR practitioners' use of social media in crisis planning. *Public Relations Journal, 5*(3), 1–16.

43 Solis, B., & Breakenridge, D. (2009). *Putting the public back in public relations. How social media is reinventing the aging business of PR*. FT Press.

44 Solis, B., & Breakenridge, D. (2009). *Putting the public back in public relations. How social media is reinventing the aging business of PR*. FT Press.

45 Coombs, W. T. (2011). *Ongoing crisis communication: Planning, managing and responding*. Sage Publications.

46 Auer, M. R. (2011). The policy sciences of social media. *The Policy Studies Journal, 39*(4), 707–736.

47 Schultz, F., Utz, S., & Goritz, A. (2011). Is the medium the message? Perceptions of and reactions to crisis communication via Twitter, blogs and traditional media. *Public Relations Review, 37*, 20–27.

48 Schultz, F., Utz, S., & Goritz, A. (2011). Is the medium the message? Perceptions of and reactions to crisis communication via Twitter, blogs and traditional media. *Public Relations Review, 37*, 20–27.

49 Hanna, R., Rohn, A., and Crittenden, V.L. (2011). We're all connected: The power of the social media ecosystem. *Business Horizons*, [online] *54*(3), 265–273.

50 Coombs, W. T. (2011). *Ongoing crisis communication: Planning, managing and responding*. Sage Publications.

51 Coombs, W. T. (2011). *Ongoing crisis communication: Planning, managing and responding*. Sage Publications.

52 Borremans, P. (2010). Ready for anything: Support and enhance your crisis communication plan with social media. *Communication World*, 31–33.

53 Borremans, P. (2010). Ready for anything: Support and enhance your crisis communication plan with social media. *Communication World*, 31–33.

Case Study 9: The Costa Concordia Disaster (2012)

The *Costa Concordia* disaster refers to the January 2012 sinking of the *Costa Concordia* cruise ship after hitting underwater rocks in Tuscany.[1] Carrying about 4,200 individuals, which included cruise staff, the ship was on a first-leg course around the Mediterranean. The captain of the ship took a detour and opted to pass through Isola del Giglio. Unfortunately, the ship hit underwater rocks near the island, resulting in events that led to the sinking of the ship. Thirty-two lives were lost as a result of the accident that could have been averted if the captain and crew had taken precautions and stayed on course and if they had reported the real situation as it happened.[2] This case study looks at the role of communication in crisis response. For instance, how does poor crisis response worsen situations and problems that one can be in? If communicated early, can a crisis be averted and the situation salvaged?

On the night of January 13, 2012, the *Costa Concordia*, a cruise ship that belonged to and was being operated by Costa Cruises, began its seven-day cruise around the Mediterranean Sea. The cruise ship was supposed to visit a total of six ports over the course of the journey. However, before the ship could reach its first port, the captain opted to perform a "salute" to the locals at the island of Giglio.[3] The cruise ship company admitted that a similar salute had been performed the previous year. However, during the first performance, the captain had had the authorization of the company and the salute had been done during the day. The ship was also quite a distance from the island during the first performance. In contrast, the salute conducted by the captain of the ill-fated ship was done at night without the authorization of the cruise ship company. The company reported that the captain intentionally left the computer-programmed route that it was required to take.

Ultimately, the ship hit coral reefs, as the captain tried to avoid other reefs. Before the accident, the captain had also turned off the ship's alarm, which was guided by the navigation system. Had the alarm been on, it would have rung when the ship came too close to the rocks or other foreign bodies that could be of harm. The impact between the rocks and the ship took place about 26 feet below the water. The impact resulted in a substantial tear in the ship's hull. Immediately, the captain was warned that the tear was substantial enough to let water into the ship. Investigators revealed that the tear was around 70 meters wide.[2] Water quickly rushed into the ship, submerging the generators and engines in the process. Soon afterwards, the ship suffered its first blackout. The ship began sinking despite the captain's alleged efforts to steer to the nearest port.

The Team's Response and Consequences

Soon after the accident and resultant power outage, the passengers started communicating to outsiders about the occurrences in the ship. However, the captain assured them that everything was well and that the ship had only suffered

Case Study 9: The Costa Concordia Disaster (2012)

a blackout that would soon be sorted out.[4] However, when the situation began becoming dire, the passengers contacted relatives regarding the impending danger. Word reached the port authorities, who immediately contacted the captain of the ship to inquire about the situation. However, the captain insisted that the ship had only suffered a minor setback.

The captain also alleged that the setback in the form of the blackout had only taken place for 20 minutes and that the crew was working on getting the power back on. The captain denied the reports that the passengers had been told to put on their life jackets. All this time, the ship's condition was worsening and on the verge of sinking. The captain finally opted to call for an evacuation one hour after the ship had its accident.[5] Many were saved by the lifeboats that were sent from the port after reports emerged that the ship was finally sinking.

Despite the efforts made to save all the passengers, about 300 passengers were stuck as the efforts to save them got underway. The captain opted to abandon ship despite the orders given to him by the coast guard to stay on the ship and help rescue all the passengers that remained on board. The captain refused to obey the orders. In the end, 32 passengers lost their lives.

It is evident that the captain's actions and lack of honesty aided in worsening the situation. First, the captain knew the extent of the damage that had been caused firsthand. However, he opted not to call or inform the port authorities of the apparent damage that had occurred. The captain also misinformed the passengers of the extent of the damage, and when the port authorities called, the captain also denied the allegations that the ship was experiencing any problems. Had the captain pointed out the problems at the first instance, the port would have organized a faster evacuation that would have helped in reducing or eliminating the casualties. This case can be used to illustrate how a poor crisis response can worsen the situation. It highlighted the need to respond to a bad situation honestly. If the captain had provided an adequate and honest response, the passengers might have been saved.

Endnotes

Case Study 9: The Costa Concordia Disaster (2012)

1 BBC News. (2014). Costa Concordia: What happened. Retrieved from http://www.bbc.co.uk/news/world-europe-16563562

2 BBC News. (2014). Costa Concordia: What happened. Retrieved from http://www.bbc.co.uk/news/world-europe-16563562

3 Daily Mail Online. (n.d.). Costa Concordia accident: Pictures of cruise ship sinking off coast of Italy "in Titanic-like scene." Retrieved from http://www.dailymail.co.uk/news/article-2086527/Costa-Concordia-accident-Pictures-cruise-ship-sinking-coast-Italy-Titanic-like-scene.html

4 NY Daily News. (n.d.). 5 convicted for Costa Concordia shipwreck. Retrieved from http://www.nydailynews.com/news/crime/5-convicted-costa-concordia-shipwreck-article-1.1404333

5 NY Daily News. (n.d.). 5 convicted for Costa Concordia shipwreck. Retrieved from http://www.nydailynews.com/news/crime/5-convicted-costa-concordia-shipwreck-article-1.1404333

Pressure Groups and Public Participation

The role of pressure groups and public participation in crisis management cannot be underestimated. Research has shown[1] that public participation plays a central role in crisis management; when a disaster strikes, the impact can be greatly reduced if individuals, authorities, and communities join hands to overcome the crisis. Just like public participation, pressure groups also play a pivotal role in the management of crises, particularly political crises. Despite the fact that pressure groups never field any candidate during the election process, they participate in the development of policies that promote peaceful coexistence and help in the management of crises like political instability.

PUBLIC PARTICIPATION

The use of citizen or public participation in the management of crises, including disaster mitigation and response, is not new. Public involvement in disaster management dates back many years. Local governments regularly involve the general public in crisis management whenever a crisis happens. As opined by Chen,[2] citizens offering their services for free as emergency response personnel because of a shortage of professionals dates back to World War II.

The goal of public participation in community-based disaster management, or simply the management of any community crisis, is to transform at-risk or vulnerable communities into disaster-resilient communities.[3] Public participation is extremely critical in the management of crises within the community. The use of the community-based disaster management (CBDM) approach boosts individuals' capacity to respond efficaciously to emergencies since it provides them with a high level of accessibility, control of resources, and basic social services. This public or community participation is viewed in the context of a social process.[4]

However, for the public to constructively participate in the management of crises, there is a dire need to equip them with the necessary knowledge and skills through training, education, and awareness-building about vulnerable groups, institutions, and other related agencies.[5] In this regard, Maskrey[6] contended that the fundamental justification of a CBDM approach includes the empowerment of local communities to deal with any crisis or disaster, reducing the risks further, in addition to leading to a sustainable decrease in disaster risk over a period of time.

According to the United Nations,[7] public participation through CBDM is extremely critical because it fosters the development of various initiatives and crisis management programs implemented solely at the local and community levels as opposed to local or community ownership. A considerable number of community participation programs have been very effectual in the management of crises, leading to a significant reduction of losses whenever a disaster or crisis happens. Pandey and Okazaki[8] tended to refute the effectiveness of public participation programs through CBDM by asserting that the successes of public participation are regularly diminished because of a lack of efficacious capacity-building and participation by the local community or the general public.

Many crises that happen justify the significance of involving the general public in crisis management. In addition to lowering the likelihood and impact of crisis or disaster within their respective areas, involving the community also helps in the reduction of the amount of budget allotted for crisis management. This allotment may then be diverted to other development programs that boost economic growth and development. Buckle[9] opined that the techniques used in the implementation of public participation programs in crisis management vary from country to country because of differences in socio-economic, cultural, and health-related issues. These differences imply that it is extremely difficult to effectively implement a uniform or universal public participation approach that fits the different community aspects. While Jahangiri[10] contended that public participation is critical in crisis management, the type of public participation, coupled with their respective contributions, is likely to differ depending on the features of each given country.

There is a plethora of stakeholders who are actively involved in the CBDM process and who ensure that public participation in crisis management is successful. Stakeholders may be divided into two pertinent groups: outsiders and insiders.[11] Insiders, who are the organizations, individuals, and stakeholders located within the community, have a prime role to play in the management of organizational crisis to reduce the risks that are likely to be stimulated by disasters. The committee responsible for the management of a crisis within the community should mobilize the public to participate in the management of the crisis.[12] Outsiders are represented by the agencies and sectors that are based outside the community, though they are part and parcel of the public participation programs geared toward lessening community vulnerability to disasters, as well as enhancing the community's ability to manage disaster risk. While the outsiders do not constitute public participation, research has shown[13] that their involvement in crisis management provides the general public with the necessary tools and the other required infrastructural facilities for helping the general public in the reduction of community vulnerabilities, while at the same time improving capacities. The outsiders, like the government, promote public participation in crisis management through the provision of material, technical, and financial support to shape successful crisis management models. Rodríguez and Aguirre[14] contended that, for public participation to be an effectual program in crisis management, disaster management and education ought to integrate the outsiders' and the insiders' views.

Where both the insiders and outsiders get involved in the management of the crisis collaboratively, the entire process of crisis management is likely to be highly efficacious compared to when only one actor is involved. It is important to note that, as far as public participation is critical in crisis management, support from outsiders (technical and financial) becomes imperative in crisis management. The provision of financial support enables public participation to implement best practices to lower the intensity of disasters.[15] Therefore, it is crucial to note that in their respective roles as institutions known for providing support, such as technical expertise, financial resources, and political influence to develop policies that impact the lives of citizens positively, outsiders must always be willing to provide support of this nature, so as to foster public participation in crisis management.

Johnston[16] asserted that international research about recovery stresses the significance of not only engaging in a stronger local government, but also developing a cohesive system of integrated private, public, and volunteer groups to deal effectively with a crisis within a community. In circumstances where a significant part of the workforce is heavily engaged in the private sector, the responsibility for developing resiliency within the public sector ought not to be left to the public alone. Instead, crisis management ought to be a collaborative process.

Palen and Liu[17] stressed the role of public participation in crisis management, looking further at how information technology has significantly boosted public participation in crisis management. They contended that the integration of information and communications technology (ICT) not only makes the role of public participation more visible, but also widens the scope of their engagement in crisis management. Social scientists who study disasters have documented the nature of post-disaster public participation as largely altruistic and active. The first responders at the site of a disaster scene are rarely trained professionals, but instead individuals from the local and surrounding communities often tasked with providing first aid to victims.[18]

In cases involving structural collapse, a majority of the individuals who are saved are saved by the emergent volunteer groups, as well as local people. This implies that the locals or the general public normally play an important role in saving a majority of the people affected by a disaster or a crisis, hence playing a crucial role in the entire process of crisis management. It is for these reasons that many people believe in the role of public participation in disaster management.

Pressure Groups and Crisis Management

A pressure group is described as an organization that never fields candidates for political elections, but always seeks to influence the legislation and policies of the government. In other words, pressure groups can also be described as being interest groups, protest groups, or lobby groups. In many instances, the term *pressure groups* is avoided because it portrays the groups as having the aim of using pressure to achieve their objectives, which is not necessarily the case. There is a clear difference between pressure groups and political parties, in that political parties always seek support to achieve victory within their countries. There are a number of pressure groups that can be classified as insider groups, outsider groups, sectional groups, or cause groups.

Insider Groups

These are the pressure groups that have direct access to government cabinet secretaries and high-end officials; thus, they can establish professional relationships that in turn help them in creating viable government policies. In many cases, there is always a section of government ministries that will be responsible for strengthening such established links between the government and the pressure group. Insider groups are usually professionals; therefore, in most instances, they are engaged by the government for legislative and crisis management tactics. A notable example is described by NFU during an outbreak of foot and mouth disease, where professionals assisted in managing the situation.

Outsider Groups
These are the pressure groups that are always far away from the government and have never wanted to stay close to the government, but at times, they are completely unable to reach the government. Such groups might have existed for a very long time within their states, but the government has never and will never seek their opinions on crisis and defense policy management; for example, the CND pressure group has been established over several years but has never been engaged by the government on policy-making. This countryside alliance has championed the interests of rural populations for a long time while strongly throwing support behind fox hunting, but has never been sought to advise the government in the UK.

Sectional Groups
These are the pressure groups charged with representing the needs of a section of the social groups within the community, such as industrial workers, teachers, and lawyers. Their major aim is always improving the working and living standards of their members, and they have been successful historically in many instances; their success can be alluded to in the prevention of the privatization of the London Underground and the United States Postal Service.

Cause Groups
Cause groups can, at times, be split into two distinct segments: the local groups who are always against changes in their areas, and the second group, which tackles wider

issues that may be of longer duration with many impacts on individual lives.

THE ROLE OF PRESSURE GROUPS IN CRISIS MANAGEMENT

In the past, foreign policy existed as a feature isolated from the struggles of the different interest groups, and such were the characteristics of domestic politics: foreign policy was constituted of relatively small cohorts of officials within the State Department and the White House who came up with policies and implemented them without necessarily considering the views of interest groups. For once, the numbers of foreign policy-centered think tanks, lobby groups, and money-fetching political action committees have increased remarkably over the last few decades. For some time, ethnic lobbies, religious organizations, and human rights activists have taken stands on the issues of foreign policy in a better way, thus making foreign policy part and parcel of the pressure groups' domestic political agendas. Additionally, many of these pressure groups have become powerful to the extent that they come up with foreign policies that are later adopted by the government.[19]

On the verge of a political crisis, pressure groups act as important links between citizens and their government, as they will always keep the government accountable and responsive to the needs of its citizens; such undertakings are quite widespread during election periods. Pressure groups are instrumental in the expression of the different needs and views of minority groups within the community; such minority groups would be neglected by the government at times.[20] While applying their expertise, pressure groups have always provided the government with very crucial information concerning the emerging issues of the time.

The major aim of pressure groups is to influence the people in leadership to make decisions that are favorable to them; pressure groups are generally not after the power of political offices, rather, they struggle to influence the decisions made by such offices. In most cases, pressure groups compete with each other with a main agenda of gaining fame; however, sometimes the groups will operate together to achieve a common goal.

Pressure groups exemplify the general opinion of the common citizen and public participation in national politics during election periods. Protest groups also act as sources of specialist information and knowledge that is always considered valuable for decision-making purposes. For instance, Mind and Mencap are groups that campaign on behalf of citizens with mental problems and disabilities; they have often been invited by the government to attend briefings to provide solutions. In return, such groups have contributed immensely to national decision-making, making them eligible for government funds and other financial assistance.[21]

Endnotes

Pressure Groups and Public Participation

1 ISDR, U. (2005, March). Hyogo framework for action 2005-2015: Building the resilience of nations and communities to disasters. In *Extract from the Final Report of the World Conference on Disaster Reduction (A/CONF. 206/6)*.

2 Chen, L. C., Liu, Y. C., & Chan, K. C. (2006). Integrated community-based disaster management program in Taiwan: a case study of Shang-An village. *Natural Hazards, 37*(1-2), 209-223.

3 Victoria, L. (2002) Community based approaches to disaster mitigation. *The Asian Disaster Preparedness Center (ADPC)*.

4 Jahangiri, K., et al. (2011). A comparative study on community-based disaster management in selected countries and designing a model for Iran. *Disaster Prevention and Management, 20*(1), 82-94.

5 López-Marrero, T., & Tschakert, P. (2011). From theory to practice: Building more resilient communities in flood-prone areas. *Environment and Urbanization, 23*, 229-249.

6 Maskrey, A. (2011). Revisiting community-based disaster risk management. *Environmental Hazards, 10*, 42-52.

7 United Nations. (2011). Revealing risk, redefining development. *Global Assessment Report on Disaster Risk Reduction* (GAR). Retrieved from www.preventionweb.net/english/hyogo/gar/2011/en/home/

8 Pandey, B., & Okazaki, K. (2005). Community based disaster management: Empowering communities to cope with disaster risks. *Regional Development Dialogue, 26*(2).

9 López-Marrero, T., & Tschakert, P. (2011). From theory to practice: Building more resilient communities in flood-prone areas. *Environment and Urbanization, 23*, 229-249.

10 Jahangiri, K., et al. (2011). A comparative study on community-based disaster management in selected countries and designing a model for Iran. *Disaster Prevention and Management, 20*(1), 82-94.

11 Victoria, L. (2002) Community based approaches to disaster mitigation. *The Asian Disaster Preparedness Center (ADPC)*.

12 Victoria, L. (2002) Community based approaches to disaster mitiga-

tion. *The Asian Disaster Preparedness Center (ADPC).*

13 Victoria, L. (2002) Community based approaches to disaster mitigation. *The Asian Disaster Preparedness Center (ADPC).*

14 Rodríguez, H., & Aguirre, B. (2005). Education, sustainable development, and disasters: An interactive and collaborative approach. *Preliminary paper #350,* University of Delaware, Disaster Research Center.

15 Victoria, L. (2002) Community based approaches to disaster mitigation. *The Asian Disaster Preparedness Center (ADPC).*

16 ISDR, U. (2005, March). Hyogo framework for action 2005-2015: Building the resilience of nations and communities to disasters. In *Extract from the Final Report of the World Conference on Disaster Reduction (A/CONF. 206/6).*

17 Palen, L., & Liu, S. B. (2007). Citizen communications in crisis: Anticipating a future of ICT-supported public participation.

18 Palen, L., & Liu, S. B. (2007). Citizen communications in crisis: Anticipating a future of ICT-supported public participation.

19 Wiarda, H. J., & Skelley, E. M. (2006). *The crisis of American foreign policy: The effects of a divided America.* New York: Rowman & Littlefield.

20 Australian Politics. (n.d.). *Pressure groups and democracy.* Retrieved from: http://australianpolitics.com/democracy-and-politics/pg/pressure-groups-and-democracy

21 Trueman, C. (2015, May). *What are pressure groups.* Retrieved from The History Learning Site: http://www.historylearningsite.co.uk/british-politics/pressure-groups/what-are-pressure-groups/

Case Study 10: Pink Slime Crisis (2012)

In March 2012, Beef Products Inc. (BPI) fell under criticism along with the lean finely textured beef (LFTB) product, a constituent in approximately 70% of ground beef in America, the meat from a cow cadaver after the primary portions of beef had been detached and separated—that is, bones and tissues placed in a sweltering centrifuge—supposedly bore some microorganisms despite treatment with ammonia, which gave birth to the criticism of the meat product.[1]

At the end of March, BPI was coerced into phasing out three and a half of its four plants because of a decrease in demand for LFTB. Two decades before it was christened "pink slime," this beef byproduct was a trivial staple in fast food, tacos for school lunches, and the meat in most supermarket freezers.[2] Federal regulators never failed to voice safety concerns about it. Not one single incidence has been connected to outbreaks of foodborne diseases or other illnesses. Interestingly, some commentators waxed poetic about the phenomenon in an uncertain world.[3] For this reason, the firm that processed this beef and its byproducts was blamed for ignorance, and a public backlash arose.

A logistics error at BPI led to the sending of 13 cartons of tainted LFTB to consumers rather than to the targeted rendering plant. The company saw the need to recall them as soon as it caught the blunder, though none of it was returned and it was presumed to have been eaten without causing any cases of disease.[4] United States Department of Agriculture (USDA) scientist Gerald Zirnstein toured a BPI facility as part of an inquiry into the contamination. He coined the term *pink slime* in an email conversation with colleagues. He did not view the product as ground beef and considered putting it in ground beef to be an example of false labeling. That same year, the USDA, the department that purchases food for the school lunch program, released a short notice questioning whether LFTB was in their best interest "from the perspective of quality."[5] The notice concluded that BPI should consider appropriate labeling.

CRISIS IN THE INDUSTRY

What the beef industry refers to as LFTB and faultfinders call "pink slime" refers to a filler byproduct that is made by passing scraps from meat cuttings through a processor that eliminates the fat from the trimmings. The beef is typically treated with ammonia to destroy bacteria such as *E. coli* and salmonella tophi.2 The process has been the subject of suspicion and endless debate irrespective of the claims that it is harmless to life.

After the beef industry increased procedures for food safety and hygiene in the aftermath of the Jack in the Box *E. coli* outbreak of 1993, Eldon Roth started coming up with a pH improvement model to limit the amount of microorganisms in beef and beef products. Roth's notion utilized treatment by the use of an ammonium hydroxide gas that consequently paved the way for the advancement of LFTB.[6] The public health organization STOP, which does not generate money, and which dealt with foodborne illnesses and the mother of a child who died as a result of the 1993 Jack in the Box *E. coli* outbreak, wrote opinions for *Food Safety News* supporting the BPI food safety initiatives.

The supermarket Safeway announced that it would stop selling LFTB products because of consumer concerns. Supervalu Inc. announced that it would do the same in all of its retail stores, and so did Kroger and Food Lion. Walmart said it would begin tagging LFTB products to give customers alternatives. In 2003, officials in Georgia returned around 7,000 pounds of LFTB after state penitentiary cooks complained of strong ammonia gas odors in the 60-pound chunks of the product that were meant to be given to inmates.[7]

Officials assumed the meat was accidentally tainted with ammonia, given that its treatment with ammonia was not documented. The same year, a BPI study questioned the process of product containing LFTB with a high pH of 9.5, though the pH of meat typically stands around 6. Company email exchanges indicated that the pH levels would be lowered.

GOVERNMENT REACTION

Federal regulators never announced safety concerns about the product. No individual or institution directly linked LFTB to foodborne illnesses or disease outbreaks. In fact, in the preliminary stages, many food safety activists commended it as technological genius in the world of raw meat, which is often associated with health risks.

Despite the deafening public outcry, USDA officials vouched for BPI's meat. They stated that it had never been linked to any specific diseases because the government began carrying out tests on it in 2009. The authority, through a government spokesperson, announced that, of the samples that BPI gave to the USDA for school lunches in the previous 24 months, all tested negative for either salmonella or lethal strains of *E. coli*.

Lawmakers, however, started claiming that the USDA should stop schools from giving out pink slime in lunch meals. They wanted companies to begin marking the meat that contained LFTB, to which some companies willingly agreed.[8]

THE MEDIA AND PRESSURE GROUPS

The media and pressure groups played a central role in the pink slime crisis. Media from all over the spectrum joined in the debate. Mainstream media like television and electronic media became awash with the details and discussions about the controversy. Another dimension was added by social media, which provided a powerful platform for debate. None of the typical suspects engendered the uproar.

Instead, the revelation was made by a Texas mom who was enthusiastic about improving school food. From her kitchen website "The Lunch Tray," Bettina Elias Siegel urged her readers to "put a stop to pink slime" in school meals and quickly introduced an online written request. One week later, the signatures had topped 200,000. A moniker, "Yuck," went viral, and the factor repelled consumers.

This informed the decision of supermarket chains like Kroger and Food Lion to abandon the product. Wendy's produced newspaper and magazine advertisements guaranteeing that it had never used the product before. Even the slow-moving government bureaucracy leapt into action by permitting schools to make choices about whether to stop or continue using it in their lunches.[9] This media campaign influenced both small and large systems, for example, public institutions.

The affair damaged the prospects of BPI, making it suspend operations indefinitely in some of its plants, though it pledged to keep on paying workers for the period of closure. The meat processor AFA Foods applied for insolvency protection that same month, citing lowered demand and desire for lean beef as factors. At the same time, in March, beef supply and demand reached a 10-year low for the month.

The fallout shows the strength of social media and other media to transform organizations in the same manner that political players and business fraternities respond to pressure exerted by the public. They become vulnerable to slights that taint their reputations. Some consumer groups watched the events unfold with a blend of approbation, wariness, and maybe even remorse.

PRESSURE GROUPS

Some pressure groups also weighed in on the controversy by playing varied roles in the events. There were lawyers, prominent journalists, health experts, and scientists groups and syndicates. Jamie Oliver exposed pink slime to the national discourse on his show, *Jamie Oliver's Food Revolution*. He did it in front of his live viewers by taking a piece of finely textured beef and then illustrated his opinion on the process of making the product by throwing the trimmings into heating equipment, and later sprinkling them with water. The audience was shocked to the point of gasping when he drained the trimmings and began mincing them.[10] Soon after, McDonald's stopped using the product.

An advertising lawyer from Harvard called M. Siegel, who is also a renowned blogger, has discussed the issue in an interview hosted by *The New York Times* after her article, stating that she came to the realization that the USDA had not dropped pink slime from school lunches was published. Consequently, she revitalized the petition, and when the ABC News ran episodes on pink slime the next day, the narrative took off. "Pink slime" became one of the trendiest topics on the Internet.

By the close of the first week show, Siegel had resorted to using caffeine and adrenaline. After nine days, the USDA announced that it was allowing schools to make decisions on the choice to continue or stop using the product.[11] Siegel became exhausted and felt particularly overwhelmed until Oliver resurfaced with a plug for her petition. He shared a tweet and the petition with his more than two million Twitter followers. BPI founder Eldon Roth reacted by taking out a full-page advertisement in *The Wall Street Journal* to denounce the crusade of what he termed lies and false statements directed at his company.[12] However, he declined to comment on most of the articles about the controversy.

CONTRARY OPINIONS

A *New York Times* report established that the USDA originally did not test BPI's beef products, presuming the ammonia gas made it free of pathogens. Federal school lunch officials tested it all the same, found *E. coli* and salmonella on several occasions between 2005 and 2009, and pulled it before it was delivered. But when the most current controversy surfaced, many supported BPI's side of the story.[13]

USDA officials had vouched for BPI's meat. They explained that it had not been directly or indirectly associated with any disease outbreaks since they had started testing it in late 2009. A renowned Seattle lawyer who had built a career on suing meat-manufacturing companies showed his support for the group by asserting that BPI's lean beef was not dangerous for human consumption.[14] He said that the product was not any more or less unsafe than anything else in a hamburger. In so saying, the implication was that the food additive was safe for consumption and that if there was any danger associated with it, then it must be from other materials used in making the hamburgers, as was the popular narrative.

Endnotes

Case Study 10: Pink Slime Crisis (2012)

1 Nestle, M. (2013). *Food politics: How the food industry influences nutrition and health* (Vol. 3). Univ of California Press.

2 Nestle, M. (2013). *Food politics: How the food industry influences nutrition and health* (Vol. 3). Univ of California Press.

3 Willett, W. (2013). *Nutritional epidemiology*. Oxford: Oxford University Press.

4 Simon, D. R. (2013). *Meatonomics: How the rigged economics of meat and dairy make you consume too much–and how to eat better, live longer, and spend smarter*. Conari Press.

5 Simon, D. R. (2013). *Meatonomics: How the rigged economics of meat and dairy make you consume too much–and how to eat better, live longer, and spend smarter*. Conari Press.

6 Nestle, M. (2013). *Food politics: How the food industry influences nutrition and health* (Vol. 3). Univ of California Press.

7 Willett, W. (2013). *Nutritional epidemiology*. Oxford: Oxford University Press.

8 Willett, W. (2013). *Nutritional epidemiology*. Oxford: Oxford University Press.

9 Simon, D. R. (2013). *Meatonomics: How the rigged economics of meat and dairy make you consume too much–and how to eat better, live longer, and spend smarter*. Conari Press.

10 Simon, D. R. (2013). *Meatonomics: How the rigged economics of meat and dairy make you consume too much–and how to eat better, live longer, and spend smarter*. Conari Press.

11 Simon, D. R. (2013). *Meatonomics: How the rigged economics of meat and dairy make you consume too much–and how to eat better, live longer, and spend smarter*. Conari Press.

12 Willett, W. (2013). *Nutritional epidemiology*. Oxford: Oxford University Press.

13 Willett, W. (2013). *Nutritional epidemiology*. Oxford: Oxford University Press.

14 Nestle, M. (2013). *Food politics: How the food industry influences nutrition and health* (Vol. 3). Univ of California Press.

Do Ethics Matter?

In crisis management, business ethics is seen as an unhinged practice; ethics is an improvisational matter. The ethical improvisational nature becomes plain when an organization is faced with a management crisis and an ethical response to crises should be followed. Managers should look for ways to enable themselves to adapt to the crisis as well as exercise a bit of moral imagination. Ethical crisis management should be structurally grounded. Each organization should adopt certain sets of ethical principles and core principled structures, along with organizational mission and vision statements, core values, and codes of conducts.

For an organization to respond to a crisis, it should show ethics as far as collaboration is concerned. Senior management should come together and collaborate with all concerned personnel. Collaboration can eliminate challenges and hindrances brought about by the different viewpoints of individuals. In crisis management, knowledge is paramount. The management team must apply some knowledge that shows their ethical obligation toward their duties. They should also be knowledgeable about the organization's values and shareholders' interests.[1] For managers to face a crisis, it is necessary for them to be comfortable talking about their moral and ethical responsibilities.

It is worth noting that ethical leadership in crisis management matters a lot. By showing their ethical principles, leaders act as role models in dealing with an organizational crisis. Most organizational crises are brought about by personal disagreements. In such a situation, ethics is important since the leaders have a responsibility for creating a safe environment, and their juniors look to them to handle the situation fairly and carefully. Crisis management requires ethical decisions from managers. Ethical leaders are more informed about their organizations; thus, they present high self-efficacy and they have a strong relationship with their juniors. Ethical leaders build a culture of ethics in the workplace, thus reducing the likelihood of crisis occurrence. Again, they influence other employees to behave ethically in the case of a crisis. It is evident that ethical leadership should start from top management and trickle down the hierarchy. The behavior of top management affects juniors directly.[2]

Some crises arise when the management team engages in well-known activities to extend harm and risk to stakeholders. Such actions are usually done without proper precautions. They include crises of deception, management misconduct, and skewed management values. Ethics becomes important during crisis management because it enhances fair economic gains, as managers do not neglect social values and stakeholders' interests. In addition, they certify that they do not favor unjustifiable economic gains. Lopsided values emerge from the classical business creed, ensuring that stakeholders' interests are not neglected. Misguided decisions can disregard the interests of key people, such as the community, employees, and customers.[3] However, ethics comes in to favor the idea that everyone is respected and all the underlying interests are satisfied.

When a crisis occurs, it is important for organizations to establish measures to continue planning for how to recover from the mess. Ethics supports continuity planning by actively pursuing and promoting organizational resilience. Ethical experiences facilitate the recognition of skillful and purposeful learning opportunities in undesirable situations. They also facilitate the development of behaviors and routines that change key operations to support advancement. Strong leaders supported by ethical guidance communicate with stakeholders and the public, influencing the realization of an effective decision.[4] They inform the public and employees about potential hazards likely to create a catastrophic impact.

Ethics encourages managers to take corrective actions during a crisis. They guide organizational leaders in the application of prior experience and learning orientation toward influencing changes to benefit the business' operations. This means that ethics promotes communication and coordination with the stakeholders and public to deal with issues whenever they emerge. Moral behaviors and ethical actions prevent the extension of negative impacts to critical areas of the organization, such as reputation and management. It is evident that a good understanding of the crisis handling process supports effective management. Ethics facilitates the realization of a long-lasting solution in the three phases of the arc: crisis recovery, avoidance, and mitigation.

Business ethics focuses on solving arising issues in a company and facilitates the smooth flow of operations. It enables the elimination of challenges that hinder the integration of ideas and the meeting of organizational objectives.

CRISIS MANAGEMENT:
THE ART OF SUCCESS AND FAILURE

Ethics considers issues as being right or wrong depending on the business context. Every organization should strive to realize economic benefits and meet social expectations. The realm of behavior extends beyond the law to influence different activities in the organization. Ethical responsibilities strive to discourage questionable behaviors by obeying the law. In addition, they avoid undesirable behaviors even when they are legal. It is not possible to develop laws to consider all unethical business activities. For instance, some companies deal with legal products that are perceived to be unethical in key contexts. Business ethics guarantees that businesses take on philanthropic responsibility by contributing money and time to society.

Ethics supports corporate governance and facilitates the establishment of an effective business culture. Every company should develop codes of ethics to support the establishment of ethical behaviors. The process enhances productivity by ensuring that conflicts are well handled. Established codes provide guidelines to be followed during the crisis management process. The process promotes public relations and the improvement of business relationships with workers.[5] Well-established ethical codes extend many benefits to stakeholders and companies in various ways. Business ethics becomes particularly important during crisis management by guiding employees when the ethical course is not obvious right away. The process enables companies and influences employees to develop positive values and a desirable culture. It also helps establish an environment of excellence and integrity.

During a crisis, business ethics improves communication and the achievement of customers' and workers' expectations. It offers room for honest, frequent, and open communication among employees, and consequently improves reconciliation and understanding between rival parties. In addition, ethics reduces inconsistent and subjective management standards. Ethics establishes the responsibilities and rights of workers and guards against preferential and capricious treatment.

Leadership competencies are important factors when dealing with crisis management. The ability of leaders to apply innovative ideas during organizational restructuring facilitates the achievement of the required results. The ethics of the leaders enables them to make unbiased decisions and focus on areas that can extend many benefits to the organization, employees, and stakeholders. They facilitate the building of a trusting environment where everyone is motivated to support crisis management. The process encourages the participation of all involved parties toward the successful elimination of problems. It becomes easy to reform the organization's mindset and ensure that the interests of all employees are in line with those of the business. The consideration of morals and ethics makes it easy to identify obscure and obvious vulnerabilities affecting the organization. Workers and managers are encouraged to make rapid and wise decisions and gain courage when making decisions.[6] Ethics makes every process a learning opportunity and attests that similar problems will not affect the organization.

Leadership actions influenced by ethics reflect the organization's competency during crisis management. The crisis management test demonstrates organizational leadership structures and determines how well an organization can handle issues that arise during crisis management. Developing effective human resources is essential when establishing organizational capacity through executive leadership. For instance, unequal human capital theory suggests that an organizational crisis can emerge from discrimination lawsuits. These discrimination lawsuits can damage reputations, influence negative stakeholder reactions, and threaten corporate survival.[7]

Ethics and moral behaviors boost the development of an effective organizational culture that inspires everyone to work hard toward organizational growth and conflict resolution. Ethics motivates workers to gain an interest in issues that determine organizational growth and success.[8] Ethics guides the decisions and behaviors of all the stakeholders in the organization and thus encourages the faster and more effective development of solutions.

Business ethics evaluates the morals and principles that determine and guide management decisions. It is evident that ethical issues determine organizational obligations to suppliers, employees, customers, and the public. Therefore, failure to consider morals and ethics during crisis management can create many negative outcomes. Business ethics deals with situations when key obligations become inconsistent with strategic or economic choices, or where they develop conflicts with each other.[9] Although ethical beliefs are voluntary, they are extremely important for organizations dealing with a management crisis. In addition, they are applied to every aspect of conduct in a business, including individuals and the business as a whole. They are important during crisis management because they follow institutional values and personal beliefs. Managers guided by ethical principles take action to support their organization and represent society.[10] Businesses depend on their reputations to achieve consistent and clear expectations concerning ethical standards toward molding the behaviors of their workers.

Ethics provides a better platform for supporting organizational communication and ensuring that employees offer required services to customers. The process enables the organization to deal with the threats or issues that are likely to affect its operations. Ethics helps organizations handle issues related to the element of surprise, organizational threats, and limited decision-making time.[11] Soliciting questions and feedback facilitates the application of codes to support open, honest, and frequent communication among workers. Most crises arise because of disagreements. The problem can be eliminated by ethics, as it minimizes inconsistent and subjective management standards.[12]

Crisis management deals with issues before they occur and impact the organization in a negative manner. Ethics forms a critical part of crisis management by establishing techniques and skills for solving the existing problem. It starts with the identification of the problem, assessing issues, improving understanding, and establishing measures to handle challenging situations. It involves a situation-based management system entailing clear responsibilities and roles.[13] The ethical response to a crisis involves crisis assessment, prevention, termination, and handling. The process focuses on prevention and the establishment of adequate and rapid responses. It means that failure to consider moral behaviors and ethical aspects can make it difficult to realize success during crisis management.

CRISIS MANAGEMENT:
THE ART OF SUCCESS AND FAILURE

During crisis management, ethics helps organizations comply with all government regulations. For instance, the landmark Sarbanes-Oxley Act of 2002 expects public organizations to develop codes to guide senior financial officers.[14] The process facilitates the development of businesses' reputation and public trust. Ethical codes enable organizations to demonstrate the companies' values in remaining socially responsible to workers and investors. This means that ethics facilitates the establishment of a long-lasting solution during the crisis management process. As part of crisis management, ethics improves employee pride, morale, and loyalty. It increases the chances of recruiting quality, well-skilled workers who have what it takes to support organizational growth.[15]

In conclusion, crisis management is a challenging process because new issues arise, challenging the organization's ability to deal with the problem. However, ethics plays a critical role in the promotion of market efficiency, particularly where existing laws are inefficient and weak. It rewards the most ethical workers by recognizing hard work and commitment from the workers. It also improves everyone's efficiency, and thus eliminates the chances of realizing failures and conflicts. It is important for organizations to consider moral behaviors and ethical aspects when dealing with crisis management because they provide guidance and motivate everyone to work hard toward solving the arising issues. It is the sole method ensuring that the interests of workers are in line with those of the organization and supporting the development of corrective measures during crisis management.

Endnotes

Do Ethics Matter?

1 Avey, J. B., Palanski, M. E., & Walumbwa, F. O. (2011). When leadership goes unnoticed: The moderating role of follower self-esteem on the relationship between ethical leadership and follower behavior. *Journal of Business Ethics*, 98(4), 573–582.

2 Carroll, A., & Buchholtz, A. (2014). *Business and society: Ethics, sustainability, and stakeholder management.* Cengage Learning.

3 Hagman, H. C. (2013). *European crisis management and defence: The search for capabilities* (No. 353). Routledge.

4 Avey, J. B., Palanski, M. E., & Walumbwa, F. O. (2011). When leadership goes unnoticed: The moderating role of follower self-esteem on the relationship between ethical leadership and follower behavior. *Journal of Business Ethics*, 98(4), 573–582.

5 Avey, J. B., Palanski, M. E., & Walumbwa, F. O. (2011). When leadership goes unnoticed: The moderating role of follower self-esteem on the relationship between ethical leadership and follower behavior. *Journal of Business Ethics*, 98(4), 573–582.

6 Avey, J. B., Palanski, M. E., & Walumbwa, F. O. (2011). When leadership goes unnoticed: The moderating role of follower self-esteem on the relationship between ethical leadership and follower behavior. *Journal of Business Ethics*, 98(4), 573–582.

7 Drennan, L. T., McConnell, A., & Stark, A. (2014). *Risk and crisis management in the public sector.* Routledge.

8 Ferrell, O. C., & Fraedrich, J. (2014). *Business ethics: Ethical decision making & cases.* Cengage Learning.

9 Lerbinger, O. (2012). *The crisis manager.* London: Routledge.

10 Avey, J. B., Palanski, M. E., & Walumbwa, F. O. (2011). When leadership goes unnoticed: The moderating role of follower self-esteem on the relationship between ethical leadership and follower behavior. *Journal of Business Ethics*, 98(4), 573–582.

11 Boulos, M. N. K., Resch, B., Crowley, D. N., Breslin, J. G., Sohn, G., Burtner, R. . . . & Chuang, K. Y. S. (2011). Crowdsourcing, citizen sensing & sensor web technologies for public & environmental health surveillance

and crisis management: Trends, OGC standards & application examples. *International Journal of Health Geographics, 10*(1), 67.

12 Ferrell, O. C., & Fraedrich, J. (2014). *Business ethics: Ethical decision making & cases.* Cengage Learning.

13 Drennan, L. T., McConnell, A., & Stark, A. (2014). *Risk and crisis management in the public sector.* Routledge.

14 Ferrell, O. C., & Fraedrich, J. (2014). *Business ethics: Ethical decision making & cases.* Cengage Learning.

15 Drennan, L. T., McConnell, A., & Stark, A. (2014). *Risk and crisis management in the public sector.* Routledge.

Case Study 11: Egyptian Crisis (2013)

On November 22, 2012, Mohammed Morsi, the Egyptian president, issued a constitutional proclamation that had six articles. In his presidential decree, the following was highlighted:

1. The Prosecutor General was dismissed
2. The trials and investigations about the murders and attempted murders of the demonstrators who were killed during the revolution of 2011 were reopened
3. All the people who held executive or political positions in the previous regime were implicated
4. The dissolution of the Constituent Assembly and the Consultative Council were prevented
5. Decrees by the president from oversight by the judiciary were shielded

The above proclamations almost stirred an uprising, with demonstrations held on November 23rd and 27th of that same year in numerous locations throughout the country. The demonstrators accused the president of trying to exercise dictatorship, as he had also claimed that he had turned out to be the "new pharaoh." The demonstrations were accompanied by huge counter-demonstrations by the supporters of the president at the University of Cairo. Consequently, Egypt was plunged into a serious political crisis that was accompanied by extreme polarization between secularists, liberals, and leftists on the one hand and Islamists on the other hand.[1]

Morsi decided to ignore the effects of the decree and pressed the Constituent Assembly to draft the constitution in a hurry. As soon as the constitution had been drafted, the president put the draft up for a referendum in two weeks' time. The opposition continued protesting. The protests eventually became street clashes in which firearms, knives, and stones were used. The protests resulted in the deaths of seven people and numerous other people were injured. Among the major reasons that caused serious opposition was the fact that there was no trust between the different political factions, which provoked doubts about the intentions of the Muslim Brotherhood with respect to the introduction of the extreme measures by the president.[2]

This case study seeks to discuss the unethical behaviors and violence caused by President Morsi and his Muslim Brotherhood in solving the crisis facing them, and how the unethical behavior brought the Brotherhood down. The case study is an illustration of the benefits of ethics in governing a country and the damage that can result if a leader tries to survive a crisis using unprincipled means.

THE UNETHICAL BEHAVIORS THAT RESULTED IN THE CRISIS

The constitutional proclamation by President Morsi on November 22 was an effort to hasten the period of transition that had begun with President Mubarak resigning on February 11, 2011. Morsi realized that, with the dissolution of the Constitutional Assembly, the country would go into a new crisis, and thus would interrupt the course of transition, which would imply that the president had failed. Morsi needed a political settlement with the military, and he therefore had to hasten his policies to protect his leadership. He knew that abolishing the Assembly would not only lengthen the constitutional vacuum, but would also imply that the country would have to start from the beginning and re-ignite the confrontations with the various political forces in the country.

Just a few months before, Tahrir Square had erupted in cheers after Egypt voted for its first democratically elected president. Now the square was packed to capacity with civilians who were cheering the ousting of President Morsi by the military. After the ousting of President Morsi, the constitution was suspended, and a senior judiciary official was made the interim leader as they waited for new elections, while Morsi was placed under house arrest.

When Morsi became the president of Egypt, he charmed civilians by telling them that he was not afraid, because he was a democratically elected president, "one of the people." That phrase was frequently used by the Muslim Brotherhood as a claim for legitimacy, and a statement that the leader represented real Egyptians. The phrase was meant to show that the leader was not just representing the city dwellers or the upper-class society, but the millions of citizens who were living in the villages, slums, and small towns.

Just a few weeks after taking office, Morsi announced that several senior military officials had been forced to retire. These officials included the defense minister, Field Marshal Tantawi, who had headed the Supreme Council of

CRISIS MANAGEMENT:
THE ART OF SUCCESS AND FAILURE

the Armed Forces (SCAF). SCAF was also forced to dissolve after it had ruled the country for about 18 months during the transition between the election of Morsi and the overthrow of President Hosni Mubarak.[3]

In the coming months, Morsi, along with his Freedom and Justice Party, failed to maximize on the popular goodwill that they had in the initial stages of forming the new government. As a matter of fact, the acts committed by this new government only seemed to push everyone away. Among the sectors that felt alienated by the new government were the army, the electorate, and the liberals who had reluctantly voted for the government (the only other choice that the liberals had was to return Mubarak into leadership, something that they strongly loathed).

In most of the situations encountered by the government at that time, Morsi appeared to be an incompetent leader who was basically a dictator. Take, for example, his announcement that his position as president was not subject to any judicial review. What Morsi meant was that he was above the law. Mass demonstrations ensued outside the presidential palace, and Morsi had to retract the announcement.[4]

On another occasion, Morsi announced massive taxation, which included significant increases in the prices of common food staples. Just like after the previous unethical announcement, this announcement was followed by an uproar from civilians, and the president had to retract his announcement at about 2 a.m. on his Facebook page.

After the two announcements, things went from bad to worse, with the ruling party getting itself involved in one crisis after another. Civilians experienced shortages in gas

Case Study 11: Egyptian Crisis (2013)

and outages of electricity, and worst of all, there was a threat of a huge water crisis. The prices of basic products rose at an exponential rate, while the level of unemployment in the country continued to increase. Tourists from other nations avoided the country since the government had failed to bring about stability and order.[5]

In a move that was a reflection of the former president's style of leadership, the general prosecutor of the state charged Bassem Youssef, a man who was popularly known as the Egyptian Jon Stewart, with having insulted Islam and the president. Youssef's program had skits that usually mocked President Morsi.

As the trial was taking place, there were also organized sexual assaults that were carried out on women, and these organized mass assaults went unchecked. The government was also frequently accused of deploying Muslim Brotherhood bandits to beat up demonstrators from the opposition.[6]

The turning point of the above events came in June 2013, when there was a conference about the crisis in Syria. At this meeting, Morsi sat silently as the radical clerics of Salafi called the Shiites infidels. A few days before the conference, Morsi had called for military intervention in Syria.[7]

Just a few days after the conference, four Egyptian Shiite men were lynched in Giza by a mob. This highlighted the rise of sectarian tensions in the government under Morsi, and these events resulted in mass violence that was highly criticized by the international community.

The above events followed the signing of a petition to have fresh general elections, as people had already given up on the government that they had elected just a few months before. As a matter of fact, people started withdrawing money from their bank accounts, others left the country, and the rest stockpiled food in preparation for a foreseeable calamity. Eventually, the military ousted Morsi after they had given him a 48-hour ultimatum to solve his political crisis.[8]

CONCLUSION

Upon the election of Morsi as the Egyptian president, he was very popular and admired by almost the whole Egyptian population. However, the tactics used by his government to solve crises made him the most unpopular man in Egypt. The mass arrests of people who were questioning his leadership and policies were highly unethical. Morsi should have at least allowed civilians to demonstrate peacefully and let them express their reasons for dissatisfaction; however, Morsi chose to be intolerant of such unrest and chose the unethical means of either killing or imprisoning people who questioned him. The forced retirement of the military officials was highly unethical, as it only meant that Morsi wanted to create a government that was totally loyal to him without any bit of loyalty to the previous leadership. Firing the officials was a clear indication that he was up to no good for the people of Egypt. Morsi also used his Muslim Brotherhood thugs to conduct unsuspecting raids on the civilians who seemed to be discontent with his leadership, and to sexually assault women. The cold-blooded killings and arrests of peaceful demonstrators and the increasing taxes on staple food products were among the unethical deeds that resulted in the failure of a government that had previously been popular.[9]

Using ethical means to govern the country, as well as involving the opposition and the general public in the

Case Study 11: Egyptian Crisis (2013)

creation of policies, would have let the government live longer. Additionally, the use of force and dictatorship while managing crises has proven to have dire effects on the management of a country.[10] When unethical means are used to govern people, or even to force them to comply with policies, the repercussions are very clear. Eventually, some external force or the people themselves will overcome the powers that be, just like they did in Egypt. It is important to note that using unethical means in leadership does not necessarily mean the use of force; for example, the action by Morsi to raise taxes on food products was unethical, without a doubt, because he did not follow the right procedures to raise taxes, the taxes were too high, and people were facing extreme levels of unemployment.

Endnotes

Case Study 11: Egyptian Crisis (2013)

1 Lakhal, S. Y. (2014). Morsi's failure in Egypt: The impact of energy-supply chains. *Middle East Policy*, *21*(3), 134–144.

2 Lakhal, S. Y. (2014). Morsi's failure in Egypt: The impact of energy-supply chains. *Middle East Policy*, *21*(3), 134–144.

3 Lakhal, S. Y. (2014). Morsi's failure in Egypt: The impact of energy-supply chains. *Middle East Policy*, *21*(3), 134–144.

4 Lakhal, S. Y. (2014). Morsi's failure in Egypt: The impact of energy-supply chains. *Middle East Policy*, *21*(3), 134–144.

5 Salman, S. (2014). For freedom or security? A critical appraisal of Egypt's unfinished revolution. *Situations: Project of the Radical Imagination*, *5*(2).

6 Curtis, L., Florance, C., Lohman, W., & Phillips, J. (2014). *Pursuing a freedom agenda amidst rising global Islamism*.

7 Abaza, M. (2014). Post January revolution Cairo: Urban wars and the reshaping of public space. *Theory, Culture & Society*, 0263276414549264.

8 Lakhal, S. Y. (2014). Morsi's failure in Egypt: The impact of energy-supply chains. *Middle East Policy*, *21*(3), 134–144.

9 Molyneux, J. (2015). Lessons from the Egyptian Revolution. *Irish Marxist Review*, *4*(13), 18–32.

10 Molyneux, J. (2015). Lessons from the Egyptian Revolution. *Irish Marxist Review*, *4*(13), 18–32.

Case Study 12: BP Oil Spill (2010)

The Deepwater Horizon oil spill refers to an accident in the petroleum industry involving the British Petroleum (BP) company in the Gulf of Mexico. The oil spill event happened on April 20, 2010 and affected the Cuban and Mexican coasts on a large scale. After the oil rig exploded, crude fuel flowed for 87 days before disaster management teams capped the pipes on July 15, 2010.[1] The explosion killed 11 people, whose bodies continue to be missing. In addition, the oil rig discharged approximately 4.9 million barrels of crude oil into the ocean. The efforts to contain the largest oil spill in the world's history involved the use of different techniques, but some of the techniques, such as controlled burns and oil dispersants, resulted in more damage.[2] However, the spill lasted a long time and had an adverse impact on aquatic ecosystems, beaches, fishing activities, tourism, and the local populations that depended on the ocean. Despite the obvious large-scale adverse effects of the oil spill, BP did not respond appropriately to the crisis. Evasion, scapegoating, and denial of responsibility marked the company's responses to the disaster and therefore undermined BP's corporate image and commitment to ethical business operations.

Transocean Ltd. operated the oil rig that exploded in

the Gulf of Mexico, but BP oil was the owner. The ownership-operatorship situation provided BP with a loophole to shift the blame onto Transocean. According to Tony Hayward, the CEO of BP, the oil rig belonged to Transocean and the people on site were the employees of Transocean, and therefore the accident did not belong to BP.[3] Given the fact that investigations had not yet commenced on the accident, the CEO's act amounted to scapegoating by forcing responsibility on Transocean, yet both companies had economic interests in the oil rig. The CEO again demonstrated the company's unwillingness to accept responsibility when he declared that the quantity of oil spilled and dispersant used was "relatively tiny," especially when compared to the "very big size" of the ocean.[4] Hayward's evasion of responsibility continued after stating that the environmental impact of the oil spill would be "very, very modest." The statements and reactions of the CEO represented BP's views and responses since the CEO is the main face of the company and speaks on its behalf. According to Corkindale,[5] BP focused on maintaining an army of PR professionals and media advisers to spin its way out of the crisis.

On many occasions, BP tried covering up the actual damage caused by the oil spill on the Mexican coast.[6] For example, the company did not provide the true quantity of oil leaking onto the ocean floor every day until scientists and environmentalists demanded proof of their figures. Videos released regarding the leak proved that the company had lied to the public.[7] Another area that remained gray for a long time involved the extent of the damage on the environment and sea life. For example, BP insisted that the damage would be minimal even though thousands of dead fish could be seen floating on the ocean and many locals could not use their beaches or go out to fish.

The company's crisis management practices during the disaster were under par for many reasons. BP's management failed to follow the company's internal guidelines regarding damage control.[8] For example, BP's damage control policy states that the company will not make any statement containing a promise that property, ecology, or anything else will be restored to normal during a disaster. Corkindale[9] wrote that BP took extreme risks, while at the same time ignoring expert advice and overlooking safety issues regarding its operations in the sea. The company's failure to respond with sufficient speed and attention highlighted the flawed culture of the organization.[10] As the crisis continued to unfold and BP failed to address it effectively, the company's share prices and value started declining in the major exchanges in which its shares trade. At no point did BP talk about compensating the people whose livelihood depended on the ocean, but who now faced many challenges and health risks. The company waited until a hearing was scheduled to set up a fund aimed at compensating the affected communities and attempting to restore the environment damaged by the disaster.

After the oil spill, environmentalists and members of the public across the world criticized BP's response to the disaster. On June 22, 2010, Lee Perkins created a Facebook page in which he rallied more than 688,500 people to boycott BP and its products.[11] On July 3, 2010, a consumer group by the name of Public Citizen had gathered more than 22,000 pledges from consumers to not purchase BP products for at least three months, hoping for a better response from the company.[12] Besides online protests, millions of people gathered in major U.S. cities to protest BP's actions and response to the disaster. Musicians and musical bands did not shy away from criticizing BP's actions and boycotting its products. In particular, Lady Gaga, Korn, the 2010 Mayhem Festival, Rise Against, Creed, and Disturbed pledged that they would not use any of BP's products in their worldwide tour concerts. In practice, the public image of a company or the attitudes of consumers about a company are very important factors in its success. Influential people and groups such as musicians and environmental activists often influence consumers' purchasing decisions. Calls for boycotts can negatively affect the sales of a company because consumers will turn to companies perceived as being better than the affected company. Companies with questionable public images always lose their competitive advantages over other companies. In this case, BP's reaction to the disaster raised many questions concerning the morality of the company.[13] For example, the oil spill resulted in extensive damage to the environment, but BP chose as its first reaction to ignore the tragedy and took no corrective action toward the problem or working closely with the stakeholders affected by the issue.

In conclusion, disasters are sometimes inevitable for companies operating high-risk business activities, such as drilling for oil from the seabed. However, it is important for every company to comply with the rules and regulations pertaining to its business. Moreover, companies should go a step further to ensure that they remain proactive before and after unexpected disasters take place. BP's failure to handle the Deep Horizon oil spill in the best possible way placed the company's reputation on the line. Backlash from the public can result in poor sales that may have adverse effects on the company. Therefore, it is important for businesses to take responsibility for their actions and to respond promptly to disasters that pose threats to different stakeholders. Proper disaster management practices always limit the damage and ensure that the company's reputation remains intact.

Endnotes

Case Study 12: BP Oil Spill (2010)

1 Mejri, M., & Daniel, D. E. (2013). Crisis management: Lessons learnt from the BP Deepwater Horizon spill oil. *Business Management and Strategy, 4*(2), 67.

2 De Wolf, D. (2013). Crisis communication failures: The BP case study. *International Journal of Advances in Management and Economics, 2*(2).

3 Webb, T. (2010). BP's clumsy response to oil spill threatens to make a bad situation worse. Retrieved from http://www.theguardian.com/business/2010/jun/01/bp-response-oil-spill-tony-hayward

4 De Wolf, D. (2013). Crisis communication failures: The BP case study. *International Journal of Advances in Management and Economics, 2*(2).

5 Corkindale, G. (2010). Five leadership lessons from the BP oil spill. Retrieved from https://hbr.org/2010/06/five-lessons-in-leadership-fro

6 De Wolf, D. (2013). Crisis communication failures: The BP case study. *International Journal of Advances in Management and Economics, 2*(2).

7 Mejri, M., & Daniel, D. E. (2013). Crisis management: Lessons learnt from the BP Deepwater Horizon spill oil. *Business Management and Strategy, 4*(2), 67.

8 De Wolf, D. (2013). Crisis communication failures: The BP case study. *International Journal of Advances in Management and Economics, 2*(2).

9 Corkindale, G. (2010). Five leadership lessons from the BP oil spill. Retrieved from https://hbr.org/2010/06/five-lessons-in-leadership-fro

10 Corkindale, G. (2010). Five leadership lessons from the BP oil spill. Retrieved from https://hbr.org/2010/06/five-lessons-in-leadership-fro

11 De Wolf, D. (2013). Crisis communication failures: The BP case study. *International Journal of Advances in Management and Economics, 2*(2).

12 Mejri, M., & Daniel, D. E. (2013). Crisis management: Lessons learnt from the BP Deepwater Horizon spill oil. *Business Management and Strategy, 4*(2), 67.

13 Mejri, M., & Daniel, D. E. (2013). Crisis management: Lessons learnt from the BP Deepwater Horizon spill oil. *Business Management and Strategy, 4*(2), 67.

Organizational Culture as a Source of Crisis

During the 1980s, organizational culture was considered the best determinant for any organizational success. Several academicians and experts argued that there was a need to develop a very strong organizational culture to achieve success within organizations. Even though there is a correlation between organizational efficiency and culture, one cannot deny the fact that every organization exhibits a strong social structural make-up through which employee behavior is driven, as observed within business and political entities. While looking at this matter, I am going to dwell mostly on the existing relationship between organizational cultures and their ultimate effects on the behaviors of employees and their drive toward success. Despite the significance of organizational culture in a company's success, sometimes it becomes the source of a crisis, which ultimately interferes with the company's competitiveness at both the local and international levels.

Over time, it has been quite difficult to have a single definition in reference to the concept of organizational cultures. The existing literature has not settled on any single definition, though the factors that surround culture have been highlighted as being integral in organizational success.[1] A number of people have employed the term *culture* in coming up with descriptions of the different patterns of multicultural attributes and their consistency that impact the organization. For instance, when people define culture as "the way we do things here," they tend to factor in the countless consistent ways through which individuals solve issues, perform duties, treat employees and customers, and resolve their conflicts.[2]

According to White,[3] culture refers to a set of mechanisms that create cross-individual attribute consistency. In such a situation, culture becomes the norms, informal values, and set of beliefs influencing group and individual behaviors within an organization by regulating their interactions with one another, as well as with individuals outside their organizations. Despite the role of culture in shaping the organization's market share and competitiveness, such culture may sometimes be the primary cause of organizational crisis, even more so in circumstances where it is not properly aligned with the objectives and goals of the organization or where the culture conflicts with the interests of different stakeholders.

An organizational crisis can be examined based on several aspects of its outcomes, including spoiling the organization's reputation; destroying the financial performance of the organization; causing harm to the health of employees, the environment, consumers, and surrounding communities; or destroying the public image and trust in the organization. An organizational crisis can then be defined as the unexpected but specific and inconsistent events capable of creating very high levels of panic and uncertainty, or rather a threat to the organizational objectives of service delivery and success.[4] Similarly, Venette[5] attempted to define an organizational crisis as being the transformation process where the old system is no longer able to be maintained or becomes outdated, hence acting as a source of the crisis.

An organizational crisis refers to the loss of balance within one of the organizational systems, thus having a greater impact on the company's path of existence, as well as that of achieving its goals. The organizational corporate culture is a fabric of several rules of behavior and values existing within and outside the company that is always shared by all the employees within the organization for the purpose of binding them together.

There is a reciprocated unintentional relationship between organizational crises and corporate culture. In the event that the corporate culture within the organization is not that strong, then an organization could break down through its subsystems in the case of a crisis; thus unveiling the values and existing relationships that are hidden behind the organizational culture would be essential.[6] On the other hand, in some cases, the organization's corporate culture can be linked to the launch of the crisis causal chain directly, showing that the absolute cause of the crisis is an imbalance within the organization's systems, accelerating the crisis development process.

The major causes of organizational imbalances are inclusive of a lack of or insufficient corporate culture, lack of inclusion, and the formulation of the corporate culture in a more systematic manner, as well as the absence of transformational practices under changing organizational conditions. The organization's corporate culture is made up of individuals within the company and with the consideration that each and every one of them seems to have different and original thoughts; every corporate culture appears to be quite unique in its own way. Similarly, there is a great influence on people's thoughts and actions, thereby making it quite impossible to act quickly against changing organizational conditions and environments, thus ultimately leading to changes within the organization's corporate structure and culture.[7]

During shifts in organizational culture, there come very significant changes subsequently; in smaller organizations, such changes are detected after two to three years, while in larger companies, they could take up to ten years before being realized. The literature has highlighted the various characteristics of corporate culture that are believed to be the source of crisis within an organization. Some organizational features, such as a lack of clear strategy to guide change implementation, can be a potent source of crisis within the organization.

ORGANIZATIONAL CULTURE AS A BARRIER TO CHANGE AND IMPROVEMENT

One cannot deny the fact that organizational changes are typically met with lots of resistance from organizational members. This is because not all members may be willing to embrace change, as they might fear that change implementation could be disastrous for their job security. There is a form of conflict that has increasingly developed between the organization's surroundings and the real world, and which incorporates the corporate culture. Even though it takes a smaller frequency of occurrence, the impact is significant to the organization. For instance, the changeover of the Czech community to a market economy from a planned economy, which is part of the corporate culture, created a crisis, as many organizations have been unable to cope with the transition to date. However, most of the crises that are being experienced in the corporate world have been attributed to the conduct of executives and company owners, based on their personal interests over a short time and their asset-stripping nature, causing them to ignore the changes taking place in the corporate culture.[8] When a new reward system is to be implemented to support a strategy or direction change, employees' cultural mechanisms and values supporting the older system tend to remain deeply rooted, thus creating a conflict with the new system. This, therefore, becomes a fierce battle affecting the cultural and structural strength of the organization.

COMPANY ENLARGEMENT AND DIVERSITY

Existing stronger company cultures will always create uniform and consistent behavior among employees; this aspect is known as the cross-individual consistency of behavior. Even though this may be desirable in many ways, it may work against the organizational objectives while other competitors can use workplace diversity for competitive advantages in more or less than two strategies. First, strong organizational cultures are created through the recruitment of new employees, and such a selection would be done based on the individuals who may be deemed fit for the organization. Thus, through this, diversity is always limited. Second, when employees are looking for potential employers in the corporate world, they will always avoid organizations with strong cultures that have no alignment with their values.[9]

Similarly, strong organizational cultures will always

be barriers to diversity in that the culture will mostly work to create homogeneity within the corporate workforce. A simple reason organizations should strive for diversity in the workforce is based on the premise that diverse decision-making teams will always be the source of strong organizational culture, thus helping the company thrive in marketplaces with lots of diversity.[10] All the benefits achieved through diversity in the recruitment process may be lost while trying to fit new employees into a strong organizational culture.

When organizations are established, each has a definite corporate culture accompanied by different attempts at implementing business plans, as well as the entrepreneurial fervor that is reflected in the stakeholders' culture. Together with organizational enlargement, an increased number of employees and the recruitment of new employees who may be lacking an intimate relationship with the company through the early stages will cause organizational changes, and the failure to understand such shifts in organizational cultures may be the source of crisis in many situations.[11]

BARRIERS TO COMPANY MERGERS AND ACQUISITIONS

Organizational mergers have been cited as one of the most notable causes of organizational failures in a high percentage of organizations; organizational goals are practically not met on time since the original organizations are unable to adopt unfamiliar mixed strategies to deal with the challenges and conflicts arising between the two conflicting organizations. Merger problems will always occur when the plans for the merger are the products of two distinct departments being expected to work and deliver as a single unit. For instance, the concepts of dress codes, team decision-making, and leadership styles are highly affected by mergers.

In most cases, mergers are accompanied by the temporary suspension of employees or permanent termination when some positions in the newly merged divisions are no longer required; this will lead to communication breakdowns between the employer and employees, thereby stimulating conflicts, unwillingness to cooperate, and mutual controversies.[12] In general terms, the merger of companies is always linked to changes in various organizational strategies, coupled with the development of new corporate cultures. Through such, the resultant culture may create a communication crisis.

THE PRESENCE OF SUBCULTURES IMPOSING NEGATIVE IMPACTS ON THE ORGANIZATION

Despite the fact that corporate culture is at times developed intentionally in certain situations, it is never monolithic and may have sprouted many subcultures within departments and professional groups. Within a number of the existing subcultures, there could be major deviations from the mainstream organizational culture based on the developed personal interests opposing the culture of the company and aimed at striking forward.[13] This will finally result in a lack of cooperation with and support for company strategies and goals, affecting the company's goal implementation and loyalty. On the other hand, such a situation may cause intentional problems and also deliberate ignorance of different problem-solving techniques, thus leading to organizational crisis.

MAJOR CHANGES IN COMPANY OWNERSHIP STRUCTURES

Any notable changes in the ownership and management systems of organizations will always bring about variations, not only in the goals and objectives, but also in the need for an alteration in the company's corporate culture. While trying to exercise such demands of organizational changes, conflict may arise between the fresh management group and the conservative personnel that have been in place since the initial establishment of the company.[14] Such conflicting interests between the two sets of management groups will always lead to a threat to organizational goals and policies, thus creating a crisis situation.

COMPANY PROCESS REENGINEERING/CHANGE IN COMPANY STRATEGY/TRANSFORMATION

Every change and transformational process within organizations will always call for full support from executives, together with the majority of employees. In the event that the organizational culture is not aligned with the objectives and goals of the organization, the probability that the change will not be successfully implemented is very high. In the case that management is successful in the implementation of such inconsistent changes, then they are always short-lived and the entire organization will always lean back on the old routines, creating a crisis in the transformation process.[15]

USE OF MANAGEMENT STRATEGIES INSTEAD OF LEADERSHIP STRATEGIES

In cases in which managers have created bureaucratic structures of rule, a situation of in-company management where decisions are centralized, the company will always be concerned with internal efficiency and processes, while in leadership, company management is always dictated by the various outcomes of the company.[16]

Apparently, institutions where management is highly inclined to embrace a positive corporate culture are more likely to see greater success. While assessing the business world, it is obvious that organizational culture is among the major factors taken into consideration to achieve competitive advantages within marketplaces. It is therefore clear that, in the event that a company becomes successful in continuous improvement, the chances of experiencing a crisis are reduced.

Endnotes

Organizational Culture as a Source of Crisis

1 Kilmann, R., Saxton, M., & Serpa, R. (1986). Issues in understanding and changing culture. *California Management Review, 28*, 87–94.

2 Frost, P. (1985). *Organizational culture.* Beverly Hills: Sage Publications.

3 White, K. (1999). *Organizational culture.* Hove, East Sussex, UK: Psychology Press.

4 Seeger, M., Sellnow, T., & Ulmer, R. (1998). Communication, organization, and crisis. *Communication Yearbook, 21*, 231–275.

5 Venette, S. J. (2003). *Risk communication in a high reliability organization* (Doctoral dissertation, North Dakota State University).

6 Svedin, L. (2009). *Organizational cooperation in crises.* Farnham, England: Ashgate Pub.

7 Zuzak, R. (2001). Corporate culture as a source of crisis in companies. *Agricultural Economics-UZPI (Czech Republic).*

8 Zuzak, R. (2001). Corporate culture as a source of crisis in companies. *Agricultural Economics-UZPI (Czech Republic).*

9 White, K. (1999). *Organizational culture.* Hove, East Sussex, UK: Psychology Press.

10 Herriot, P., & Pemberton, C. (1995). *Competitive advantage through diversity: Organizational learning from difference.* London: Sage Publications.

11 Venette, S. J. (2003). *Risk communication in a high reliability organization* (Doctoral dissertation, North Dakota State University).

12 Jick, T. D. (1979). *Process and impacts of a merger: Individual and organizational perspectives* (Doctoral dissertation, ProQuest Information & Learning).

13 Zuzak, R. (2001). Corporate culture as a source of crisis in companies. *Agricultural Economics-UZPI (Czech Republic).*

14 Seeger, M., Sellnow, T., & Ulmer, R. (1998). Communication, organization, and crisis. *Communication Yearbook, 21*, 231–275.

15 Svedin, L. (2009). *Organizational cooperation in crises.* Farnham, England: Ashgate Pub.

16 Kilmann, R., Saxton, M., & Serpa, R. (1986). Issues in understanding and changing culture. *California Management Review, 28,* 87–94.

Case Study 13: J.C. Penney Hiring an Outsider CEO (2012)

J.C. Penney experienced increased online business activities in 2010. The company was unable to handle its customers efficiently during its Cyber Monday sale. As a result, numerous customers were unable to place orders, illustrating the company's inability to transform into an online shopping environment. The company's internal challenges in adapting to online retailing led to poor consumer experiences, resulting in asset and customer losses. J.C. Penney hired Ron Johnson as the new CEO in November 2011, in an effort to regain its lost competitive glory.[1] Johnson sought to eradicate conventional discount coupons with his new "fair and square" pricing policy that drove customers away. By eradicating weekly sales and the coupons loved by customers, Johnson had forsaken the core element that attracted consumers to the store.

Jonson's first move was to reinvent J.C. Penney into a new brand with new pricing strategies and models. He believed that changing the company logo, store layout, and return policy would enhance the consumer-shopping experience, strengthening the company's position in a competitive market.[2] Johnson developed a new three-tiered pricing system named "fair and square." The pricing system was broken into month-long values, everyday prices, and best prices. The everyday prices were symbolized by the daily prices reduced by 40%. The month-long values showed that product prices were changed each month and coincided with special events, such as Father's Day or Back to School. The Best Price Fridays were symbolized by the blue tag on the logo indicating clearance prices on the first and third Fridays of every month.[3] The company sought to establish itself as a high-quality retailer offering discounted prices compared to its competitors. As a result, the store's famous Doorbuster sales, held on Black Friday, the busiest shopping day after Thanksgiving Day, were eradicated. Customers were usually treated to extremely low prices on over 400 items from 4 a.m. to 1 p.m. In addition, Johnson eliminated the use of words such as *sale* and *clearance* in the store, arguing that all items were priced at the best price every day.[4] The new practice drifted away from the store's shopping culture. The new pricing strategy eliminated the listing of the manufacturer's suggested retail price (MSRP). Sales and MSRPs were projected to show customers the value of the prices, attracting more customers who believed they were saving on the offered price. The fair and square pricing strategy eliminated the use of ".99" on price tags and adopted the ".00" pricing strategy, which was not appealing to consumers. The new pricing strategies contravened the cultural shopping experience of consumers who shied away from the store while preferring other retailers.

Month-long values and Best Price Fridays upheld a slight emphasis on the low pricing strategy commonly used by retailers to maximize average product prices for consumers with diverse price preference. Price-conscious customers often wait for offers, discounts, sales, clearance, and coupons so that they can get a bargain. Less price-sensitive consumers buy when it is convenient for them and rarely purchase during clearance sales or doorbuster specials. The dominance of high-low sales in the contemporary retail market compels the more price-sensitive consumers to wait for sales and compare prices across retail stores.[5] The new J.C. Penney pricing strategy eliminated the distribution of cash coupons to customers via email, weekly circulars advertising special offers, direct mail, and its famous Red Zone Clearance aisles. Instead, the company used a high-quality, heavy content catalog to publish its monthly offers. The new pricing strategy was abrupt and drastically implemented, causing customer shock that resulted in reduced sales.

The True Value sales strategy adopted by Johnson was in replacing the traditional coupons and offering discounts to customers who felt they had lost the previous bargaining experience. Customers often feel that true value is relative, whereby discounted items or items on sale are believed to offer truer value compared to low-price items. Abolished discounts meant "more expensive" to customers who relied on discounts and sales to purchase items. Customers also felt the fair price policy benefited the stakeholders instead of consumers. Johnson failed to understand that it is fruitless to change a company without changing its renowned culture.

Johnson's new company brand and price culture resulted in more losses instead of profits. J.C. Penney had its own established style, which was liked by customers. The inflated prices with discounts attracted customers who felt like winners after purchasing. Johnson failed to understand

CRISIS MANAGEMENT:
THE ART OF SUCCESS AND FAILURE

what customers wanted and introduced low prices, which customers associated with poor quality.[6] Johnson's failure to test what J.C. Penney shoppers wanted in advance resulted in his detrimental decisions. As a new CEO, Johnson ought to have taken the time to study what J.C. Penney consumers wanted to create happy and loyal consumers. The company's use of discounted prices, coupons, and clearance sections attracted and retained customers; hence, their abolishment made customers lose their connection with the store's culture, and they started shopping elsewhere.

Initially, sales clerks at J.C. Penney were awarded commissions based on their sales. This had created a culture of aggressive sales. Johnson eliminated sales commissions, as he believed that aggressive selling did not complement his new fair and square pricing. This reduced employee morale and commitment to making sales. With sales commissions, customers were greeted at the entrance by a sales representative who took them through the shopping experience.[7] The lack of employee motivation resulted in poor customer service and human relations, which led to reduced sales.

J.C. Penney changed the store's promotions and presentations by adding new brands. Johnson expanded on the store changes by adding more brands and replacing outdated fixtures, and he also changed the marketing strategy by reducing the 590 annual sales promotions to creating a monthly catalog of 96 pages. He argued that this strategy reduced the company's annual marketing budget of $1 billion to $960 million.[8] The new marketing and promotional strategy came with merits and flaws. The addition of new brands, new store layouts, and new storefronts attracted new customers. The catalog advertisements left

Case Study 13: J.C. Penney Hiring an Outsider CEO (2012)

the impression that the store is more luxurious and pricy than its competitors, and the rebranding of the store alienated loyal customers since it looked too expensive for them.

Johnson's rebranding of J.C. Penney created an identity crisis within consumers. Drastic reductions in prices made consumers unsure whether the store was a high-end department store or a low-end discounter. The low pricing intended to attract more customers was confused for low quality by existing customers. The new pricing strategy contradicted the store's traditional pricing culture, which the customers were used to and preferred. Loyal customers felt that the store was focused on attracting new customers while abandoning old customers, compelling them to shop elsewhere.

The introduction of Ellen DeGeneres, a talk show host and comedian, as the store's spokesperson garnered a lot of emotion among the store's loyal consumers. DeGeneres appeared in television commercials and store-themed skits for her talk show. A conservative group of loyal customers asked its members to boycott J.C. Penney because they felt that Degeneres' homosexuality did not fit well with the store's image as a traditional shopping store.[9] Although the store survived the controversy, it lost a number of loyal customers.

The drastic loss in revenue experienced by J.C. Penney under Johnson's leadership resulted from unfavorable management methods, damaged stakeholder relationships, and marketing strategy flaws. Stakeholders play a crucial role in exploiting new technology, the creation of value, and creating effective marketing strategies and adapting human resource policies for competitive gain. Johnson rapidly introduced new changes in the organization with respect to cost reduction and increased return on investment. Reduced advertisements in the bid to save on company revenue failed to retain existing customers because they created a new culture that drove loyal customers away. Johnson failed to effectively manage the store by imposing a new, stringent culture without considering what customers or employees felt about his new marketing strategies. Effective management needs to find dynamic alternatives in solving company issues instead of just fixing one variable. J.C. Penney had a culture of trained professionals engaging customers with a welcomed message, which was eradicated by Johnson and replaced with a professional relationship.

In conclusion, Johnson failed to understand and build upon the J.C. Penney brand. Instead, he chose to introduce a new brand that was not received well by the company's loyal customers. Johnson failed to take the time to learn what customers loved about the store and chose to implement what he thought worked best without doing a market test. The company's new marketing strategy was not effectively communicated to consumers, who responded with decreased sales.

Endnotes

Case Study 13: J.C. Penney Hiring an Outsider CEO (2012)

1 Werema, G., Banafe, A., Luter, S., Beltran, J., Franscioni, Hagedorn, M., Pak, J., & Press, E. (2013). JC Penney, INC: The impact of rebranding on internal and external communication. *Center for Management Communication.*

2 Werema, G., Banafe, A., Luter, S., Beltran, J., Franscioni, Hagedorn, M., Pak, J., & Press, E. (2013). JC Penney, INC: The impact of rebranding on internal and external communication. *Center for Management Communication.*

3 Werema, G., Banafe, A., Luter, S., Beltran, J., Franscioni, Hagedorn, M., Pak, J., & Press, E. (2013). JC Penney, INC: The impact of rebranding on internal and external communication. *Center for Management Communication.*

4 Ofek, E., & Avery, J. (2013). J.C. Penny's "fair and square" pricing strategy. *Harvard Business School.*

5 Ofek, E., & Avery, J. (2013). J.C. Penny's "fair and square" pricing strategy. *Harvard Business School.*

6 Smith, B., & Villarreal, K. (2015). Hire, fire, re-hire: The case of J.C. Penney's decision to fire CEO Ron Johnson. *Journal of International Academic Research for Multimedia Disciplinary, 3*(7), 190–197.

7 Ofek, E., & Avery, J. (2013). J.C. Penny's "fair and square" pricing strategy. *Harvard Business School.*

8 Clifford, S. (2012, January). J.C. Penney to revise pricing methods and limit promotions. *New York Times,* B1.

9 Ofek, E., & Avery, J. (2013). J.C. Penny's "fair and square" pricing strategy. *Harvard Business School.*

Case Study 14: The BBC-Jimmy Savile Sexual Abuse Case (2012)

THE SEXUAL ABUSE

A report detailing the sexual abuse cases that were perpetrated by Jimmy Savile, a television and radio personality and charity fundraiser who hosted the BBC television show (Jim'll Fix It) between May 1975 and June 1994, is inclusive of both adults and children. The youngest of the documented victims was 8 years old, and the oldest was a 47-year-old woman. The venues that were outlined by the police as being the most frequently used for the offenses that spread over a span of 50 years featured 450 complaints against Savile. An estimated 214 crimes were documented in 28 police force areas.[1] Out of these crimes, about 34 incidents dealt with rape and penetration without the consent of the victims.

The number of incidents as given by the victims was a clear indication that Savile had been a most prolific sexual offender. It is highly unlikely that an individual could mastermind so many sensitive criminal activities without being detected. After his death, a series of allegations of the crimes emerged. Apparently, there had not been sufficient evidence, or the victims may not have had to come forward when Savile was still alive, in light of the likelihood of failing to make a strong case against him. This was primarily due to the celebrity status that he had.

The revelation of the abuse of children prompted several other victims to come forth and make claims of crimes committed against them. Among the hospitals where the abuse cases were reported was the Great Ormond Street Hospital. Another offense was recorded at the Wheatfields Hospice. Around 15 cases were related to schools. The first of the allegations presented against Savile dates back to 1955, and the very last dates back to 2009, when he was in his early 80s.[2]

The peak years for the offenses were those between 1966 and 1976. The number of allegations of sexual abuse that have been made against Savile since October 2012, after his death, is estimated to be about 450. Out of this number, 73% were under the age of 18, mostly between age 13 and 16.[3]

ORGANIZATIONAL CULTURE WEAKNESS

Jimmy Savile's sexual scandal case was a real failure by the British Broadcasting Corporation (BBC) to utilize the essence of organizational culture at the workplace. From the published cases, it is apparent that some of Savile's colleagues knew about his sexual abuse tendencies but never filed formal reports. As an entity, the BBC should have had the mandate of taking charge of all the activities going on in the premises.[4] For all organizations, frameworks should be put in place to ensure that they keep track of the activities that their employees engage in while on duty. To further improve on the desired efficiency, it is of essence that strategies are put in place to review the activities that staff members engage in while off duty.

Case Study 14: The BBC-Jimmy Savile Sexual Abuse Case (2012)

In reviewing the essence of organizational culture, the one at the BBC highlights a weakness in that there was not a framework designated to engage staff members in active team building. Such would be the forum in which to share the challenges faced in the course of overseeing the assigned organizational duties.[5] The airing of professional challenges can also be a platform where individuals can get close to one another and establish relationships. The relationships that are established could also be social, depending on the extent of the interaction. This would be the primary determinant of the essence of sharing, so that some of the crimes like the one Savile had could be easily detected and managed at an early stage.

A well-established organizational culture at the BBC would have been essential in eradicating the emergence of anomalies, as depicted in the cases of sexual abuse. There should have been a pre-determined code of conduct to be used in overseeing the primary behaviors of employees. Once there is an outlined code of behavior at the workplace, everyone within the confines of the organization would be obliged to abide by the regulations.

In an organizational setup, the essence of culture needs to be reviewed frequently to ascertain that all the ongoing practices are working in conjunction with the organization's primary objectives. This would be the determinant of due success.[6] The BBC, therefore, failed in not putting out a required code of conduct.

LAX LEADERSHIP AND RIGID MANAGEMENT AT THE BBC

In the wake of the revelations of the series of sex scandals involving one of the top hosts at the BBC, Jimmy Savile, lax leadership by the BBC management has been revealed. This is a result of the failure to take any notable action toward resolving the issue or seeking justice for the victims. It has been established that those in charge were lacking and were never significantly sanctioned.[7]

The case is proof of the rigid management chains within the organization. However, even given the potency it had for tarnishing the image of the corporation and the entire network, there was no attempt to engage in an investigation to determine the actualities of the case and what to do if the allegations were true.

To further highlight the essence of the lax leadership at the BBC, there were no reported charges of a cover-up in the course of the investigation of abuse by its employee. After such a crisis, the expectation is that there would be individuals held answerable so that the investigation would have a solid base. There should have been members of the management team to discuss the ethical codes of the organization that were in play during the time frame the abuse took place.[8]

There were no remarkable dismissals from the top positions, which should have been the key to solving the crisis. The only move that was made is the reassignment of top officials. Some resigned, others were completely blameless. Even though the CEO agreed that there should have been better steps taken to address the issue, he never thought that the repercussions were enough to earn some individuals' dismissals.[9] When an organization fails to take action to deal with a crisis of this magnitude in the organizational ranks, this is lax leadership.

Case Study 14: The BBC-Jimmy Savile Sexual Abuse Case (2012)

Endnotes

Case Study 14: The BBC-Jimmy Savile Sexual Abuse Case (2012)

1 Cowell, A. (2014, June). *U.K. inquiry finds "Truly Awful" sexual abuse by TV host at medical facilities.* Retrieved from http://www.nytimes.com/2014/06/27/world/europe/britain-jimmy-savile-sexual-abuse.html?_r=0

2 Cowell, A. (2014, June). *U.K. inquiry finds "Truly Awful" sexual abuse by TV host at medical facilities.* Retrieved from http://www.nytimes.com/2014/06/27/world/europe/britain-jimmy-savile-sexual-abuse.html?_r=0

3 Cowell, A. (2014, June). *U.K. inquiry finds "Truly Awful" sexual abuse by TV host at medical facilities.* Retrieved from http://www.nytimes.com/2014/06/27/world/europe/britain-jimmy-savile-sexual-abuse.html?_r=0

4 Cowell, A. (2014, June). *U.K. inquiry finds "Truly Awful" sexual abuse by TV host at medical facilities.* Retrieved from http://www.nytimes.com/2014/06/27/world/europe/britain-jimmy-savile-sexual-abuse.html?_r=0

5 Johnson, C. E. (2013). *Meeting the ethical challenges of leadership: Casting light or shadow.* Sage Publications.

6 Daft, R. (2014). *The leadership experience.* Cengage Learning.

7 Kellerman, B. (2012, December). Lax leadership. Retrieved from http://barbarakellerman.com/lax-leadership

8 Kellerman, B. (2012, December). Lax leadership. Retrieved from http://barbarakellerman.com/lax-leadership

9 Kellerman, B. (2012, December). Lax leadership. Retrieved from http://barbarakellerman.com/lax-leadership

Crisis as an Opportunity

In the modern world, most veteran businesses have faced a lot of crises that they had never encountered before, owing to the fact that the business marketplace and environment is slowly being digitized. The origin of such crises may be from the limited capacity of such businesses, cost pressures, and a lack of total capacity to meet the market demands of their consumers. A number of large business enterprises have had to face strategic challenges that are related to the segmented, digitized environment, with a lot of portfolio and overhead maintenance to provide room for expected innovations and developments, as there is no more time to be wasted and action needs to happen immediately.

In many of the instances identified in the research literature, entrepreneurs are expected to make dramatic changes on the models of operation. A number of individuals are unaware of their roles in business and management, while leaders can also be unaware of their roles from creating visions to come to reality. Enterprises charged with addressing changes usually operate using two extreme models: the methodological approach, which basically aims at minimizing the risks associated with a crisis but will take a long time during the transformation period; or the rip-the-bandage methodology, which focuses on significant tasks while managing risks using sophisticated strategies. The latter approach is valuable in that it is very quick and puts fewer burdens on organizational operations; however, its increased associated risks always cause a re-work, which also comes at inflated costs.

HOW DO ENTERPRISES TURN A CRISIS INTO AN OPPORTUNITY?

For enterprises to be able to successfully turn crises into opportunities and manage the development of a big change, a number of strategies may be explored that focus on the needs of the business and consumers at large; this involves addressing how the expected change and the related risks will affect the customer being served by the enterprise. It is prudent to identify critical activities and roles to assist in the establishment of a methodological approach in the areas that need to be focused upon, together with the improved organizational changes.

Every individual has a role to play within the organization during the change process so that resistance is not met. It is also important to standardize and integrate the different processes by developing an integration platform; this is probably the main reason a number of large enterprises have been able to grow through mergers while others could not.[1] Over time, employees will create stopgap strategies while assisting fragmented systems; thus, it is important to establish standardized platforms across the organization and ensure that everyone has been coordinated with proficiently.

In the event that an enterprise has a large workforce, there is a probability that it may become lax and thus be unable to adjust to the new systems of doing things, slowing down the pace of adopting the latest methodologies and emerging technologies. In addressing such challenges, it is important to bring in fresh approaches, as well as infuse the workforce with the significant expertise that is missing.

STRATEGIES OF CRISIS CONVERSION TO FORM OPPORTUNITIES

To turn crisis into opportunity, managers need to possess a number of characteristics to triumph over the challenges that come with crises. Such attributes include the following.

Staying Positive

Negative events in a crisis must be perceived in a more confident manner to avoid the stress and health complications that come with them. When the panic of 1857 struck the business marketplace, John D. Rockefeller was only two years into his first job. In a real sense, he could have become very stressed owing to the unfortunate circumstances that struck him, but he rather chose to perceive the events in a different manner than his peers. He viewed the employment challenges as an opportunity to gain knowledge and experience—a form of baptism by the market conditions. Rockefeller was literally inclined to see opportunities in every disaster.

Having gone through the employment crisis, Rockefeller was able to gain control of over 90% of the oil market stakes within 20 years. Today, entrepreneurs just like Rockefeller are living in times marred with economic and market turbulence; therefore, judgment should not be based on the events that have clouded the environment, this sentiment for instance should be considered as well, that came into existence out of unpromising surroundings, and which became great examples of how to act under pressure and change predicaments into viable opportunities.

CRISIS MANAGEMENT:
THE ART OF SUCCESS AND FAILURE

Thinking Differently

It is important to have a different model of thinking to be able to fight a crisis. For example, Steve Jobs, the Apple inventor, was quite dismissive of negative phrases such as *It can't be done*. He ordered to be supplied with a special kind of glass for his first batch of Apple phones, but his employees were unsure if they could make such a delivery before the deadline, which they considered quite aggressive. However, within 24 hours, they managed to transform their machines into glassmaking behemoths, and within the first half of the year, they had established enough machinery for the production of enough glass for the whole first batch. The point here is about addressing a crisis that Jobs' employees thought would never be solved; he insisted on pushing them past their belief that they would not be able to create the necessary materials for their new products within the short deadline. Therefore, it is possible for inspired managers to make the right choice based on their first judgments and discard the negative protests that make some people believe that obstacles can never be cleared out of the paths to success. Just like Jobs, perhaps many managers have the ability to create something new; digitized companies such as Google and Facebook banked on the concept that no one had ever done anything like they had—this was a key motivation in their work, making them the owners of powerful new business entities.

Reassessing the Rules

In this case, it is practical for managers to continue reexamining the basic rules and not to follow them with blind eyes. Samuel Zemurray, who was the owner of an upstart fruit company, was unable to create a bridge that he had wanted to build across a river in Central America. This was based on the fact that government agencies had taken bribes from United Fruit, which was one of the most powerful entities in the United States during that period. Zemurray went ahead and instructed his engineers to construct the bridge against the rules he had been issued by the government; they made up a provisional pontoon that would enable them to connect to other regions within a short time. Later, United Fruit complained; Zemurray answered that it was merely a collection of old wharfs. Such ingenuity is also evident when looking at the Tesla and Uber companies. There comes a time in the business world when one needs to take an audacious action against the rules and go against oppressive laws and regulations to complete required business tasks.

Anticipating/Thinking Negatively

This technique is also known as the pre-mortem strategy and has been widely used by many popular fruit companies and startup businesses, according to the *Harvard Business Review*. This technique was brought into existence by Gary Klein, a psychologist, while attempting to describe the concept of advanced hindsight, but it is not a new concept. Much credit is owed to the prehistoric Stoics, who had a better name for the process: the premeditation of evils. Through the application of that concept, managers will attain the ability to go beyond their competitors, who are often shocked by negative outcomes and thus fall back in devastation because they had never imagined such occurrences.[2]

CRISIS MANAGEMENT:
THE ART OF SUCCESS AND FAILURE

Loving Your Fate (*Amor Fati*)

In the process of dealing with a crisis, it is much better to respect the reality and try to deal with the possibly unalterable results as well as fate at large; when Thomas Edison's production and research college burned down, he never grew angry or desperate; rather, he was reenergized and even more vigorous. About three weeks after the incident, part of the factory had been built back up and was operational, all because he believed in accepting fate. Possibly, other managers can emulate the example set by Edison in the event that they lose their customers and investors.[3] When Jack Dorsey was replaced as Twitter's CEO, he was not disturbed or paralyzed; he moved on successfully and founded the highest-paying processing firm.

THE USE OF BRAVE IDEAS TO TURN CRISES INTO OPPORTUNITIES

While projecting the potential harm from the crises that an organization may go through, it is prudent for stakeholders to drive their main ideas so that the organization may move from a risk-driven position to a forward-driven one with an opportunity mindset. Even though such ideas are often painful and difficult to execute, the results are always desirable and can shape the future of the organization.[4] During a crisis, the problem being experienced will always drive the content of the messages and ideas to be communicated to the public, but there are a number of elements that need to be considered when developing such ideas.

The idea being communicated should be honest; in the event that an idea has not been founded on honesty, it does not qualify as being a brave idea and, as such, the best it can do is reduce the damage by a small percentage. In most cases, crises are rare happenings, and in the event that they occur, there must be somebody who drove it to happen, and there must always be that portion of the problem that was contributed to by the company. For example, following the hacking of the Sony website in 2014, Sony's aggressive behavior with the media reduced the media's interaction with people in charge inside the company regarding the information leakage. However, the approach Sony took indicated that they had distanced themselves from any responsibility leading to the leakage. They later ensured that their actions to resolve the matter were covered by the mainstream media for several weeks after the event.[5]

An idea should be bold; the concept of reframing and controlling issues becomes a critical step in turning a crisis into opportunity; thus, the boldness of the general idea needs to be communicated to the public. The information should be bolder than most organizations would have released to uphold the status quo; for example, following the recent mass shooting in South Carolina, Nikki Haley, the governor of South Carolina, stood by African-American democrats and protested while calling for the removal of the Confederate flag from the South Carolina governor's residence.[6] This move was not only pushed by the anger directed toward her by the residents of South Carolina over the mass shootings, but also by a desire to ensure the removal of the Confederate flag from all places within the state, with her being portrayed as being on the right side of the matter.

CRISIS MANAGEMENT:
THE ART OF SUCCESS AND FAILURE

CRISES AND OPPORTUNITIES IN EDUCATION AND DAILY LIVES

In the course of life, an individual may be faced with several types of crises, but one has the ability to go through such instances by ensuring that the threat is converted into an opportunity with the aim of avoiding the negative consequences of the crisis. For instance, in Asia, university education is valued such that whoever does not qualify for a position to learn in such institutions will always be considered a failure in life, and will have low living standards. However, individuals who miss out on university enrollment will usually work out various ways of satisfying themselves, such as becoming businesspersons with the aim of living a desirable life while averting the crisis of missing out on a university education.

In analyzing Shakespeare's *Romeo and Juliet*, we see that the play brings out a good example of an opportunity that comes with a crisis. The meeting of Romeo and Juliet is preceded by love, which later leads to marriage, which forms the climax of the play and leads to their untimely deaths. The two families had been feuding for a long time; the deaths of their children were instrumental in ending the long war that had raged between the two families. The deaths of Romeo and Juliet formed the crisis; it served as an opportunity to end the bitter relationship that had developed between the families so that they could continue the cordial relationship they had once enjoyed.

AMERICA AND THE GREAT DEPRESSION: CRISIS AND OPPORTUNITY

Each crisis we meet is just an opportunity in disguise; for instance, during the Great Depression in the U.S., the situation was a great threat to the economic and political stature of the U.S. However, the U.S. had strategies that assisted in addressing the predicament, turning it into several opportunities. During the period of the Great Depression, all the states had run out of money and were unable to meet their expenses; this made the U.S. the sole debt owner, but it was incapable of recovering the money, leading to a number of companies closing down, thus inflating unemployment figures since companies were unable to meet the wage demands of their employees. The major factor that led to the closure of so many companies and sparking unemployment was based on their lack of prior investments to enable them to meet their employees' salary demands and expenses.

Later on, the government established long-lasting solutions to the problems; it hired a number of workers to work on road, bridge, and other infrastructure construction projects; these workers had to buy food to live. Through this, the issue of unemployment was solved. In this case study, it is evident that the U.S. took advantage of the crisis that had been created by the Great Depression to build up the country while improving the living standards of its citizens.

CONCLUSION

In the fields of business and politics, there are different forms of crises that arise every day, and such may be the beginning of an entity's downfall; it is therefore important to note that dealing with an arising crisis within the shortest framework is significant in preventing further damage from such threats. In this section, I have made strides to assess the various sources and types of crises as well as the possible ways through which such crises may be turned into

CRISIS MANAGEMENT:
THE ART OF SUCCESS AND FAILURE

viable opportunities. Basically, a crisis is just an opportunity wrapped in problems, and the perception and urgency accorded to the threat will be quite instrumental in saving the face of organizations and political entities by providing genuine lessons and practical experiences. However, when a crisis is not addressed in a timely manner and changed into an opportunity, then it will be the source of an organizational curse and downfall. In the business world, entrepreneurs like Steve Jobs and Thomas Edison worked on their threats and weaknesses to shine as business moguls who once invested where none others had.

Endnotes

Crisis as an Opportunity

1 Coatney, L. (2015, September). *Turning crisis into opportunity: How to make good on big change.* Retrieved from Information Services Group: http://blog.isg-one.com/turning-crisis-into-opportunity-how-to-make-good-on-big-change

2 Edison, T. (2014, April). *Turning crisis into opportunity: 5 ways to deal with hardship.* Retrieved from Entrepreneur: http://www.entrepreneur.com/article/232848

3 Edison, T. (2014, April). *Turning crisis into opportunity: 5 ways to deal with hardship.* Retrieved from Entrepreneur: http://www.entrepreneur.com/article/232848

4 Weaver, C. (2015, July). *Using brave ideas to turn crisis into an opportunity.* Retrieved from APCO Worldwide: http://www.apcoworldwide.com/blog/detail/apcoforum/2015/07/10/using-brave-ideas-to-turn-a-crisis-into-an-opportunity

5 Weaver, C. (2015, July). *Using brave ideas to turn crisis into an opportunity.* Retrieved from APCO Worldwide: http://www.apcoworldwide.com/blog/detail/apcoforum/2015/07/10/using-brave-ideas-to-turn-a-crisis-into-an-opportunity

6 Weaver, C. (2015, July). *Using brave ideas to turn crisis into an opportunity.* Retrieved from APCO Worldwide: http://www.apcoworldwide.com/blog/detail/apcoforum/2015/07/10/using-brave-ideas-to-turn-a-crisis-into-an-opportunity

Case Study 15: The Norway Terrorist Attacks (2011)

The Norway terrorist attacks that took place in 2011 was one of the deadliest attacks Norway ever known.[1] Norwegians encountered a dramatic turn of events that year as one lone wolf attacked twice on the same day. The attacker, identified as Anders Breivik, was a Norwegian right-wing extremist in his early thirties. He was outspoken against the Islamic religion and immigration into Norway. The focus of the attack was mainly against government activities allowing immigrants into the country and the spread of Islam, which he considered a threat to civilization.[2]

Breivik's first attack was a vehicle explosion near the prime minister's office building and other government buildings. The explosives consisted of a highly flammable mixture of fertilizers and fuel oil in the back of a minivan. The van's position clearly targeted government offices, which the attacker considered the core of the country's leadership. More than 10 people were killed that day, and 209 were injured. Hours later, Breivik launched a second attack in Buskerud at a summer camp organized by the right-wing Norwegian ruling party.[3]

Breivik managed to pull off the two attacks dressed as a police officer. The police uniforms used in the attacks were homemade, with a badge bought online illegally.

Breivik boarded a ferry to the island where the summer camp was held and opened fire on innocent civilians. Among the injured were personal friends of the Norwegian prime minister and a step-brother of the royal family's princes.[4] This was one of the most brutal massacres since World War II. The success of the attacks was largely blamed on the slow response of the police.

PREPARATIONS FOR THE ATTACK

Breivik was never considered a terrorist threat to Norway because of his clean criminal record and never demonstrated his violent nature, not even while participating in online debate forums.[5] Breivik claimed to have started his terrorist ambitions in the Czech Republic in early 2002. He considered the Czech Republic and Norway the best places to shop for heavy weaponry because of their less-restrictive gun laws. The two states were well-known for their reluctant laws on drugs and weapons trading. This created an opportunity for Breivik to get access to very sensitive and sophisticated weaponry.

Before that time, Breivik started expressing his frustrations and his negative attitude toward Islam and immigration in online debate forums. In 2009, these frustrations drove him to organize the attacks,[6] but he managed to conceal his violent intentions from the public. Prague was the best place to start looking for support materials, such as guns and explosives. Also known for its illegal drug trade and arms sales, it was the ideal place to get the necessary materials he wanted to use for the attack. Breivik's main target weapons he was looking for were heavy weaponry, which were difficult to find in Prague. He later managed to get access to badges and police uniforms through an illegal online purchase. He failed to get access to heavy weaponry because it drew more attention to him, which scared him off and made him consider other places and other weapons.

Breivik was a determined person and would do almost anything to get what he wanted. He even went as far as forming his own company to get access to chemicals, fertilizers, and other explosive materials without attracting attention. Breivik also managed to get training by visiting firing ranges, a requirement for licensed gun owners. Some skills were derived from gaming software, which enhanced his combat skills.[7]

THE OSLO BOMBING

Breivik was an extremely intelligent and patient person. He used his brilliant skills to coordinate different attacks in different locations. The bombing in Oslo demonstrated how careful and cautious he was in successfully achieving his goals.[8] He drove a minivan next to the prime minister's office and other government buildings. A receptionist in the building noticed his suspicious activity despite his police uniform and gun. The receptionist considered his behavior odd and tried calling for security guards.

Seven seconds later, Breivik managed to get to his getaway vehicle, parked on the other side of the street. After his departure, the bomb in the van exploded, causing serious damage to the surrounding buildings and many casualties, the explosion brought the city's transportation system to a halt.

THE UTOYA MASSACRE

Hours after the attack in Oslo, Breivik arrived at Utoya dressed as a police officer with false identification documents. This gave him easier access to the camp and authority over the people. Fake police uniforms and documentation are easy to access through online sellers. Breivik's behavior at the camp aroused suspicions, which led to him signaling for and asking people to gather around. Soon after this, he pulled out heavy weapons, which he used to open fire on the unarmed civilians. Breivik started shooting at everyone in the camp indiscriminately, causing many deaths and casualties. Without remorse, he started focusing his attention on those trying to flee the island by swimming away.

The bombing in Oslo and the massacre in Utoya formed one of the worst terrorist attacks in the history of the European nations. International organizations such as The North Atlantic Treaty Organization (NATO) and the United Nations, plus European nations, condemned the attacks and expressed their support for the Norwegian government and people.[9] To fully address the attacks, the prime minister and the monarch arranged for an investigation on the matter. Later on, a report was forwarded to the prime minister's office, concluding that the attack could have been prevented by the Norwegian police department. The report also insisted that more security and emergency measures were needed to prevent attacks.

HOW THE GOVERNMENT HANDLED THE CRISIS

During this period, the Norwegian government and its people demonstrated a great deal of responsibility and calm throughout the crisis. The role of the government and the Norwegian community as a whole was of significance to the victims of the crisis. The government made the effort to motivate the Norwegian people against terrorism by praising the

Case Study 15: The Norway Terrorist Attacks (2011)

country's democratic values, liberty, and unity. The government continuously urged the people to shun violence and remain resilient throughout the crisis. In 2006, before the attacks, the Norwegian government, in coordination with other European states and organizations, organized a 30-hour terrorism simulation exercise.[10] The exercise was meant to protect Norwegian citizens against future terrorist attacks. As many as 4,000 people participated in the event, including 50 organizations that were the main organizers and sponsors of the program. Students and teachers posed as journalists and editors to shed some light on the role of the media during a crisis. Based on this exercise, the Norwegian government and citizens were able to manage the situation, which helped in overcoming the crisis during the 2011 attacks.

With the aim of avoiding declarations inconsistencies, government agencies, in coordination with the royal family, were able to share information during and after the attacks that symbolized unity and also created calm within the country. The Norwegian prime minister took the leadership role by serving as the chief communicator, using all the media channels as instruments of communication with the people. Despite the calm nature and organized government communication channels, the Norwegian police were still criticized for failing to prevent the attacks, even after having all the evidence required to act and arrest Breivik. The government was also criticized for defending the police department for their failure and providing inaccurate information about the number of victims of the attacks.

The Muslim community during this period also took the responsibility to react swiftly to the attack by holding a meeting condemning the attackers and offering assistance to the government and victims of the attacks. At that time, international media outlets around the world were concluding that the attack was conducted by an Islamic terrorist group. However, the government of Norway and its local media channels unanimously refused to speculate on the possibility of a jihadist group. The communicated message was clear and focused on solving the issue rather than escalating the war of words.

Norway's internal cooperation and lack of division in this situation demonstrated the nation's strength and unity while experiencing tragedy. The calm and composed nature was a way to show the world that terrorist activities did not threaten their values and cultures as a diverse, industrialized country. The government constantly maintained focus and praised the country's cultural diversity. The government insisted on not defaming or discriminating against minority groups around the country and sought to provide an example of a civilized nation in terms of a crisis.

The non-verbal communication from the Norwegian people and leaders spoke louder than words. Images of royal family members and leaders visiting victims in hospitals and homes showed the strength and unity that existed among the Norwegian citizens. Music bands and artists performed for the mourners to cheer them up, and the march of a funeral service from a mosque to a church was a symbol of unity and solidarity.

GOVERNMENT OPPORTUNITIES AFTER THE GOOD INITIATIVES

The government of Norway has been reluctant to improve its laws and policies regarding the security of the country.

Case Study 15: The Norway Terrorist Attacks (2011)

Widespread gun sales and drug trafficking have become traceable causes affecting the lives of Norwegian citizens, and necessary measures need to be taken to address such vital issues. Based on the investigation conducted by the Norwegian government, Breivik used all the overlooked laws in both Norway and its neighboring countries. He took advantage of the loopholes the system had and used them to take other people's lives.

The Norwegian government is considering possible strategies to improve the security situation in Norway and also to cooperate with its neighboring countries in the sharing of counterterrorism intelligence. The inter-agency communication that took place during the crisis enabled different government agencies to continue sharing information regarding terrorist activities and prevent future attacks. This has strengthened the intelligence-gathering process, making it easier for Norway to counter terrorism activities more quickly.

The immigration issue has become a sensitive issue to address, and many European countries are being continually challenged by the increase in refugees seeking immigration status in Western countries. This has made it impossible to control rogue terrorist sympathizers hiding among them. Norway is now developing policies to control an immigration crisis that is taking a toll on the country. Controlling the immigration rate improves the security of the country and also makes it possible to identify potential threats.[11]

The unity demonstrated during the crisis has also transformed how people view one another and has improved security situations in many parts of the Norwegian community. People are now sharing information with one another and with the relevant authorities regarding suspicious activity. People are taking the responsibility to protect others by reporting activities that are considered a threat to society. Regulatory authorities are finding it easier to get information about a threat and act on it quickly.

The Norwegian government witnessed the value that the 2006 simulation program brought with respect to how it impacted the 2011 attacks. People were able to follow procedures that reduced the death toll. The government has also set aside possible strategies and budgets to fund such programs, which can help citizens during attacks. This experience has shown that advanced planning and training can pay off during an actual event.

Endnotes

Case Study 15: The Norway Terrorist Attacks (2011)

1 Starla, M. (2011). *Tragedy in Norway: Oslo bombing.* Cambridge, UK: Cambridge University Press.

2 Starla, M. (2011). *Tragedy in Norway: Oslo bombing.* Cambridge, UK: Cambridge University Press.

3 Wong, C. (2013). *Oslo bombing: Victims story.* New York: Associated Press.

4 Wong, C. (2013). *Oslo bombing: Victims story.* New York: Associated Press.

5 Godfrey, H. (2012). *Utoya and Oslo terrorist attacks.* New York, USA: Yale University Press.

6 Godfrey, H. (2012). *Utoya and Oslo terrorist attacks.* New York, USA: Yale University Press.

7 Wong, C. (2013). *Oslo bombing: Victims story.* New York: Associated Press.

8 Wong, C. (2013). *Oslo bombing: Victims story.* New York: Associated Press.

9 Godfrey, H. (2012). *Utoya and Oslo terrorist attacks.* New York, USA: Yale University Press.

10 Wong, C. (2013). *Oslo bombing: Victims story.* New York: Associated Press.

11 Godfrey, H. (2012). *Utoya and Oslo terrorist attacks.* New York, USA: Yale University Press.

Business Recovery and Continuity

In the contemporary business environment, business organizations are increasingly pursuing approaches and techniques that ensure business excellence. In an attempt to ensure business excellence following a crisis, various business organizations have developed and implemented strategic focuses in the contexts of mission, vision, and objectives. Risks are rated among the critical issues that ought to be managed to foster business operation performance. The success of any business organization is largely dependent on its ability to manage uncertainties and risks to ensure that the best possible decision is made in respect to managing business risks. Sporadically, risks might be sufficient to build a crisis that could eventually turn disastrous if left unattended.[1]

Business risks take many forms, including safety risks, political risks, social risks, and business risks. Risks, irrespective of form or nature, are more likely to cause business havoc, which eventually leads to financial losses. However, no business organization can boast of being immune to crises, because some crises are inevitable. Nonetheless, it is imperative that business organizations develop superb recovery plans or techniques to ensure that crisis effects are not prolonged. Competition in the contemporary business environment is extremely stiff, implying that business organizations aspiring for success in such a tumultuous environment must be able to come up with potent measures to ensure business continuity following a crisis.[2]

Business interruption is one of the worst things that can happen to any organization. This is because business interruptions can lead to a diminished corporate image and loss of revenue, which can dent business continuity. Business continuity and recovery plans become very pertinent in the subsequent success of the business following the crisis; to restrain possible drawbacks, organizations should be provide a powerful framework for building resilience with the ability to ensure efficacious responses geared toward safeguarding the interests of key stakeholders. In addition, they should maintain building stronger brand loyalty and reputation as well as value-creating activities.[3]

Safeguarding organizations following a crisis has become increasingly critical in the smooth continuity of business organizations. The complexity of contemporary threats, coupled with the mounting sophistication of interdependent and interlinked operating environments, has triggered new approaches for ensuring the successful continuity of business organizations. The traditional methods of disaster recovery planning (DRP) and crisis management (CM) have proven to be limited in terms of their ability to provide efficacious strategies that integrate the environmental, technical, and human components of modern operating environments.[4]

Against the backdrop of the ever-escalating resultant threats and technical complexity, a narrow focus on reactive approaches to both natural and technical disasters has underpinned the need for holistic and strategic approaches for organizational preparation and protection.

According to IBM,[5] disaster recovery is the basis for building business resilience following a crisis. While characteristically linked to pandemics, natural disasters, and national emergencies, recovery following a crisis entails the capacity to efficaciously recover from almost any events deemed disruptive, and which might impact the organization's operations, workforce, applications, business processes, or infrastructure.

Recovery following a crisis is extremely pertinent in disaster continuity. Disaster recovery not only ensures that the organization is prepared for any eventual disaster, but also makes sure that the business organization in question complies with the rapidly changing regulatory requirements that could also be a source of crisis. By conducting effectual recovery, business organizations will be able to regain their original glory and attract a considerable market share that in turn boosts their competitive advantage in both the local and global business environments. Despite the significance of business recovery plans, it is imperative that management reevaluates other pertinent factors, such as global business expansions or mergers, which are equally likely to influence the capability of the business organization to effectively respond to disasters. It is essential that the continuity plan be reevaluated to ascertain whether it is capable of standing the test of time. Developing a recovery plan following a crisis is indispensable because it facilitates the maintenance of brand equity and, hence, smooth business continuity.[6]

DISASTER RECOVERY AND BUSINESS CONTINUITY PLANS

Business continuity and disaster recovery plans are renowned business tools used for the purpose of facilitating the resumption of normal business operations in the most effective, structured, and prioritized manner. With the full implementation of business continuity and disaster recovery plans, the organization's chances of survival become greater, while the future impacts of business crises, in terms of financial loss and business operations, are greatly minimized.[7]

A business continuity plan is not only formal, but also a comprehensive process developed by business organizations to provide a framework for business continuity following a disaster. Business continuity plans ought to be effectively integrated within the organization's thinking and culture. The 2007–2008 financial crisis hit business organizations hard, and as a result, they were forced to develop recovery and business continuity plans to ensure their effective recovery from the crisis. Only business organizations that developed superb recovery plans were able to regain their original glory within a short time frame.[8]

THE USE OF CONTINUITY AS A STRATEGIC BUSINESS TOOL

No one can deny the assertion that the frequency and number of disasters have increased considerably in recent times. The 21st century has been characterized by different business crises, forcing most business organizations to turn away from their simplistic planning techniques and embrace new techniques capable of effectively addressing the needs of the present challenging business environment. The probable losses, coupled with costs from operational downtime resulting from crises or disasters, underscore the need to develop more holistic and strategic crisis mitigation strategies for the purposes of safeguarding organizations from possible future disruptions.[9]

Business organizations must develop strategies to ensure that their activities remain operational even after a crisis. As opined by Snedaker,[10] an organization's capacity to protect its functions by ensuring their continuity following disruptive events has increasingly become a propitious organizational objective. In this respect, superb planning, coupled with efficacious crisis management strategies, plays a crucial role in the success of a business following a crisis.

As an evolution from crisis management and disaster recovery approaches, business continuity has emerged as a critical aspect of recovery planning that provides holistic approaches to protecting the organization following a crisis. In addition to branching out from the conventional method of treating a crisis as a solitary occurrence, business continuity broadens the scope to integrate with organizational persistence of recognizing the need for preparation, a delineation of the causes of the crisis, and the development of a superb reaction strategy for dealing with potential problems.

In contrast to the risk management approaches, business continuity focuses primarily on pertinent business practices.[11]

THE ROLE OF BUSINESS CONTINUITY MANAGEMENT IN PROMOTING ORGANIZATIONAL RESILIENCE

The significance of business continuity management (BCM) following a crisis rests in its ability to develop excellent organizational resilience, which buffers the organization against any future crisis. Additionally; through the identification of organizational exposure to both external and internal threats, BCM often seeks to offer an efficacious recovery, protection, and continuity of the organization's business functions.[12]

BCM makes use of a combination of management and planning to satisfy its set organizational goals and objectives for the purposes of long-term value creation. The fact that BCM's critical objective is to protect the key functions of the organization implies that it is capable of supporting the development of the organization's resiliency. This, in turn, enables the business to not only endure, but also absorb the consequences resulting from disruptive events.[13]

Janssen and Ostrom[14] highlighted that, by giving an organization the ability to absorb the impact that comes with change from its external and internal operating environments, organizational resilience following a crisis becomes a crucial value-enhancement tool. Figure 4 demonstrates the relationships between BCP, BCM, DRP, and CM. Despite the fact that their objectives are alike in terms of purpose, partial variances in the context of their methodologies and focuses could be remarked.

Figure 4: The typology of continuity efforts

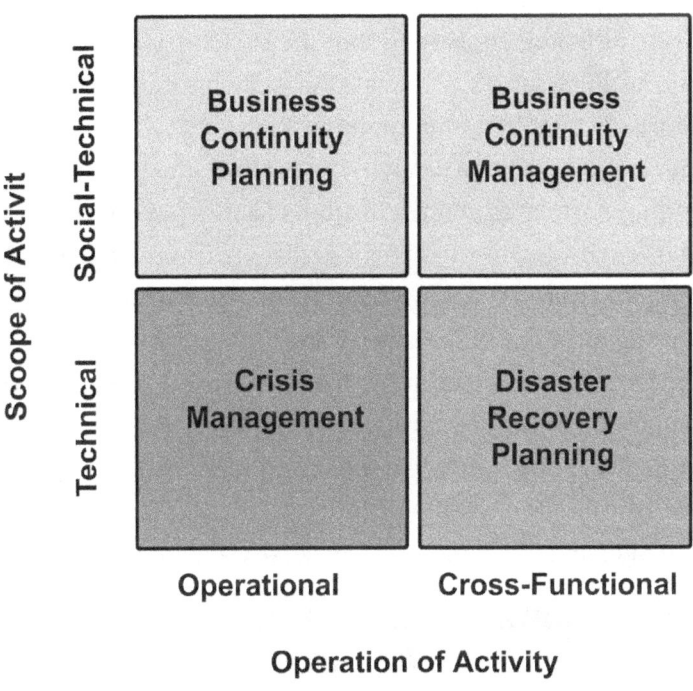

Operation of Activity

Source: Herbane et al., 2004[15]

Figure 4 demonstrates some of the limitations of characterizing organizations as having an exclusive focus on technical operations. From the figure, it is clear that a narrow focus offers an organization the ability to only react to, but not to limit or anticipate losses from, events deemed disruptive. Nonetheless, Herbane[16] posited that organizations taking deliberate steps are more likely to move into the upper left (BCP) and lower right (DRP) quadrants as a result of planning for technical interruptions across the entire organization. By moving beyond the technical into the social-technical, the organization will be moving toward realizing its goal despite the crisis that may have befallen it.

Herbane[17] contended that the successful implementation of BCM serves a crucial role in terms of checking the degree of adoption and implementation by senior management. A crisis always renders an organization dysfunctional, and in most cases when a business lacks a superb recovery plan, such a business is likely to lose its competitiveness in the global arena. In this respect, in circumstances where the organization is seeking to boost its competitiveness in the face of unknown threats likely to threaten its solvency, reputation, or future survival, research shows that for BCM to be successfully implemented and effectually utilized, it needs to follow a top-down approach that relies upon senior management to champion its necessity and purpose.

ADVANTAGES THAT COME WITH BUSINESS RECOVERY

There is a plethora of benefits that business organizations are likely to reap as a result of implementing tools that ensure faster recovery following crises. Among these benefits are rapidly gaining market share, which eventually gives the business a competitive edge over its rivals. This eventually translates into organizational profitability. The ability of the business to recover rapidly from threats and crises depends on the type of recovery tool being employed. According to Herbane,[18] BCM fosters faster recovery, as well as restoration practices that eventually result in recovery advantages (improved competitive advantage).

The BCM tool is highly appropriate for organizations whose operations are deemed time-sensitive. Rapid business recovery not only accelerates a return to business, but also lessens the threat of reputation damage during the post-crisis phase.[19] Moreover, Rosenkopf and Nerkar[20] opined that ensuring faster recovery following a crisis compared to one's competitors serves as a source of business opportunity and hence, a competitive ability. Adequate organizational recovery along with the aftermath experiences promote effective resource utilization, BC knowledge, and the deployment of healthier strategy. In so doing, management will be able to reduce downtime while at the same time strengthening the organization's resilience to crises, which further enables the organization to boost its competitive advantage in both the local and global markets.

ORGANIZATIONAL CULTURE AND POST-CRISIS MANAGEMENT

Organizational culture is an important component of organizational success. Therefore, modification of the organizational culture following a crisis is a move in the right direction as far as the management of future crises is concerned. In line with organizational culture, Lewis[21] posited that the process of group thinking may develop in situations where the organization begins to believe that their size or certain features they might possess makes them immune to disasters.

This form of organizational culture should be done away with if the business is serious about making itself resilient against future organizational crises. In some instances, management or executives may hold a firm belief that insurance covers them from all possible risks without necessarily taking into consideration the fact that insurance may not indemnify them against the loss of business reputation or market share, or tarnished brands.[22]

Research shows that organizations that are prone to crises always tend to display the characteristics documented above more than organizations that are deemed crisis-prepared organizations. While all individuals or organizations are likely to employ the use of the group think mechanism (such as that the organization is fully insured), the difference concerns the degree or the extent to which it is utilized. Altering this type of organizational culture (or mindset) is not an easy job, as it can sometimes trigger resistance. Additionally, in such circumstances, the implementation of the best practice business continuity modus operandi may not be the best approach. The manager faced with such a situation must first be able to understand the fact that all organizations are different and, therefore, a technique that works in one organization may not necessarily work in others.[23]

Most of the executives tasked with tackling the issue of business continuity following a crisis are eager to realize quick wins while striving to espouse successful business strategies that have been adopted elsewhere, without considering the suitability of the action taken. Therefore, it is imperative that a business organization modifies its organizational culture to demystify the old thinking that business insurance covers everything. Such old thinking should be done away with, and management, together with the other employees, needs to understand that there are other things, such as business reputation, that are not covered by insurance.

LEADERSHIP AND POST-CRISIS BUSINESS RECOVERY AND CONTINUITY

The role of leadership in post-crisis business recovery and continuity cannot be underestimated. Research shows that the type of leadership embraced within an organization is critical in the subsequent success of the organization. According to Spreitzer and Quinn,[24] leadership may be conceptualized as a collective phenomenon in which varied individuals come together to ensure organizational success. Leadership competence, which is key in a business organization, refers to the skills, knowledge, and abilities facilitating an individual's ability to perform a given task. As documented by Denis, Lamothe, and Langley,[25] leadership is considered a dynamic process by which roles progress over time, further illustrating that leadership influences go beyond the focal organizational boundaries.

In a crisis situation, leadership is deemed dynamic and collective, and therefore calls for leaders to have sense-making skills and accurate perception to determine the appropriate courses of action.[26] In this respect, it is expected that crisis leadership competencies, including activities such as communication, decision-making, managing multiple constituencies, creating organizational capabilities, and developing human capital, are critical during post-crisis organizational management and continuity. Implementing the above competencies helps the organization to successfully recover following a crisis.

Levitt and March[27] posited that organizational members and leaders ought to learn that codes inferences based on past business experiences into routines that eventually guide business behavior. The effectual management of organizational crises is highly dependent on the nature of the leadership behavior exhibited by members to actively engage in strategy formulation, as well as knowledge acquisition, with the sole objective of resolving organizational crises. As the business organization changes and becomes increasingly multifaceted, it becomes extremely critical to come up with a set of skills that can help them preclude, as well as effectually respond to, organizational crises.[28]

Transformational leaders are more likely to come up with proactive strategies for successfully driving the business into the right path following a crisis. According to Wang and Belardo,[29] development and learning are the genesis of what many consider crisis leadership. Crisis leadership competencies are especially pertinent in managing strategic, operational, and human resource functions following a crisis. Therefore, in that respect, it is clear that leadership plays a central role in post-crisis organizational management and business continuity, further justifying the need for management to foster a work environment that inculcates a competency-based approach to post-crisis business management.[30] This entails the identification of the key activities and tasks required during post-crisis situations, including the skills, knowledge, and abilities needed to successfully recover from the crisis.

By building the skills, capabilities, and knowledge required to successfully drive the organization following a crisis, leaders nurture a culture where the organizational members are empowered to think critically and systematically following a crisis to ensure quick recovery. The profitability of the business is of paramount significance, and therefore, organizations must ensure that potent strategies and measures are laid down for success following recovery.[31] Developing a superb business culture is a key ingredient for ensuring successful business recovery and continuity following a crisis.

Wang and Belardo[32] contended that a crisis management culture calls for a comprehensive analysis that takes into consideration leadership competencies, such as skills, abilities, and knowledge, as the leadership quality is critical during the post-crisis management stage. The quality of the decisions made, as well as the strategies developed, is closely related to business success.

Endnotes

Business Recovery and Continuity

1 Ōyama, T. (2010). *Post-crisis risk management: Bracing for the next perfect storm.* Singapore: John Wiley & Sons.

2 Glendon, A. I., Clarke, S., & McKenna, E. F. (2006). *Human safety and risk management.* Boca Raton, FL: CRC/Taylor & Francis.

3 Glendon, A. I., Clarke, S., & McKenna, E. F. (2006). *Human safety and risk management.* Boca Raton, FL: CRC/Taylor & Francis.

4 IBM. (2015). *Build a viable plan for disaster recovery and crisis management.* Retrieved from https://www-935.ibm.com/services/au/gts/pdf/disasterrecoverycrisisplanningsolution.pdf.

5 IBM. (2015). *Build a viable plan for disaster recovery and crisis management.* Retrieved from https://www-935.ibm.com/services/au/gts/pdf/disasterrecoverycrisisplanningsolution.pdf.

6 IBM. (2015). *Build a viable plan for disaster recovery and crisis management.* Retrieved from https://www-935.ibm.com/services/au/gts/pdf/disasterrecoverycrisisplanningsolution.pdf.

7 Snedaker, S., & Rima, C. (2014). *Business continuity and disaster recovery planning for IT professionals.* Waltham, MA: Syngress.

8 Snedaker, S., & Rima, C. (2014). *Business continuity and disaster recovery planning for IT professionals.* Waltham, MA: Syngress.

9 Snedaker, S., & Rima, C. (2014). *Business continuity and disaster recovery planning for IT professionals.* Waltham, MA: Syngress.

10 Snedaker, S., & Rima, C. (2014). *Business continuity and disaster recovery planning for IT professionals.* Waltham, MA: Syngress.

11 Lee, M. (2006). *New directions? A view from multiple perspectives.* Unpublished Thesis. Queensland University of Technology.

12 Herbane, B., Elliott, D., & Swartz, E. M. (2004). Business continuity management: Time for a strategic role? *Long Range Planning, 37*(5), 435–457.

13 Herbane, B., Elliott, D., & Swartz, E. M. (2004). Business continuity management: Time for a strategic role? *Long Range Planning, 37*(5), 435–457.

14 Janssen, M. A., & Ostrom, E. (2006). Resilience, vulnerability and adaptation: A cross-cutting theme of the International Human Dimensions Programme on Global Environmental Change. *Global Environmental Change Part B: Environmental Hazards, 16,* 2.

15 Herbane, B., Elliott, D., & Swartz, E. M. (2004). Business continuity management: Time for a strategic role? *Long Range Planning, 37*(5), 435–457.

16 Herbane, B., Elliott, D., & Swartz, E. M. (2004). Business continuity management: Time for a strategic role? *Long Range Planning, 37*(5), 435–457.

17 Herbane, B., Elliott, D., & Swartz, E. M. (2004). Business continuity management: Time for a strategic role? *Long Range Planning, 37*(5), 435–457.

18 Herbane, B., Elliott, D., & Swartz, E. M. (2004). Business continuity management: Time for a strategic role? *Long Range Planning, 37*(5), 435–457.

19 Smith, D., & Sipika, C. (1993). Back from the brink: Post crisis management. *Long Range Planning, 26*(1), 10.

20 Rosenkopf, L., & Nerkar, A. (2001). Beyond local search: Boundary spanning, exploration, and impact in the operational disk industry. *Strategic Journal Management, 22,* 19.

21 Lewis, G. W. (2006). *Organizational crisis management: The human factor.* Boca Raton: Auerbach Publications.

22 Lewis, G. W. (2006). *Organizational crisis management: The human factor.* Boca Raton: Auerbach Publications.

23 Lewis, G. W. (2006). *Organizational crisis management: The human factor.* Boca Raton: Auerbach Publications.

24 Spreitzer, G., & Quinn, R. (2001). *A company of leaders: Five disciplines for unleashing the power of your workforce.* San Francisco: Jossey-Bass.

25 Denis, J., Lamothe, L., & Langley, A. (2001). The dynamics of collective leadership and strategic change in pluralistic organizations. *Academy of Management Journal, 44*(4), 809–837.

26 Walsh, J. (1995). Managerial and organizational cognition: Notes from a trip down memory lane. *Organization Science, 6*(3), 280–321.

27 Levitt, B., & March, J. (1988). Organizational learning. *Annual Review of Sociology, 14*, 319–340.

28 Garcia, H. (2006). Effective leadership response to crisis. *Strategy and Leadership, 34*(1), 4–10.

29 Wang, W., & Belardo, S. (2005). Strategic integration: A knowledge management approach to crisis management. *Proceedings of the 38th Hawaii International Conference on System Sciences* (pp. 252–260). Big Island, Hawaii: IEEE Computer Society.

30 Wooten, L. P., & James, E. H. (2004). When firms fail to learn: The perpetuation of discrimination in the workplace. *Journal of Management Inquiry, 13*(1), 23–33.

31 Senge, P. (1990). *The fifth discipline.* New York: Doubleday.

32 Wang, W., & Belardo, S. (2005). Strategic integration: A knowledge management approach to crisis management. *Proceedings of the 38th Hawaii International Conference on System Sciences* (pp. 252–260). Big Island, Hawaii: IEEE Computer Society.

Case Study 16: How Germany Recovered from the 2008 Financial Crisis

The international crisis of 2008 had an adverse effect on every nation. Most business processes were drawn back and profit margins were minimized. Among the most affected countries was Germany, given the stalling of the economic status that took center stage. However, there have been a lot of improvements over the years that have subsequently resulted in the overall improvement of the economic state. The growth in the gross national product has been stellar over the years, resulting in the developments noted in the state of the economy.[1]

The onset of the economic crisis in Germany started in September 2008, upon the highlighted insolvency of Lehman Brothers. The force of the impact was massive; after six months, the export and import trades had fallen by well over 20%. The most affected was the prolific German automobile industry. The number of vehicles produced in that month when compared to the same month in the previous year was a reduction of nearly 34%.[2]

There have been constant improvements. As of mid-2011, the economy was at the brink of full recovery in light of several noticeable trends. The level of financial recovery that has been recorded showed that Germany is the largest national economy in the EU. It was far above all the records made by other nations that affected by the 2008 turmoil; Germany recorded $285 billion in trade surplus, the highest in the world in 2014. The primary consideration of this exploration is to give an account of the steps taken by Germany after the economic recession that ultimately made it an outstanding economic example.[3]

INTERVENTION OF THE FEDERAL GOVERNMENT

The majority of the improvements that have been realized in the economy in Germany have been due to the intervention of the federal government. The commitment that has been shown by the state appears to be more intense than the same commitment shown by other states.[4] This has been at the epicenter of the economic improvement.

Several business programs were initiated by the government in the quest to revitalize falling estates. The values of most of the projects were estimated in billions of euros. This has been the principal determinant of the improvements observed in the course of business performance. Some of these have always acted in the capacity of capital that is invested into the economy.[5] The returns from investment have always been reimbursed into the business schemes so that there is a further bolstering of the basics of the economy. Thus, there has been inevitable growth of the economy given the fact that frequent investments have yielded a self-sustainable economic standing.

After the recession was declared, efforts were made by the federal government to focus on the renovation of buildings so that there could be a boost in public sector investments. A move was also made to promote car scrapping premiums so that a given number of stipends were paid to individuals for agreeing to have their vehicles scrapped. This move was crucial to the resurgence of the motor vehicle industry in terms of making materials available to add to the material base that was relied on for primary manufacture processes.[6] This was at the forefront of the considerations that could be said to have led to great improvements in the automobile industry.

The other factor that effectively resulted in the reclamation of the economic condition of Germany ahead of the other nations that were affected by the economic recession lies in the rescue package that was designed for banking institutions. Once banks are secured, financial management is bound to be seamless and will contribute to the development of the economy. The improvement of the state of the banks points out the need to monitor financial expenditures so that all relevant plans can have a seamless transition.[7] The sustainability of the banking institutions was crucial in the prevention of further distortion in the financial sector.

Favorable Employment Laws

Besides the intervention of the federal government in occasioning overall improvements in the economy after the recession, the other pertinent factor that was key in boosting business performance was the favorable employment laws that were enacted. It is only logical that the scope of success and the economic sustainability that can be enjoyed by a nation are attributable to the workforce that it bears. Most states rely directly on the input of the workforce if there are to be any notable returns in revenue from the input. As such, the capacity of success could be sufficiently related to how well the workforce in various sectors of the economy is committed to service and the delegation of duties that are apportioned to them.[8]

This was crucial in the ultimate improvements in the German economy after the recession of 2008. In a review of employment law, two years after the recession, flexible work hours and shorter work periods were introduced. Once there was a review of the flexibility of the terms of employment, it was inevitable that employee turnover would match the expectations that are billed.[9] As such, the performance of individuals was critical in raising the stakes of the returns due to the improved state of the economy, and it has been a vital component of the bid by Germany to rebuild after the economic recession.

Such modifications to employment law successfully led to the prevention of mass redundancy during the crisis. These are the measures that allowed businesses to respond quickly in the post-recession era, so that the input has created an inevitable demand for market products in foreign markets.[10] The availability of the markets was also essential in building market sustainability, with markets assured and labor readily available in light of the satisfaction instilled by the new employment law. There was a swift transition of the raw materials used in production through the designated channels, until the point where they were ready for consumption.

German businesses offered a range of products so that the many different entities were well-positioned in the markets to achieve sustainability. This has also been vital in edging out competing nations in the sale of the various products in the export business. Sustainability has also been the result of meeting the needs of the consumers in emerging markets to further widen the scope of influence of the German products. Such economic dynamism has led to endless success in building a strong base for the economy that has been realized after the onset of the recession.[11]

Influence of Family-Owned Businesses

Some mid-sized businesses have been the core of Germany's economic resurgence. Most of these business sectors are owned by families and are as vital as an additive to the economic growth, given the large number of people that are employed by them. Out of the entire workforce, up to a total of 65% are employed by such businesses. The increasing number of these businesses has been crucial in contributing to the economy. These business entities have a distinguishing feature that further cements their status in the country's ability to sustain economic growth and stability.[12] These entities have long-term thinking approaches that lay down a step-by-step framework to be used in overseeing operations. These strategies ensure that the continuity of operations is not interrupted, and that there is a constant generation of value from the ventures that are pursued.

From the factors reviewed above, it would suffice to draw the general conclusion that preparedness and proper planning were crucial for the rise of Germany in the quest to emerge from the recession. This is the key difference when compared to the unpersuasive initiatives that have been achieved by other states of a similar caliber as Germany. Germany's sustainability of operations has also managed to translate into the best-practice modalities to further raise the stakes for success.

Endnotes

Case Study 16: How Germany Recovered from the 2008 Financial Crisis

1 Reinhart, C. M., & Rogoff, K. S. (2014). *Recovery from financial crises: Evidence from 100 episodes* (No. w19823). National Bureau of Economic Research.

2 Greenglass, E., Antonides, G., Christandl, F., Foster, G., Katter, J. K., Kaufman, B. E., & Lea, S. E. (2014). The financial crisis and its effects: Perspectives from economics and psychology. *Journal of Behavioral and Experimental Economics, 50*, 10–12.

3 Storm, S., & Naastepad, C. W. M. (2015). Crisis and recovery in the German economy: The real lessons. *Structural Change and Economic Dynamics, 32*, 11–24.

4 Reinhart, C. M., & Rogoff, K. S. (2014). *Recovery from financial crises: Evidence from 100 episodes* (No. w19823). National Bureau of Economic Research.

5 Greenglass, E., Antonides, G., Christandl, F., Foster, G., Katter, J. K., Kaufman, B. E., & Lea, S. E. (2014). The financial crisis and its effects: Perspectives from economics and psychology. *Journal of Behavioral and Experimental Economics, 50*, 10–12.

6 Kickert, W. (2012). State responses to the fiscal crisis in Britain, Germany and the Netherlands. *Public Management Review, 14*(3), 299–309.

7 Karanikolos, M., Mladovsky, P., Cylus, J., Thomson, S., Basu, S., Stuckler, D., & McKee, M. (2013). Financial crisis, austerity, and health in Europe. *The Lancet, 381*(9874), 1323–1331.

8 Kickert, W. (2012). State responses to the fiscal crisis in Britain, Germany and the Netherlands. *Public Management Review, 14*(3), 299–309.

9 Shiller, R. J. (2012). *The subprime solution: How today's global financial crisis happened, and what to do about it.* Princeton University Press.

10 Karanikolos, M., Mladovsky, P., Cylus, J., Thomson, S., Basu, S., Stuckler, D., & McKee, M. (2013). Financial crisis, austerity, and health in Europe. *The Lancet, 381*(9874), 1323–1331.

11 Hendrikse, R. P., & Sidaway, J. D. (2014). Financial wizardry and the Golden City: Tracking the financial crisis through Pforzheim, Germany. *Transactions of the Institute of British Geographers, 39*(2), 195–208.

Case Study 16: How Germany Recovered from the 2008 Financial Crisis

12 Karanikolos, M., Mladovsky, P., Cylus, J., Thomson, S., Basu, S., Stuckler, D., & McKee, M. (2013). Financial crisis, austerity, and health in Europe. *The Lancet, 381*(9874), 1323–1331.

PART TWO

Miscellaneous Crisis Case Studies

PART TWO

Case Study 17: Refugees in the EU 2015 Crisis

INTRODUCTION

The European Union (EU) crisis of 2015 has been one of the most complicated experiments that the governments of the union have encountered so far, with its history being in the beginning of the Arab Spring movement; a large number of refugees have entered European countries from African and Middle East countries due to the inhabitable conditions existing within their countries of origin. This chapter, therefore, is concerned with the causes of the high number of refugees creating a crisis in European countries, while making attempts to dig deep into their root causes, the impacts on the receiving countries, and initiatives that have been put in place to control the crisis.

Refugees in the EU 2015 Crisis Explored

The European migrant crisis of 2015 came into existence due to the surge of migrants and refugees who were moving to the EU by crossing the Mediterranean Sea into southeast Europe. A number of them were managing applications for asylum. The refugees involved in the crisis originated from Middle Eastern countries (Iraq and Syria), Africa (Nigeria, Sudan, Somalia, Gambia, and Eritrea), Asia (Pakistan, Bangladesh, and Afghanistan), and the western Balkans

(Kosovo, Serbia, and Albania). Based on the statistics from the United Nations High Commissioner for Refugees, as of December 2015, refugees and migrants since the beginning of 2015 were 50% Syrians, 20% Afghans, and 7% Iraqi nationals, with over 60% of the migrants and refugees being adult men.[1] The term *European refugee crisis* became a widespread connotation in April 2015, a time during which a boat that had been ferrying migrants through the Mediterranean Sea to Europe sank and killed over 1,200 people.

The continuous wars in many countries within Africa and the Middle East inflated the total number of refugees across the world to close to 60 million by the end of 2015. This was the highest number since the end of World War II. During the massive overseas migrations, a number of governments within the EU refused to offer financial aid to the rescue operations, which were being driven by Italy via Operation Mare Nostrum, which was later replaced by Frontex's Operation Triton in November 2015, when the flow of refugees began to increase across northern Europe, Germany, and the Balkan states.[2] Since April 2015, the EU has been struggling to manage the ever-increasing number of refugees creating a humanitarian crisis by enhancing the different border operations within the Mediterranean region, among other strategies used to cope with the crisis.

PRESSURE AND THE EFFECTS OF THE REFUGEE CRISIS ON EUROPEAN COUNTRIES

Impact on the GDP

It is estimated that over three million refugees will flow into Europe by the end of 2017, according to the European Commission. It has been suggested that an influx of refugees in such an uncontrolled manner will have a relatively small impact on the economy of the countries receiving them, while causing a rise in the GDP to a margin of between 0.2 and 0.3%, which would rise above the baseline come 2020. However, the European Commission has taken note of the fact that such impacts would vary in different countries; with this perspective, Germany would be more adversely affected by the crisis than the other transit states through which the migrants pass.[3] The high number of refugees will impact public spending with the need to spend more; the labor force will increase with people who have skills similar to those already existing within the EU, and such a coherent labor force will be instrumental in the regulation of employment rates.

The Impact on Public Finance
According to an article by *The Economist* (2015), having analyzed a study of the Organization for Economic Co-operation and Development (OECD), there is an estimated net financial contribution from the refugees and migrants within the over 27 countries that they have managed to settle in so far. The direct contributions of the refugees tend to be smaller than the contributions realized by native citizens; this is, however, attributed to the fact that they remit fewer taxes, but this is never connected to the fact that they claim higher benefits; rather, it is because of their lower employment rates with respect to women. To drive an increased financial contribution, they should be empowered in the employment field so that their labor force contributions can be realized. Therefore, the overall conclusion of the article on the concept of migration is based on the fact that migra-

tion is never a source of drain, but neither does it bring about gains to the public fiscal basket.

While looking at the debate on the contributions of refugees to the financial debt in Germany, Mark Schieritz[4] cites the analysis by Essen with the claim that, by the end of 2015, the cost of maintaining refugees and migrants would rise to up to 10 billion euros, with that figure increasing progressively in 2016. Such projections were similar to the German government projections, which had placed the cost of individual refugees at 1,200 euros annually. However, amid the excess expenditures that have been linked to the crisis brought about by the refugees, the surplus within the German annual budget will improve from its current 0.3% of the GDP in 2015 to about 0.6% in 2016. This is connected to the fact that all the extra spending did not just disappear, but rather acted as a stimulant on the internal economic demands in Germany. The ease of access that the refugees have to the labor market will establish a greater opportunity for them to make notable contributions to welfare sustainability in Germany.

As Holger Schmieding asserted, it is expected that there will be a small demand for integration; the excess spending charged to issues related to migration and refugees will be responsible for the improvement of the GDP values from the current 0.3% to an aggregate of 0.4% annually.[5] This may not only be applicable to Germany, but also to other countries where the migrants and refugees are received and accepted; therefore, a number of countries will ultimately quote the existence of refugees to have been one of the determining factors for their exceeded annual fiscal budgets. To achieve a balance, a short-term stimulus demand of about 0.2% of the Eurozone GDP for 2015–2016 needs to occur.

Case Study 17: Refugees in the EU 2015 Crisis

The Impact on the Labor Markets

Having noted the huge wave of refugees that arrived in Germany during the summer period, Lidia Farre[6] attempted to make a correlated analysis of the labor market impacts of migration; she based her argument on the notion that, in many instances of immigration, there are very minimal or no impacts on the wages of native citizens. It is evident that a number of migrants and refugees often possess lower educational qualifications and work experience; thus, they play a great role in the displacement of habitual residents with few manual work occupations, which in turn have higher levels of remuneration and specialization. According to Farre, many studies have shown an existing complementary relationship between the native women workers and their migrant counterparts; in several situations, the majority of the immigrants secured job opportunities within the service sectors with more precise consideration of the delivery of care to the elderly and children within the entire community. This denotes an increased provision of labor within domestic services to allow for the substitution of unpaid labor hours for remunerated work hours, thereby causing notable progress within professional careers.

While discussing the concept of the winners and losers of the refugee wave, Hans Werner stated that the uptake of a low-skilled workforce would keep the salaries offered to the semi-skilled workforce under intense pressure, as has always happened in the U.S.[7] This is usually common to individuals who have been involved in migrations to newer states; in such situations, the winners are always the qualified workers who will definitely benefit from the falling labor costs within the simple tasks framework. The idea of a minimum wage inhibits the conceptual integration of immigrants and refugees into the labor market. Furthermore, Werner brings about a proposal that the minimum wage ought to be reduced while coming up with compensation through the activation of individual wage subsidies; such a measure would ensure that many people will take part in performing work, but at lower costs than the unemployment subsidies.

Initiatives to Combat the Refugee Crisis in the EU

Having realized that the refugee crisis of 2015 has become a widespread problem within European countries, there is a great need to keep coming up with new solutions to combat the problems that accompany such crises.[8] Currently, Europe is on the verge of challenges emanating from the extraordinary number of refugees during 2015; to ensure that such a migration process does not become part and parcel of the operations within the continent over time, it is prudent to come up with stringent measures aimed at curbing the problem. In initial policies, it is important to indulge the spirit of togetherness and humanity throughout the EU whenever immigrants are received into their new countries; this, therefore, calls for the EU to set up humane standards that ought to be followed by all member states while addressing the refugee issues. The EU has been working on common policies to deal with asylum issues, as well as the conditions that have been set for refugees reception across the EU member states.

There is a need to ensure a course of refugee redistribution among the European states; German nationals are working diligently to welcome the refugees into Germany and are being quite instrumental in their integration into society in a manner never seen before. However, such an act of solidarity can only be viable and have a long-term advantages in the event that it happens across the European continent and is adopted by all member states; in the event that it turns out to be the case that only a handful of countries bear the burden of refugees, then the initiative will be quite short-lived and unsustainable since the strain will be aligned with selected countries only. As pointed out by Steinmeier and Gabriel,[9] there is an elaborate need for creating reforms to the Dublin Convention that go into effect immediately to open up more ways of establishing integrated and objective refugee quotas with the ability to account for the capabilities of the member states to bear them. Europe is still in dire need of managing its borders, which does not only fall on the fact of providing frontier security; this could be achieved through the establishment of new rules and regulations based on the timely and efficient registration and monitoring of the new refugees as they arrive in Europe.

There is a great need to expand the various avenues for both legal labor and educational migration; it is quite clear that not all the refugees in the European Union are asylum-seekers, with specific consideration for those across the Mediterranean pathway, which is a mixed zone of individuals in search of improved economic situations and living standards for themselves and their families. Among the group may be individuals evading prosecution for crime cases, escaping poverty, and evading poor state governance in their countries to areas where they have the hope of living freer lives full of dignity. Such groups of self-imposed refugees do not qualify for any form of state protection under the current international refugee laws or EU directives. To address this challenge, the EU has developed a crisis mitigation strategy by establishing new migration policies that have taken into consideration the fact that the older population forms an important part of the economic welfare of the EU.[10] Additionally, the member states have moved steps ahead in seeking approval for the development of visa application avenues for the purpose of the employment of the skilled workers moving with the refugees, as well as student visas for those who wish to continue with their education in such recipient states.

According to *The Guardian* and Reuters, there have been high-tech militarized border operations by Operation Triton that included the use of several aircraft and had a budget three times that of Operation Mare Nostrum; the operation has been mandated to carry out extensive border surveys and rescue operations across the Mediterranean Sea. On April 25, 2015, the EU held an emergency summit with the heads of states and reached a consensus to triple the rescue operations budget (Operation Triton), hitting 120 million euros for the fiscal year 2015/2016 to allow for improved operations just like those of the preceding operation back in 2013–2014.[11] Having commissioned the funding for the operations, EU members donated naval ships to the operations; this move was highly criticized by Amnesty International, which accused the EU of acting to save face rather than saving lives, while adding that any failures to expand the operations by the Triton rescue team would significantly undercut the commitment to the problem.

In summarizing this chapter, it is significant to note that the refugee crisis within the EU has been a result of an influx of immigrants from countries facing civil unrest and economic hardships. As of December 2015, the available statistics state that the number of refugees has hit 762,000, with numerous deaths being recorded during their period of transit through the Mediterranean pathway. The huge number of immigrants has both positively and negatively impacted the labor market and financial situations within their countries of settlement, as well as in security sectors, thus prompting the establishment of a number of initiatives to combat the dangers of such uncontrolled population movements.

# Endnotes

PART TWO: Miscellaneous Crisis Case Studies

Case Study 17: Refugees in the EU 2015 Crisis

1 Rachman, G. (2015, November). Refugees or migrants—what's in a word? *Financial Times*. Retrieved from http://blogs.ft.com/the-world/2015/09/refugees-or-migrants-whats-in-a-word/

2 Huttl, P., & Leandro, A. (2015, October). How will refugees affect European economies? *Bruegel*. Retrieved December 22, 2015, from http://bruegel.org/2015/10/how-will-refugees-affect-european-economies/

3 Calamur, K. (2015, November). The economic impact of the European refugee crisis. *The Atlantic*. Retrieved from http://www.theatlantic.com/international/archive/2015/11/economic-impact-european-refugee-crisis/414364/

4 Huttl, P., & Leandro, A. (2015, October). How will refugees affect European economies? *Bruegel*. Retrieved December 22, 2015, from http://bruegel.org/2015/10/how-will-refugees-affect-european-economies/

5 Huttl, P., & Leandro, A. (2015, October). How will refugees affect European economies? *Bruegel*. Retrieved December 22, 2015, from http://bruegel.org/2015/10/how-will-refugees-affect-european-economies/

6 Huttl, P., & Leandro, A. (2015, October). How will refugees affect European economies? *Bruegel*. Retrieved December 22, 2015, from http://bruegel.org/2015/10/how-will-refugees-affect-european-economies/

7 Huttl, P., & Leandro, A. (2015, October). How will refugees affect European economies? *Bruegel*. Retrieved December 22, 2015, from http://bruegel.org/2015/10/how-will-refugees-affect-european-economies/

8 Steinmeier, F.-W., & Gabriel, S. (2015, August). How the EU can solve the migrant crisis, in ten points. *The Telegraph*. Retrieved from http://www.telegraph.co.uk/news/uknews/immigration/11822752/How-the-EU-can-solve-the-migrant-crisis-in-ten-points.html

9 Steinmeier, F.-W., & Gabriel, S. (2015, August). How the EU can solve the migrant crisis, in ten points. *The Telegraph*. Retrieved from http://www.telegraph.co.uk/news/uknews/immigration/11822752/How-the-EU-can-solve-the-migrant-crisis-in-ten-points.html

10 Carrion, D. (2015, September). Syrian refugees are not the security threat that they are feared to be. *Chatham House*. Retrieved December

23, 2015, from https://www.chathamhouse.org/expert/comment/syrian-refugees-are-not-security-threat-they-are-feared-be

11 Sorcha, P. (2015, May). LÉ Eithne to be dispatched in migrant search on May 8th. *Irish Times*.

Case Study 18: The Chinese Stock Market Crash (2015)

The Chinese Stock Exchange, which forms the crux of this discussion, is based in the city of Shanghai, China. Inaugurated in November 1990, the Stock Exchange is state-owned, with a market capitalization of $2.3 trillion, which makes it the sixth-largest stock exchange globally. The Chinese Stock Exchange recently experienced an unexpected cash crash. The stock market crash that is currently befalling China was long overdue. Bello[1] opined that the meaningful escalation of the share prices in the Shanghai Stock Exchange from mid-2014 to mid-2015, when the composite index rose by about 150%, was a strong indicator of the impending stock exchange collapse. The prices were expected to rise significantly above the real values of the traded assets.

The Chinese stock market recorded a sharp decline, despite the potent measures that were laid down by many officials from Beijing geared toward stimulating global confidence in the country's slowing economy. In 12 months, shares had escalated to 150% of their real values, further worsening the state of the stock exchange. The Chinese move to devalue its currency (the yuan) failed to serve a good purpose, but instead worsened the situation, as it significantly intensified the worries that the country's economy was facing.[2]

CRISIS MANAGEMENT:
THE ART OF SUCCESS AND FAILURE

Bello[3] contended that, like Greenspan during the 2008 Wall Street crisis, neither foreign and local investors nor the Chinese government appeared prepared to handle the situation when the crash began. Bello[4] highlighted that the Shanghai composite index was pushed up 40%, further triggering a worldwide collapse of stock prices, something that forced Beijing to intervene for the purpose of buying market shares. However, when this move failed, Beijing was forced to devalue its currency, hoping that it would help the situation.

The fact that many Asian countries have a strong link with China implies that the effect is likely to spread among the different Asian countries, implying that many Asian countries stand to lose out in a big way if the Chinese stock market continues to fall. Allen[5] opined that, beyond the Asian markets, investors in other countries, such as Australia, have begun to feel the effect of the Chinese stock market crash. If the current situation persists, Australia is likely to experience a decline in commodity prices, leading to a decline in the demand for products, such as Australian coal and iron ore. Additionally, the Australian dollar is under immense pressure and has recorded a significant fall compared to the U.S. dollar.

CAUSES OF THE CRISIS

Today, China is on the verge of facing almost three major financial problems, though different, risks that were absolutely rooted in the substantial stimulus program dating to 2008; these critical challenges are inclusive of real estate bubbles, the presence of shadow banks, and both private and public debts attached mainly to local government debts.

Case Study 18: The Chinese Stock Market Crash (2015)

Such market risks have been highly intertwined and involve the banking sector, thus making it possible that those risks will spill over to the formal financial sectors (banks).[6] What has placed the Chinese market and policy-makers in such an awkward position is the continued gradual slowing of the growth of their GDP, among other important financial indicators. Keeping in mind that the growth rate of the Chinese economy is almost at 50% of the rate of the last decade, it will not be so easy for the country to run out of national debts, which had been used as the best strategy for growth.

The market crisis resulted from a number of factors and conditions that were both within and outside the Chinese market structures. During the year preceding the market crash, having received encouragement from the national media, several business investors inflated a bubble of investment in the stock market using their borrowed money; this excessive pumping of investments into the stock market with loaned money surpassed the economic growth rate and profit accrual by the institutions in which they had invested. Later, on the brink of a crisis, investors received communications *en masse* concerning their stocks within the bulging markets, forcing the majority of them to dispose of their shares *en masse*, thus accelerating the crash.

By July 9, the Chinese stock market had lost over 30% of its stakes within a short period of three weeks, during which time over 1,400 organizations, representing more than 50% of all listed companies, had requested a stoppage in trade, treating this as an attempt to mitigate further losses that had been predicted within the market. The Chinese stock market continuously lost value, even though several efforts had been instituted by the government to mitigate the fall, to a certain extent. Following three weeks of stability, the index value fell again by August 24 by a margin of 8.48%, which also marked the largest depreciation since 2007.[7]

Even though shadow banking has not been as highly leveraged in China as it has in the United States and Europe, the regulatory aspects still remain absolutely lenient and subtle. Such banks utilize the money absorbed from the issuance of property management plans in offering credit/loan facilities to real estate and local government developers, creating a bubble in the Chinese real estate investment.[8]

Even though government authorities had been working day and night to manage the level of speculation in the real estate sector by imposing higher deposit payments, as well as regulating the state's overreliance on the real development of real estate to boost economic growth, a notable property bubble still remained, resulting in surpluses in the form of ghost city creations.

Similarly, there was an increased level and pace of both public and private indebtedness, and this was a worrying trend in lieu of the economic state of the state; according to a report by McKinsey [9] on the economic situation, Chinese total debt had accumulated to over 282% of the country's GDP in 2014. This represented both public and private/household accumulations, an increase from the 158% accumulation of the GDP as recorded in 2007. This gave China the highest recorded index among the world's major economies.

According to Chen Zhiwu,[10] if China did not get over its dangerous foreign debts, the economic road ahead would be quite bumpy compared to how it was back in 2008 and could lead to a prolonged and painful market crash. Zhiwu was quite specific on the lack of correlation that existed between short-term debts and long-term investment plans by local governments, which resulted in increased debt set-offs, accelerating the country's credit risks.

THE IMPACT OF THE CHINESE STOCK MARKET CRASH

Pettinger[11] has contended that the Chinese stock market has remained extremely volatile, witnessing a significant decline in prices since July 2015. For instance, on August 24 alone, share prices fell by an estimated 9%, considered to be among the biggest single-day falls in the history of the Chinese stock market. Some economists have documented some of the possible effects of this crisis, asserting that it is likely to pose a serious threat to the global economy. The following are some of the likely effects of the stock market crash.

Reduced Exports

One of the serious effects of the Chinese stock market crash was reduced exports. Pettinger[12] posited that the crash will escalate the consumer spending index by approximately 10% on a yearly basis. A significant number of countries see China as a potential source of exports for a good number of Western countries. Certain brands, such as Yum and Burberry, have carved out niches in the Chinese market; therefore, a decline in the share price will significantly lower the wealth of Chinese investors. Worries regarding share prices, coupled with political uncertainty and the falling prices, could disrupt the growth in consumer spending, which eventually contributes to lessened demand for exports. Considering the weak economic growth in the U.S. and the

Eurozone, a fall in exports to China could be another factor holding back growth while stimulating another slowdown.[13]

Falling Commodity Prices

Falling commodity prices are another pertinent effect of the Chinese stock market crash. According to Pettinger,[14] the slowdown in the Chinese economy is likely to cause serious repercussions for the global demand for commodities such as gas, oil, and metals. A significant fall in commodity prices will most likely lead to a fall in export revenue, particularly for commodity producers, such as Australia, Canada, OPEC (Organization of the Petroleum Exporting Countries), and African countries. In contrast, the reduced commodity prices will have pertinent benefits for consumers hailing from Western countries because they are likely to benefit from cheaper commodity and oil prices.

The Rising Dollar

The instability caused by the Chinese stock market crash could compel investors to consider looking for safe havens for their investments. As opposed to holding Asian and Chinese shares, investors may consider other countries, such as the U.S., where shares have greater stability. The rise in the demand for U.S. bonds and shares could escalate the dollar value. An escalation in dollar value could lead to a rise in the cost of U.S. exports, further leading to lower export sales. This is very dangerous to the growth and development of not only the Chinese economy, but also the global economy. If this happens, the government should react with speed to ensure that the prevailing situation is modified before things get out of hand.

Global Confidence

The spectacular fall in the Chinese stock share market prices revives the specter of the 2008 financial crisis. The decrease in the Chinese stock market appears to be reflected in other markets in different parts of the world, something that has led to global ripples and subsequent losses of confidence. Such volatility and uncertainty can discourage spending and investment significantly, leading to a global economic slowdown.

RESPONSES AND INITIATIVES TO MITIGATE THE CHINESE STOCK MARKET CRISIS OF 2015

Considering the market crisis, it was prudent to take steps to manage the situation in China to ensure that the effects did not bounce back to hit the economy and other related sectors at their worst points. The Chinese government came up with a number of initiatives to stem the crash tide; such steps included limiting the short-term selling of investment stocks by issuing arrest threats.[15] However, this crash could not be stopped by bailing out banks through credits, but rather through the purchase of market shares to stabilize market products. The government stopped all the public donations that it had been engaging in and instead engaged in the issuance of financial assistance to market brokers to buy investment shares. This step was thoroughly backed by cash that the government received from the Chinese central bank.

Given the fact that a majority of the shareholders in the Chinese stock market are individuals, with companies only accounting for 20%, national media stations continued with vigorous campaigns in attempts to convince the Chinese to obtain shares from the stock market. Additionally, the China

CRISIS MANAGEMENT:
THE ART OF SUCCESS AND FAILURE

Securities Regulatory Commission (CSRC) instituted a half-year ban on major stakeholders and let the government have ownership of more than 5% of any organization's stakes from the disposing of stocks; this later led to an impressive rise in the stock market by over 6%. Going further with recovery strategies, about 1,300 companies, or 45% of the stocks available in the market, imposed a 6-month suspension on any trade of their stocks starting from July 8, 2015, a wise step in saving the Chinese stock market.[16]

According to Colombo,[17] a *Forbes* contributor, the measures that had been taken by the Chinese government, inclusive of the interest-reduction strategies that allowed for the attachment of personal property as collateral while obtaining a credit facility, as well as the motivation of brokerage activities in market share purchases and sales, were part of the significant steps that caused the notable shake of the market in the middle of July 2015. In his argument, Colombo asserted that, generally, the interventions by the Chinese government during the crisis were not easily predicted, and based on their outcomes, he insisted that, in the long run, the impact would be attached to the establishment of a larger market bubble.

Further Reading

> ➢ Serafino, P. (2015). *China's aftershock ripples through sales of cognac to ore.* Bloomberg.
> ➢ The Economist. (2015, August). *The causes and consequences of China's market crash.* Retrieved from: http://www.economist.com/news/business-and-finance/21662092-china-sneezing-rest-world-rightly-nervous-causes-and-consequences-chinas

Endnotes

Case Study 18: The Chinese Stock Market Crash (2015)

1 Bello, W. (2015). China's stock market crash is the latest crisis of global capitalism. Retrieved from http://www.commondreams.org/views/2015/10/02/chinas-stock-market-crash-latest-crisis-global-capitalism

2 Allen, K. (2015). Why is China's stock market falling and how might it affect the global economy? Retrieved from http://www.theguardian.com/business/2015/aug/24/china-stock-market-fall-effects-global-economy-shares-interest-rates-inflation

3 Bello, W. (2015). China's stock market crash is the latest crisis of global capitalism. Retrieved from http://www.commondreams.org/views/2015/10/02/chinas-stock-market-crash-latest-crisis-global-capitalism

4 Bello, W. (2015). China's stock market crash is the latest crisis of global capitalism. Retrieved from http://www.commondreams.org/views/2015/10/02/chinas-stock-market-crash-latest-crisis-global-capitalism

5 Allen, K. (2015). Why is China's stock market falling and how might it affect the global economy? Retrieved from http://www.theguardian.com/business/2015/aug/24/china-stock-market-fall-effects-global-economy-shares-interest-rates-inflation

6 Hess, P. (2015, November). *How likely is a financial crisis in China?* Retrieved from The Diplomat: http://thediplomat.com/2015/11/how-likely-is-a-financial-crisis-in-china/

7 Gough, N. (2015, July). Chinese shares tumble again. *The New York Times*.

8 Hess, P. (2015, November). *How likely is a financial crisis in China?* Retrieved from The Diplomat: http://thediplomat.com/2015/11/how-likely-is-a-financial-crisis-in-china/

9 Hess, P. (2015, November). *How likely is a financial crisis in China?* Retrieved from The Diplomat: http://thediplomat.com/2015/11/how-likely-is-a-financial-crisis-in-china/

10 Zhiwu, Chen. (2013). Capital freedom in China as viewed from the evolution of the stock market. *CATO Journal, 33*(3), 587–601.

11 Pettinger, T. (2015). Impact of Chinese stock market crash. Retrieved from http://www.economicshelp.org/blog/14212/growth/impact-of-chinese-stock-market-crash/

12 Pettinger, T. (2015). Impact of Chinese stock market crash. Retrieved from http://www.economicshelp.org/blog/14212/growth/impact-of-chinese-stock-market-crash/

13 Pettinger, T. (2015). Impact of Chinese stock market crash. Retrieved from http://www.economicshelp.org/blog/14212/growth/impact-of-chinese-stock-market-crash/

14 Pettinger, T. (2015). Impact of Chinese stock market crash. Retrieved from http://www.economicshelp.org/blog/14212/growth/impact-of-chinese-stock-market-crash/

15 Kollewe, J., & Duggan, J. (2015, July). China stocks bounce back after days of panic selling among investors. *The Guardian*.

16 Kollewe, J., & Duggan, J. (2015, July). China stocks bounce back after days of panic selling among investors. *The Guardian*.

17 Colombo, J. (2015, July). Watch these charts to better understand China's stock market crash. *Forbes*.

Case Study 19: The Belgian Political Crisis (2007-2011)

The Belgian political crisis was caused by diverging party politics and the future ambitions of the liberal and pro-independence New Flemish Alliance (Flanders) and the pro-unity Socialist Party (Wallonia) that made the development of a coalition government problematic.[1] Belgium is comprised of three autonomous regions: Brussels, Wallonia, and Flanders. Some 3.5 million people speak French, while 6.5 million people speak Dutch. The country is more divided than the Republicans and the Democrats in the U.S., split between the less prosperous French-speaking south and the Flemish-speaking north. The regional separation, cultural distinctions, and linguistic antagonism between the two divisions of the country have long made it problematic to develop a comprehensible majority in a parliament occupied by numerous small parties that are divided along communal lines.[2]

The period of 2007-2011 was characterized by political instability and communal relations arising from the divergent opinions on state reforms and the continued existence of the contentious electoral district of Brussels-Halle-Vilvoorde (BHV). Parties from the Flemish divide were in favor of the devolution of powers to the regions and communities, and the dividing of the unconstitutional BHV, while the French divide in the country favored retaining the status quo. After the 2010 Belgium general elections, issues of socio-economic reform, public debts, and deficit cuts were added to the debate, with the French-speaking parties proposing an increase in taxes while the Flemish parties proposed a reduction in spending as a mechanism for reducing the consumption of available revenues. The crisis was resolved in 2011 after a new government was inaugurated on the promise that they would create policies for dealing with the economic downturn and partitioning the BHV district.[3]

The victory of the alliance of the Flemish Christian Democrats and the New Flemish Alliance (NFA), who supported extensive state reform and the partitioning of the BHV in 2007, marked the beginning of the crisis in Belgium. The country endured a period of 194 days that were characterized by a heated debate between the parties, culminating in the formation of a new government. However, in 2008, the Fortis case erupted, destabilizing the government and leading to the resignation of Yves Leterme, the acting prime minister. A new, fragile state was established by the Herman Van Rompuy-led government, but ended when he left to act as the first full-term president of the European Council. The Leterme II government that succeeded this resignation fell in 2010 after failing to provide any progress in resolving the BHV issue. New elections were held in 2010; the conservative and separatist NFA won massively in Flanders, while the pro-unity Socialist Party triumphed in the French-speaking regions. Despite numerous differences relating to socio-economic and community issues, Belgium remained without a

Case Study 19: The Belgian Political Crisis (2007–2011)

functioning government for 541 days, surpassing the record of 249-day set by Iraq in 2010.[4]

Numerous efforts had been made to ensure that the political crises in the country were resolved for the long term and all these efforts did not culminate in providing a sensible route to resolving the disputes. However, with the looming financial meltdown in the Eurozone, Belgium was forced to act, and act fast. Standard & Poor demoted the country's credit rating, and borrowing remained as high as the nation's GDP, while the banking sector stood shaken and vulnerable. The euro crisis forced Belgium to forge a government that would end a period of 535 days without a proper leader. Ultimately, a new government was sworn in on December 6, 2011.[5]

Although the political crisis wrangled on in Belgium, the day-to-day life in the country went on as usual. The absence of government in the country, with all government before the 2011 agreement acting in a caretaking capacity since 2007, did not alter the bureaucracy in the country, as it continued to hum along. Schools remained open, government workers were paid, and all government activities and duties in the country remained operational. Although confrontations existed over the economic developments in the country, significant reforms were being undertaken, as exemplified by the tightening of the budget to control the country's debt levels by the 2010 caretaker government. Since the political crisis, the country has been on an upward economic development trend, with growth of 2.1% in 2012 compared to the average development of 1.5% in the EU; unemployment of 8.5%, below the EU average of 9.4%; and a doubling of foreign investment.

CRISIS MANAGEMENT:
THE ART OF SUCCESS AND FAILURE

According to Hooghe,[6] the government continued to deal with legitimate matters, such as sending troops to Libya, complying with NATO, contributing capacity to save the euro, concluding deals to save banks, and approving the budgets required for urgent needs. Thus, it is evident that in countries that have mature democracies, a power vacuum is handled in a responsible, creative, and constructive manner. The federalized and decentralized nature of Belgium enabled the country to run most of its operations in the midst of the crisis. While running the decentralized and federalized Belgium, however, the problems of the divided society persisted. Belgium's power-sharing arrangement was not stable prior to December 2011 because ethnicity was raised above other group rights, and institutional efforts were mainly concerned with an ethnic focus. The linguistic, cultural, and regional division between the Walloons and the Flemings had to be dealt with to end the racial antagonism in the country and create a peaceful, coexisting state that would allow democracy and the rule of law to thrive.

As initially indicated, the situation in the country was unfavorable for a stable democracy. To solve this problem, segmental autonomy and a grand coalition government were required. One of the elements that would provide a base for political stability was the constitutional protection of the linguistic minority. In this case, the minority would be protected from institutional change because, according to the constitution, any of these changes would require a majority in every language group. The formation of a coalition government comprised of people from all regions would ensure that the partners would have to consider the aims and aspirations of their colleagues in the other language

Case Study 19: The Belgian Political Crisis (2007–2011)

groups. In other words, decisions concerning the government's major activities would be based on a communal agreement between the representatives of all the diverse linguistic groups. Only then would all the residents of the country feel like they had representation and belonged to one country with different linguistic groups. Negotiations between the leaders of both linguistic groups needed to take place without any preset conditions.[7]

Although the decentralized nature of the government provided a medium in which a majority of operations could be orchestrated, devolving power according to ethnic backgrounds would empower ethnic division in the country, further serving to hurt any attempts to recover the nation's diminishing democracy. Furthermore, the demands of each of the divides would be a stumbling block to achieving justice.[8] Uniting the country on a linguistic basis would mean using shared cultural norms and values. In the 1960s, everyone in the country interacted in schools and other shared activities, reducing the tension between them. However, with the increasing rift between the distinct linguistic groups, pressure increased. According to Deschouwer,[9] the different linguistic groups in Belgium rarely intermarry, while the division means that the schools are separated and there is minimal interaction between them. With this kind of society, the existing economic and political conditions are difficult. To solve these issues, politicians need to rally the citizens around shared values, ceremonies, cultural practices, games and sports, and other events. Ending the struggles in the nation would be possible by ending the tension between the three major regions while establishing a peaceful coexistence platform. Intermarriage should be encouraged, and the government should promote diversity in job allocation and ensuring that there is an equitable distribution of resources in all regions.[10]

The role of uniting the different divides in Belgium does not lie solely in the hands of the Belgian government and political leaders. Although the country needs an elite professional politician who would act as a uniting factor and facilitate numerous political developments and integration in the country, the humanitarian groups in the country, the media, non-governmental organizations, and the civil society have a critical role in the peace-building practice. It is essential to note that the problems that existed in Belgium are based on the self-determination of the different groups, which could not be resolved in a court of law. Although issues such as the division of the BHV can be partially settled in the courts, the civil society can aid in the development of a solution by developing new formats of dialogue and interaction between the media and regional traditions. Other than that, the role of the civil society, in this case, is to lead by example by ensuring that they discourage all the minute forms of disintegration among the different societies in Belgium. They can facilitate political development by joining hands in combating any kind of injustice and acting in support of minority groups, while ensuring that they do not create tension that can cause further disintegration.[11]

It is critical to note that combining democracy and peace-building in a divided nation is a fundamental challenge for any strategy chosen to end the crisis. Being a stronghold of a union, the EU should have acted as a custodian and the principal player in Belgium conflict management. Conflict management implies legal and ethical responsibility. In this

Case Study 19: The Belgian Political Crisis (2007–2011)

case, anyone who is involved in the process of resolving disputes should be aware of the normative implication of the intervention chosen, for instance, concerning the grounds of legitimacy, the interrelation with political agendas such as democratization, the use of power, and the selection of action to be engaged in the process. In this regard, the EU could have served as a capable custodian that could have taken a neutral position as the chief arbitrator and custodian in the formation of a coalition government.[12]

Although the EU could provide a platform for negotiations, international humanitarian organizations and countries outside the EU could help in providing valuable ideas and knowledge that could aid in ending the political crisis in the country. However, the major tool that could be used to solve the situation in the long term is constitutional review. Constitutional reform would ensure that power and resources are shared equally among all tribes. Other than that, a constitutional review could include the minimum number of representatives that each linguistic and geographical divide should have in the government. Constitutional reform would aid respect for the rule of law and democracy, while providing a platform for public and political security reform. The constitution has the ability to provide a basis that can facilitate dialogue and power-sharing among the politicians in the country. Regardless of the strategy chosen, it is critical to ensure that it is in accordance with the traditions, beliefs, and culture of the Belgians. Providing foreign conflict resolution strategies that are against these pillars could widen the gap in the country.

Endnotes

Case Study 19: The Belgian Political Crisis (2007-2011)

1 Hooghe, M. (2012). The political crisis in Belgium (2007-2011): A federal system without federal loyalty. *Representation, 48*(1), 131-138.

2 Swenden, W. (2013). Conclusion: The future of Belgian federalism— Between reform and swansong? 2007-11: A critical juncture in the transformation of the Belgian state? *Regional & Federal Studies, 23*(3), 369-382.

3 Hooghe, M. (2012). The political crisis in Belgium (2007-2011): A federal system without federal loyalty. *Representation, 48*(1), 131-138.

4 Swenden, W. (2013). Conclusion: The future of Belgian federalism— Between reform and swansong? 2007-11: A critical juncture in the transformation of the Belgian state? *Regional & Federal Studies, 23*(3), 369-382.

5 Hooghe, M. (2012). The political crisis in Belgium (2007-2011): A federal system without federal loyalty. *Representation, 48*(1), 131-138.

6 Hooghe, M. (2012). The political crisis in Belgium (2007-2011): A federal system without federal loyalty. *Representation, 48*(1), 131-138.

7 Van de Walle, S., Thijs, N., & Bouckaert, G. (2005). A tale of two charters: Political crisis, political realignment and administrative reform in Belgium. *Public Management Review, 7*(3), 367-390.

8 Deschouwer, K. (2012). *The politics of Belgium: Governing a divided society*. Palgrave Macmillan.

9 Deschouwer, K. (2012). *The politics of Belgium: Governing a divided society*. Palgrave Macmillan.

10 Galasso, V. (2014). The role of political partisanship during economic crises. *Public Choice, 158*(1/2), 143-165.

11 Rosenthal, U., Boin, A., & Comfort, L. K. (2001). *Managing crises: Threats, dilemmas, opportunities*. Charles C Thomas Publisher.

12 Rosenthal, U., Boin, A., & Comfort, L. K. (2001). *Managing crises: Threats, dilemmas, opportunities*. Charles C Thomas Publisher.

Case Study 20: Starbucks U.K. Tax (2012)

Founded in the 1970s in Seattle, Starbucks is one of the best in coffee roasting, branding, and retail of specialty coffees worldwide. However, the corporation experienced a financial crisis after being accused of tax avoidance in the U.K. in 2008. Having won many business awards, such as 100 Best Cooperate Citizens and Most Admired Company, among others, Starbucks' prices are slightly above those offered by other domestic coffee houses, and its quality is indisputable. During the 2008 economic crisis, which is often closely correlated with the tax scandal that hit the U.K. in 2012, the company was forced to shut down approximately 600 of its coffee shops that were making little or no profit at all. Starbucks customers had begun opting for cheaper coffee brands.[1]

In an attempt to control or reduce the impacts of its involvement in the financial crisis, Starbucks awoke a controversy that resulted from tax avoidance. The commencement of the action to evade taxes happened a few days after the company's top executive was faced with questions regarding the payment of the corporate tax over the preceding three years as set by Starbucks U.S. management. According to Shang,[2] Starbucks paid no form of taxes to the U.K. government, and yet it was said to be a profitable business, even though it had caused the U.K. to lose up to £150 million in the past seven years. Whenever the company's chief financial officer was questioned about the report, he claimed that the results were so because the business sector of the U.K. was not doing as well as in past years.

Contrary to the reports that showed that Starbucks has evaded the payment of taxes for a long time, the company maintained that it has been paying taxes correctly. Howard Schultz, the company's chief executive, once said, "Starbucks has always paid taxes in the U.K., despite recent suggestions to the contrary." He further noted that "Over the last three years alone, our company has paid more than 160 million pounds in various taxes, including national insurance contributions, VAT, and business taxes." Additionally, Starbucks' spokeswoman once said, "While the subject of tax law can be extremely complex, Starbucks respects and complies with tax laws and accounting rules."

According to Shang,[3] the economic impacts of Starbucks on the U.K.'s economy went far beyond its employees and stores. The business spends many millions of pounds to supply both local and wholesale suppliers with their products, such as sandwiches, cakes, and milk, and any alteration in its operations has consequences for the company's reputation and social media. The damage was caused solely by the revelation that the company had not paid any corporate taxes to the U.K. Immediately after Starbucks implemented the idea of allowing their customers to talk about and exchange their views on the company, the varied opinions gave it more importance.

In the course of the financial crisis, the company lost some of its crucial buyers, and its reputation was damaged.

Case Study 20: Starbucks U.K. Tax (2012)

Subsequently, the business had to rebuild its name and good relationship with its customers. This would only be achieved by developing strategies that would convince the world that it cares about consistency in provision and high-quality products. According to statistics, Starbucks' score on daily brand perception fell from +0.7 to -13.9 in the past four years. The numbers implied more negative comments about the company than positive comments. Additionally, after the revelations of the tax avoidance, the company's overall reputation score dipped from +4.6 to approximately -3.0.[4]

The company implemented some ideas that customers had given in forums that allowed them to link directly with the company. The act of offering customers a podium to air their views and ideas concerning the coffee brand, and Starbucks responding to the ideas, served as the stepping stone to reigniting trust in the company. Kris Engskov, Starbucks' U.K. managing director, once wrote on a blog that the company "paid over 160 million pounds in various taxes, including Pay As You Earn for our 8,500 U.K. employees, national insurance and business rates" in an attempt to show that the company's tax arrangement was in line with the tax law and consequently boost the company's image within the community.

Upon realizing that it had to plan a powerful marketing strategy and promote it through its social media platforms, Starbucks switched to social media marketing, with the main aim of engaging more with the community rather than seeming desperate as it tried to increase sales. The "My Starbucks Idea" helped the business to fully understand the needs of its customers; had the company not been responsive to their contributions, its reputation could not have been mended. The "My Starbucks Signature" was also another initiative that enabled customers to create their own drinks and personalize them. This action showcased the company's assortment in a big way.[5]

Among the many tweets by customers was "Keep calm and make coffee"; it was viewed by the company as an encouraging tweet, meaning that they should aim at preserving the company's image as well as building the community. The integration of social media to improve its damaged public image played a crucial role in mitigating damage and helping in the management of the information that was causing so much harm to the company's identity globally.

Following the Starbucks crisis, which ruined the company's name globally, a crisis management plan was developed. The main objectives of the initiative were to protect the health, reputation, safety, and the lives of the community, suppliers, customers, and the company's partners, as well as all their shareholders; to safeguard proprietary information, property, and other assets of the company; and to restore normal business operations as quickly as possible. Additionally, the plan provided succinct and clear guidance to the esteemed partners of the enterprise after the crisis and shaped the framework to react adeptly against any unplanned form of business interruptions.

The Starbucks crisis management plan classified crisis vulnerabilities into five categories—personnel, consumer, event, supply chain, and reputation— describing the potential disasters under each category. The likelihood of occurrence, the severity of the disaster, and the effectiveness of the control measures were also assessed. The post-evaluation

Case Study 20: Starbucks U.K. Tax (2012)

stage entailed the utilization of all the collected information from customers, employees, and stakeholders throughout the assessment of the crisis. All the information was then put together and used to evaluate the effectiveness of the management initiative.[6]

The reinforcement strategy was employed by Starbucks as a means of communicating their reputation regarding their trustworthiness and their overall expertise in offering their products. The company did this by setting up a press room containing the business's offerings, including coffee beverages, Ethos-brand water, bread, and cookies. Since Starbucks had already begun changing its products, it came up with tactical selections of some of its popular products to showcase them for their quality. The core principle of using this strategy was to bolster the company's image, and it was successful. During a press conference that Starbucks hosted, it distributed a press kit that presented a unified message to all the people in attendance. The kit served the role of closing up all undesirable perceptual gaps and consequently outlining promising stakeholder expectations. Therefore, based on all the tactics and the strategies that were initiated by the Starbucks' crisis management plan, it is evident that they were effective, since the image of the company that was once ruined was restored.

CRISIS MANAGEMENT:
THE ART OF SUCCESS AND FAILURE

Endnotes

Case Study 20: Starbucks U.K. Tax (2012)

1 Shang, L. (2007). The crisis of Starbucks "brand problem." Globrand, accessed, 1.

2 Shang, L. (2007). The crisis of Starbucks "brand problem." Globrand, accessed, 1.

3 Shang, L. (2007). The crisis of Starbucks "brand problem." Globrand, accessed, 1.

4 Perera, L. C. J., Lenk, H. U., de Souza Corrêa, M., Yoshikawa, A. N., Silva, A. A. G. D., & Arasaki, R. K. (2012). Effects of the 2007 financial crisis on Starbucks. *Journal of International Business Strategy*, *12*(1).

5 Schultz, H., & Jones Yang, D. (1999). *Pour your heart into it: How Starbucks built a company one cup at a time*. Hyperion.

6 Latif, M., Gulzar, H., Bukhari, S. R., & Sameen, S. N. (2014). Starbucks sustained during economic crisis. *International Journal of Accounting and Financial Reporting*, *4*(1), 307.

Case Study 21: Sony Pictures Cyberattack (2014)

The cyberattack on Sony in 2014 significantly threatened the year's projected sales. From the first estimations, Sony Pictures was projected to lose millions of dollars since several companies were to be paid in trying to contain the situation. From the nature of the transactions that the company was involved in, the projected losses were to be inclusive of the losses that the employees were to incur.

From the beginning, the estimation of the losses was about $171 million. This estimation was later reduced to about $100 million since the solution was limited to the repair and replacement of computers and the systems used in handling security. The estimated amount spent to handle the situation was reported to be the largest in the history of the U.S.[1]

The cyberattack destroyed Sony's image and reputation because the company was not able to secure its systems and information. The sensitive information that the company was supposed to safeguard, from clients to employees, was not kept safe, and this was the major cause of the whopping amount to be paid. Being a leading entertainment company, the failure to safeguard their information was a major challenge, and a weakness used by competitors.

Sony has been known for their quality productions

and lucrative offers to clients and customers. The failure in handling the situation was a score for their competition. The cyberattack tarnished the image of the company, with less trust placed in them.[2]

The amount that was to be paid in compensation and the chances of recovering the information reduced annual profits by a large percentage. From March to December 2014, the company was to make an estimated $500 million. When the losses are deducted from the profits, the annual profits were affected by 20%. The expected duration to recover this amount is not short.

Sony, as a company, has an insurance cover that was to cater to the situation, but from the total estimates, the company could not pay the whole amount. This left Sony with little option but to take care of the larger percentage. From an economic point of view, losing a whopping $100 million in a single month would cost the company everything. For future operations, the company had two options to recover the lost amount in a proper manner. First, Sony would have to work twice as much, which can include the involvement of extra labor and ways of handling operations. Second, Sony could borrow some extra money.[3]

Since Sony is one of the best entertainment companies, other companies were waiting to learn their ways of handling issues and the secrets that make them the best. Sony has a unique marketing strategy. This strategy can be valuable to several other companies that are relevant in their fields of operation.

The dangers of leaking the information to the public and competitors could be extremely costly, depending on the information released by Sony, the most crucial information had already been hacked, and the hackers had already shared some of it with the public. For the purposes of secrecy and competition, Sony is likely to lose a lot of valuable resources from the revealed information.[4]

The Sony attacks showed that national security is at risk of cyberattacks. As one of the most trusted companies in the U.S., Sony being hacked played a big role in ensuring that the national security on cyber-crimes is well handled. With the plan created after the attack, Sony could not successfully handle the issue without the national government's help because of the sensitivity of the matter and the chances of their solution resolving the issue being small to nil. In the case that the government helps the company in resolving the whole mystery, trust can be restored, as stakeholders and customers can see the government's commitment to try to help the most influential companies.

In trying to resolve the issue, the government must work hand in hand with the company because the issue is not just specific to the company, but could affect the country as a whole. The hackers, based on the information given by the company, were not from the U.S., but from outside the country. Their success in this mission poses a challenge to all other companies plus the information security of the U.S. as a country.

From the above discussion, we see that the crisis that saw Sony's salient information leak has not been fully resolved. In the case of this crisis, the purpose of crisis management must be defined. After the definition of the purpose, the type of crisis should be determined and then outlined. The crisis type will dictate the path taken in managing the crisis.

CRISIS MANAGEMENT:
THE ART OF SUCCESS AND FAILURE

Having a crisis management plan in place makes the resolution process faster. Creating awareness through the national government and making the crisis a national problem creates critical thinking on the possible solutions. Taking full responsibility as a company without blaming the government puts Sony in a position to set the pace for finding a solution. Implementing prospective solutions, as a company and as part of a collective agreement with the state, allows for a faster solution to be reached, with all the problems handled to everyone's satisfaction. In general, the attack on Sony played an essential role in learning how to deal with various information-related issues in the company, as well as the industry at large.

Endnotes

Case Study 21: Sony Pictures Cyberattack (2014)

1 Adams, S. (2014). Did Sony do the right thing when it pulled "the interview"? *Forbes.com*, 7. Retrieved from http://search.ebscohost.com/login.aspx?direct=true&db=buh&AN=100126504&site=ehost-live

2 Murad, A. (2014). *Sony, Microsoft battle hackers as gamers question their call of duty*. Retrieved from http://www.ft.com/intl/cms/s/0/b7d-3d47a-8ce4-11e4-9f52-00144feabdc0.html#axzz3fE5G95G7

3 Crothers, B. (2014). *Sony to shutter 20 stores in US, implement staff cuts*. Retrieved from http://news.cnet.com/8301-1001_3-57619601-92/sony-to-shutter-20-stores-in-us-implement-staff-cuts/

4 Various. (2014). *Open letter to Michael Lynton, Sony Pictures Entertainment Chairman and CEO re: The interview*. Retrieved from http://www.pen.org/blog/open-letter-michael-lynton-sony-pictures-entertainment-chairman-and-ceo-re-interview

Case Study 22: FIFA Corruption Crisis (2014)

Admittedly, the world soccer governing body, the International Federation of Association Football (FIFA), has been involved in corruption and governance scandals for several years. The levels of corruption have been on the rise as the FIFA president determinedly clings to power. This exemplifies the level to which some global sports organizations pull down many nations regarding democratic governance standards. In 2014, Brazil hosted the FIFA World Cup. The event was marred by many cases of corruption. The underlying crimes behind money laundering, together with the World Cup juggernaut, demonstrated the factors fueling corruption in FIFA. Many investigative reporters and sports commentators have disclosed the level of bribery in the soccer society across the globe. They have offered detailed results from their investigative reports and brought to light instances of corruption at FIFA. However, little seems to improve every year. Against this backdrop, the following discussion provides a case study of the 2014 FIFA corruption crisis by describing crisis management initiatives, how the media dealt with the crisis, and the effects of the crisis.

CRISIS MANAGEMENT:
THE ART OF SUCCESS AND FAILURE

SUMMARY OF THE FIFA CORRUPTION CRISIS

Essentially, the 2014 World Cup in Brazil was plagued with what has currently become standard for World Cups and FIFA, including ticket scandals, claims of bribes, large amounts of money dished out to players, and high levels of greed. Other issues include sloppy ethics, and the awareness that the whole event only profited a few, while the host country pays millions of dollars and spectators scuffle to obtain tickets for one match.[1] Soccer pundits have argued that most of the senior management and executives of FIFA came from the tournament in Brazil wearing luxury watches, which were not subjected to taxation. They also had swag bags, handed over to the FIFA executives by the English 2018 World Cup bid team, comprised of $30,000 Hublot watches.[2] 2014 also saw FIFA officials involved in a scandal about the prices of tickets and hospitality packages for competition matches. Several arrests were made after the final game in connection with an investigation of Match Services AG for its role in reselling hospitality packages and tickets at a profit.[3] It is alleged that FIFA has long awarded a series of contracts to Match Services to offer IT and travel services, accommodations, and ticketing to the tournament since one of the shareholders of the company has a relationship with FIFA officials. Reports indicated that the company was reselling the packages and tickets at a profit ($100 million) instead of returning the tickets that were not used to FIFA as dictated, breaching both Brazilian law and FIFA rules that limit the sale of match tickets beyond face value. As a matter of fact, of the over three million match tickets that were available for the 2014 tournament, 445,500 tickets were allocated to Match Services.[4] Nevertheless, FIFA regulations demand that all unused or unsold tickets be returned to FIFA to make them accessible to the public.

The next corruption allegation against FIFA was that of biased awarding of the opportunity to host the World Cup. The decision made by FIFA to award Russia and Qatar an opportunity to host the World Cup in 2018 and 2022, respectively, could charitably be described as having shocked everyone. It is in the minds of everyone that Qatar is a country in which summer temperatures are extremely high. Worst still, the national soccer team of Qatar has never reached the World Cup playoffs, and the nation provides limited infrastructure to cater to the influx of supporters and fans that admittedly will double during the tournament. The recent revelations from media outlets have indicated that Qatari agents and others had perhaps orchestrated the award by giving millions of dollars to FIFA officials.[5] Without reservation, granting the World Cup to two countries that are known for their biased tax systems, unenforced money laundering rules, corrupt officials, and little freedom of the media clearly shows the corruption crisis within FIFA.

HOW THE MEDIA DEALT WITH THE CRISIS

The media plays a crucial role in informing the public about hidden vices within the community and across the globe. The same applied to the FIFA corruption crisis that took the soccer world by storm. Essentially, many mass media networks have been in the limelight for disclosing and clarifying the corruption allegations leveled against FIFA. In the corruption case involving the awarding of the opportunity to host the 2018 and 2022 World Cup, FIFA officials refused to detail the reasons for these awards. However, the media played a vital role in revealing to the public that the awards were based on bribes received from the Qatari and Russian governments. The media dealt with the issue by detailing the figures and individuals involved in influencing the awards. For instance, *The Sunday Times* published a series of articles arguing that it was apparent that Qatari agents, together with others, had seemingly orchestrated the award by doling out significant amounts of money to FIFA officials.[6]

The media also dealt with the FIFA corruption crisis by providing proof of the allegations leveled against FIFA. The media has been monitoring and documenting the dealings of FIFA officials for a long time. For instance, an email acquired from a South African newspaper showed that the former president of South Africa, Thabo Mbeki, and the FIFA president, Sepp Blatter, agreed on some deals.[7]. The same applied to the issuance of a series of contracts to Match Services to offer packages and tickets. This proof provided the basis on which some FIFA officials were arrested, while others were suspended.

The Effects of the FIFA Corruption Crisis 2014

The FIFA corruption crisis created a gap between the soccer governing body and spectators and fans. As a result, efforts to restructure FIFA's management structure and bring in genuine reforms continue to break. Studies have reported that the FIFA corruption crisis forced some officials to resign, citing frustrations from Blatter and other top officials.[8] In addition, the corruption at the top of FIFA, as experienced in 2014, reduced the incentive to handle challenges on the pitch that affect the experience of the fans, particularly match-fixing and racism. Recently, cases of racism and match-fixing have become prevalent due to a lack of accountability and responsibility on the part of FIFA officials. For example, in January 2014, Kevin-Prince Boateng, an AC Milan player, walked away from the field during a friendly match, citing racist chants from audiences; the incident hit the international news.[9] Weeks later, fans of Den Bosch, a soccer club in the Netherlands, gave Jozy Altidore, a U.S. player, the same treatment. While FIFA instituted a task force to deal with discrimination and racism, and even provided stringent penalties for offenders, FIFA leaders do not have the moral power to implement changes because of the corruption that has become part of the organization's operations.

Crisis Management Initiatives

To manage and control corruption, FIFA's structure should be completely overhauled. In the FIFA congress, every country gets a single vote. Therefore, in reality, the unrecognized national associations have the same weight in making decisions as larger organizations. However, in practice, these smaller countries or groups can easily be bribed for the awarding of minor FIFA activities. On the same note, patronage can be acquired by awarding prized VIP tickets for big events, including the World Cup finals.

Regarding enforcement, FIFA carries out inquiries into corruption allegations by itself. Worst still, it decides on the penalties for corrupt officials. Without a doubt, this is the same as the accused offering the verdict in his or her case. Admittedly, change within the organization seems unlikely. In fact, any internal resistance to the president, who apparently sits on enough evidence to prove the corruption allegations against FIFA officials, is bound to fail. Therefore, the push to handle entrenched corruption must emanate from external forces, including governments planning taxpayer-funded proposals for FIFA World Cup activities. Therefore, bidders must not only take into account the paucity of real economic gains that flow in their direction, but also the probability that they are not on the same playing field. In fact, the logical response for any responsible bidder is to not bid. Undeniably, this will minimize the independent power that FIFA enjoys.

In conclusion, corruption is a vice that has taken the soccer fraternity by storm. It has resulted in increased cases of match-fixing and racism on the field, not to mention the hiked prices of tickets. As such, stringent measures should be implemented to ensure that those involved in the corruption within the soccer world are subjected to similar penalties, fines, and sentences as others convicted of crimes. FIFA's management structure should be overhauled and an independent oversight authority established to treat the corruption in FIFA with the seriousness it deserves.

Endnotes

Case Study 22: FIFA Corruption Crisis (2014)

1 Avsar, V., & Unal, U. (2014). Trading effects of the FIFA World Cup. *Kyklos, 67*(3), 315–329.

2 Hughey, S. (2015). Social media, football, and crisis: An exploratory case study examining the FIFA World Cup addressing player concussions. *Journal of Media Critiques, 1*(4), 51–65.

3 Korosi, K., & Brown, K. (2014). Sporting events as sites of international law, society, and governance: The 2014 Brazilian World Cup. *Southwestern Journal of International Law, 21*(8), 2–28.

4 Noah, D. (2015). The series of scandals have not only tainted FIFA but undermined trust in the game as well. *Americas Quarterly*. Retrieved December 24, 2015, from http://www.americasquarterly.org/content/series-scandals-have-not-only-tainted-fifa-undermined-trust-game-well

5 Sugden, J., & Tomlinson, A. (1998). *FIFA and the contest for world football*. Cambridge, UK: Polity Press.

6 Wilson, J. (2014). *Why stamping out corruption in FIFA will not be easy*. The conversation. Retrieved December 24, 2015, from http://theconversation.com/why-stamping-out-corruption-in-fifa-wont-be-easy-34264

7 Avsar, V., & Unal, U. (2014). Trading effects of the FIFA World Cup. *Kyklos, 67*(3), 315–329.

8 Avsar, V., & Unal, U. (2014). Trading effects of the FIFA World Cup. *Kyklos, 67*(3), 315–329.

9 Hughey, S. (2015). Social media, football, and crisis: An exploratory case study examining the FIFA World Cup addressing player concussions. *Journal of Media Critiques, 1*(4), 51–65.

Case Study 23: Iraqi Failure in Crisis Management

Successful governments are founded on sound social, political, and economic development that results in peace and stability. However, many governments across the world face management challenges in terms of political and economic stability. The crisis in management in Iraq can be traced back to the reign of Saddam Hussein. His death in 2003 was hoped to be one of the steps in containing the crisis in management in Iraq. However, Iraq continues to face a crisis in management, with a number of key institutions, like government ministries, being dysfunctional as a result of war and economic sabotage.

One of the greatest causes of crisis is war. Citizens normally struggle over the country's resources, like jobs, land, business opportunities, and representation in government positions. Iraq is no different in this kind of crisis. Even though, internationally, the fall of Saddam Hussein was celebrated, in Iraq it led to a political crisis. The rift between Sunnis, Shiites, and Kurds continued, threatening Iraq's political and democratic stability to a large degree. As a consequence of the discontent following the killing of Saddam, violence has persisted in Iraq since 2003. Even though the government has been trying to contain the

CRISIS MANAGEMENT:
THE ART OF SUCCESS AND FAILURE

violence, their strategy for countering the attacks has worsened the state of affairs in Iraq further. However, despite the obvious porous relationship between the Shia and Sunni peoples, the government has remained adamant in trying to remedy the rift, and bad blood remains between the two communities. History records the differences between the Sunnis and Shiites to be a result of theological and doctrinal differences, as well as political disagreements. Security and political analysts contend that the rivalry between the two societies is mirrored in their power, status, and resource competition.[1]

Governments are the creation of political systems that require and rely on sound, established institutions to run efficiently while addressing crises and challenges. However, Iraq has weak government institutions with ceremonial powers. The backward thinking of many leaders is to blame for the weak government institutions, such as the judiciary, legislature, and executive branches. For instance, since the country is highly polarized along communal lines, appointments to such institutions are based on ethnicity rather than qualifications and experience. These ethnic appointments not only result in weak government structures, but also communal animosity, whose result is war and violence. According to the World Bank, a majority of the Iraqi civil service consists of semi-literate men that contribute insignificantly to the country's development. Nevertheless, the high levels of illiteracy in government appointments are blamed on communal thinking, which prevents qualified citizens from getting employment. Communal appointments are a tactic that is used by the government to hide bad governance while misappropriating government resources.

Case Study 23: Iraqi Failure in Crisis Management

Economically, Iraq is classified as a failed state due to massive poverty. Crisis in management is inevitable with a system that is economically constrained. Iraq is constrained in terms of manpower and money resources. For instance, it relies on other nations for both military and financial support. Despite having lucrative resources like oil, the country lacks both the manpower and economic resources to effectively exploit and harness them. Overreliance on other countries makes a country less effective. In most instances, countries that rely on other states for supplies are controlled and compromised on many grounds. Political observers and security experts construe American involvement in Iraq as a means of micromanaging it. Since the violence has taken a toll on the country's development, many Iraqi citizens are seeking education in other countries. In addition, the military incursion in Iraq by U.S. forces has given the world's most powerful state a direct line into the affairs of the war-torn nation. Even though the UN issued a noninterference policy that should safeguard the autonomy and independence of sovereign states in running their affairs, countries that rely on support from other nations lose those provisions since there are strings attached to the support they receive.[2]

Crisis in the management of a country is mirrored in several instances and various structures of government functions. However, its effects are devastating, as it takes a toll on almost all interrelated functions of the government. Legitimate governments should ensure favorable environments for business and the individual development of citizens. In addition, essential services, like security, education, and health, should be realized by all citizens, regardless of their

CRISIS MANAGEMENT:
THE ART OF SUCCESS AND FAILURE

social, religious, political, or economic positions. However, Iraq remains one of the few countries that is still unable to provide such essential services to its citizens. Many of its nationals travel abroad for security, education, and health services. Since the fall of Saddam in 2003, the nation's infrastructure has been destroyed, with little progress made in its renovation and reconstruction. There are many Iraqi nationals in other countries as refugees. Many are in the U.S. or European nations like Britain, pursuing education and careers. A survey by the United Nations Human Rights Commission (UNCR) reported that even though most of the nationals from Iraq in other countries are either working or studying, the majority landed as refugees.[3]

The effects of war are always devastating. The crisis in management in Iraq depicts the negative consequences of war and violence. Countries that have always been faced with civil war have always suffered the ignorance of insensitive leaders. Rwanda, a small nation in eastern Africa, almost completely massacred one of its tribes in 1994. The international community responded when the genocide was taking place. The spontaneous violence that rocked Iraq after the death of Saddam remains to be seen as a failure of leadership. The feelings of marginalization by the Sunnis have provided a ripe ground for radicalization and the creation of an extremist movement. However, the sectarian violence that is predominantly undertaken by Shiites under the reign of Nouri al-Maliki has not bothered to quell the discontent, but rather continues to consolidate power. A state is large and transcends the wishes and interests of an individual. In circumstances when the wishes of minorities are taken into consideration at the expense of the majority, problems

Case Study 23: Iraqi Failure in Crisis Management

are inevitable. In addition, this leads to mistrust and hate between the members of the divide. Alongside the Kurds, Iraq is split into two different sects. For instance, there are those that want to retain power, like the Shiites, and those that feel marginalized and are radicalizing to gain power, like the Sunnis.[4]

The containment of the crisis in management requires both military and political responses. It has been over a decade since the fall of Saddam, but the state of affairs in Iraq continues to move from bad to worse. Researchers and analysts have espoused various arguments and theories to describe and explain the cause of the Iraqi crisis. Nevertheless, other nations have also contributed to try to stabilize Iraq. World bodies like the World Bank continue supporting the stabilization of Iraq, and other nations donate soldiers to fight insurgents and keep the peace in Iraq. However, a destabilized society is ripe for breeding violence, gangs, and other agents of instability. The emergence of the Islamic State group is not only a threat to Iraqi stabilization, but also to world peace. Many people have been recruited in other countries and taken into Iraq to join the Islamic State. The emergence of frequent terror attacks in many countries around the world, including the U.S. and France, has demonstrated the failure in crisis management in Iraq. The violence that broke out in protesting the death of Saddam is now taking a different front, as many terror groups are trained in various parts of Iraq.[5]

Stable countries ensure that the rights of their citizens are protected through well thought-out and drafted constitutions. Iraq's constitution remains an ineffective paper booklet that most of the leaders have no respect for and are contravening in their many actions. For instance, the irrational consolidation of power and wealth by the Shiite prime minster offends the provisions of equality that the constitution provides for in the sharing of the country's resources. A majority of the Sunnis that are angered by the actions of the prime minister have developed hate for the country and are forgetting the ideals of a patriot. Whereas most of the Sunnis are challenging the government on the various inequalities that persist in the country, others are fleeing the nation. In addition, Iraq is losing a lot of manpower to brain drain in other nations. The nationals who end up in other nations as refugees and acquire education are reluctant to return home to develop their nation due to the violence and favoritism that is ripe in Iraq in most state appointments and recruitments. The end result of all these factors is slow economic growth and the provision of breeding grounds for war and other forms of insecurity. Iraq requires the contributions of all its nationals to grow politically and economically. Therefore, the exclusion of either party only contributes to instability and crisis, whose results are devastating to the country in terms of unity and stability.[6]

The failures of Iraq in managing its crisis date back to 2003 during the fall of Saddam; since then, the Islamic State of Iraq and al-Sham (ISIS) has surged into the major territories within northern and central Iraq. Most significantly, the insurgent group has managed to take over major cities within the country while additionally gaining access to and control of the major oil fields in Kirkuk and Baiji. Additionally, the group has declared all the regions under its control within Iraq and Syria to be under the Islamic state.[7] The notable crisis in Iraq has demonstrated the various loopholes that might have existed within the framework of a government's policy formulations; it is a clear indication that the U.S. policy established to save the Middle East state has failed terribly to meet its objectives. During the attempts of quelling the raging war in Iraq, the U.S. ironically achieved its purpose by destroying the social, political, and economic infrastructure, thus rendering the state worthless and more of a puppet society; the current government has no mandate to rule over its citizens, thus plunging it into more conflict and crisis.

Just like in Iraq, a failure in effective management can also be attributed to the crisis situation in Syria, emanating from the shared control of the state by ISIS. A combination of international and religious networks have failed to effectively address the challenges faced by Iraq and have elevated the conflicts between different religions and races, such as between the Sunnis and the Shiites, causing a cycle of sectarian strife.[8] Additionally, Iraq has been divided into three distinct sections: the majority Shiites control the government, the minority Sunnis are controlled by ISIS, and the Kurds control Iraqi Kurdistan. It will be very difficult for the government of Iraq to effectively regain its control over the states that have assumed a militant role; the Kurds have been reported to have been the sole beneficiaries of the crisis in Iraq.

Even though there have been several claims about the crisis management failure in Iraq, it is still important to note that any amicable solution is connected to the ability of the Iraqi citizens to sort out their problems and religious differences. It could be possible if the current and future governments create policies abolishing the sectarian and marginalization policies; on the other hand, the country should bank more on improving oneness and inclusivity while practicing participatory democracy, so that the pluralistic society in Iraq can feel accepted and appreciated. Through the modification of such existing policies, Iraq would be able to fight terrorism and segregation while securing a better future full of political and social stability and success.

CONCLUSION

In summary, the instability witnessed in Iraq can be traced to the fall of Saddam in 2003, when the U.S., under President Bush, killed him. Since 2003, Iraq has faced a number of economic and political crises that can only be remedied through bipartisan approaches. However, Iraq remains a nation that is divided along communal lines, with Sunnis in the opposition and the Shiites in government. The failure in crisis management by Iraq threatens the country's peace and stability. The once-vibrant country, in terms of its development owing to its natural resources, like oil, is disintegrating on economic and political grounds. The country loses many of its citizens to war and violence, while the few that survive the war flee to other countries. In addition, elite and educated Iraqi nationals fear returning home as they seek employment opportunities in peaceful countries. The international community is on the forefront of efforts to stabilize Iraq, with the U.S. maintaining its presence in the war-torn nation. However, due to its unstable nature, the country now provides breeding grounds for extremist groups and other terror gangs, whose actions are devastating across the globe. The Islamic state movement in Iraq is responsible for the many unfortunate incidents of security challenges that the world continues to suffer. For instance, the recent attacks in San Bernardino and Paris demonstrate the devastating effects of the failure in crisis management in Iraq.

CRISIS MANAGEMENT:
THE ART OF SUCCESS AND FAILURE

Endnotes

Case Study 23: Iraqi Failure in Crisis Management

1 Barkey, H. J., Lasensky, S., & Marr, P. (2011). *Iraq, its neighbors, and the United States: Competition, crisis, and the reordering of power.* Washington, D.C.: United States Institute of Peace.

2 Coombs, W. T., & Holladay, S. J. (2012). *The handbook of crisis communication.* Chichester, U.K: Wiley-Blackwell.

3 Cordesman, A. H. (1991). *Weapons of mass destruction in the Middle East.* London: Brassey's (UK).

4 Jørgensen, K. E. (1997). *European approaches to crisis management.* The Hague: Kluwer Law International.

5 Mazeel, M. A. (2011). *Iraq oil and gas papers 2010.* Hamburg: Disserta-Verl.

6 Seybolt, T. B. (2008). *Humanitarian military intervention: The conditions for success and failure.* Oxford: Oxford University Press.

7 Tziarras, Z. (2014, July). The Iraq crisis and its geopolitical implications. *E-International Relations.*

8 Tziarras, Z. (2014, July). The Iraq crisis and its geopolitical implications. *E-International Relations.*

Case Study 24: JPMorgan Chase Financial Crisis (2013)

JPMorgan Chase & Co. is among the oldest, best-known financial institutions in the world. It dates back to 1799 in New York City, where its earliest successor got a charter, and it is the biggest bank in the U.S., owning assets worth $2.4 trillion. The firm has its foundation in over 1,200 successor institutions, with the major ones including J.P. Morgan, Chase Manhattan, National Bank of Detroit, and First Chicago. These heritage organizations worked closely during their time to innovate in the financial and economic growth of the U.S. and the world as a whole.[1] The firms made significant changes to local regions and communities, like JPMorgan Chase & Co. does today.

The bank offers several financial services, including traditional banking roles and street-exclusive deals with big business. The services include providing car loans, credit cards, and mortgages. Chase has 255,000 employees. In the past, large banks like J.P. Morgan & Co. were in the mortgage security business before the 2008 crisis. Their mortgage securitization activities involved buying home loans from retail banks. Therefore, the firms involved in this business lost money to the borrowers who were unable to pay their mortgages. The losses caused by the incident triggered a loss of confidence in the U.S. bank and monetary systems.

The top-rated securities based on the faulty mortgages were labeled as junk, and finally big banks and investors underwent massive losses. There was a confidence crisis in the global banking and financial system as a result. This crisis led to a $700 billion bailout for the U.S. bank systems and a $188 billion bailout for Fannie Mae and Freddie Mac. Although there were other causes of the 2008 crisis, the badly packaged mortgages were the core cause.[2] JPMorgan Chase was in a mess because it bought Washington Mutual, and hence contributed to the crisis in a way. Bear Stearns was among the firms heavily involved in the business of reselling packaged subprime mortgage securities. Washington Mutual was one of the most active mortgage lenders in the retail sector. Bear Stearns was on the verge of collapsing in March 2008.

To prevent Bear Stearns from going down, JPMorgan came in and bought it, facilitated by a Federal Reserve loan of $29 billion. Chase took on all of the Washington Mutual and Bear Stearns legal exposures in the process. In January 2013, JPMorgan Chase was part of the ten-bank agreement to settle $8.5 billion with the Office of the Comptroller of the Currency and the Federal Reserve for robot signatures and other misdeeds in the foreclosure process.[3] The banks had to pay $3.3 billion to the harmed borrowers and a combined $5.2 billion to assist in mortgage deductions for the borrowers. JPMorgan Chase did not settle its share, and hence was forced to pay a lot more than the settlement price. The bank was supposed to return $546 million to the country and sell them to other firms. Public financial companies like Freddie Mac and Fannie Mae bought the mortgages.

Case Study 24: JPMorgan Chase Financial Crisis (2013)

The banks packaged some of the mortgages into private complex housing mortgage-backed securities that attracted investors from all around the globe.

The mortgage dealers did not know that the loans they were selling were bad. That is, most of the loans were subprime in that the people paid small down payments and had reduced credits. A lot more were of the "Alt-A" category of loan quality—just a bit better than subprime loans. The companies were aware of the fact that they were investing in low-quality credit risks. Chase did not admit wrongdoing, and a lawsuit threat later cost JPMorgan Chase $100 million in March 2013.

Jefferson County, Alabama, declared partial bankruptcy due to a risky arrangement of financing with JPMorgan Chase in the overhaul of the county sewer system in 2011 that left the county in extreme debt. JPMorgan Chase was blamed for the loss and hence lost $1.564 billion on June 6, 2013. Chase purportedly engaged in manipulating electricity markets in Michigan and California from 2010 to 2012, and was fined $410 million, paid to the Federal Energy Regulatory Commission. In September 2013, J.P. Morgan & Co. agreed to settle the Bear Stearns charges by paying $18.3 million. The company also paid part of $300 million on September 9, 2013 to settle charges of pushing customers into overpriced insurance for property. The bank suffered large losses after paying $920 million for the derivatives trade conducted by "London Whale" Bruno Iksil in September 2013. On September 19, 2013, the Consumer Financial Protection Bureau accused JPMorgan Chase of charged credit cards and improper billings that customers did not get, and hence was forced to pay $309 million.

CRISIS MANAGEMENT:
THE ART OF SUCCESS AND FAILURE

During the crisis, JPMorgan Chase referred to as the "innovation evangelist" by major media firms after the risks taken since 2008. A team within JPMorgan Chase pioneered credit derivatives that almost brought the monetary system down and was later played off in 2013. Although JPMorgan did not invent the derivative credit idea, it was the first to use it in a practical manner to cover a lump sum number of loans. The derivatives helped the firm to create rapid expansion in the market and to shift the risks of its business books. Although JPMorgan Chase & Co. made a mistake in packaging and lowering the mortgage standards, it did better than its competitors. After the Bear Stearns and Washington Mutual crises, there was recovery and stabilization in the financial sector.

JPMorgan Chase admits its failure in the financial sector, especially in the case of subprime mortgages. Although critics point to the company as being fraudulent during the crisis, the company admitted that its employees misled investors, costing the global banking and monetary systems. However, some of the bank's reactions during the crisis have stirred up questions among its customers.[4] For instance, since the company is big and powerful, it has cut deals to settle the charges by appeasing the crowds instead of following the long route to get the banking system properly regulated. The settlement solutions are short-term because the mortgage business is massive and incorporates millions of consumers.

The bank announced that it would add 5,000 employees for the sake of control functions. The purpose of the control plan is to protect the bank from undue business risk, to prevent misdeeds of globally standardized ethics, and to avoid violations of legal and financial rules. The control agenda has three primary functions: to prevent, to perceive, and to act in response. The business leaders who should lead are the ones who devote the most useful resources; they should hire outstanding staff and those who have the ability to respond actively and keenly to the company's business operations.

The staff who fit into this kind of department must be highly competent in the compliance, legal, financial, audit, risk, and industrial areas. For a complex organization like J.P. Morgan & Co., an effective control agenda is a huge area. The strategy would deal with several business functions, like assessing company functions, legal risks, and moderate risks; detecting and handling problems promptly; and mitigating risk via checks, balances, and education.[5] The initiative to control risk requires good management personnel. It also necessitates considerable investment in terms of time and resources, and hence it is of utmost importance that the company has a transparent culture in which its activities are carried out with integrity across all business operations.

Endnotes

Case Study 24: JPMorgan Chase Financial Crisis (2013)

1 Aliber, R. Z., Kindleberger, C. P., & Kindleberger, C. P. (2011). *Manias, panics, and crashes: A history of financial crises*. New York: Palgrave Macmillan.

2 Bernanke, B. (2013). *The Federal Reserve and the financial crisis*. Princeton University Press.

3 Bigas, H., & Institute for Water, Environment and Health. (2012). *The global water crisis: Addressing an urgent security issue*. Hamilton, Ont: United Nations University—Institute for Water, Environment and Health.

4 Malloch, T. R., & Mamorsky, J. D. (2013). *The end of ethics and a way back: How to fix a fundamentally broken global financial system*. Singapore: Wiley.

5 Vinãls, J., Pazarbasioglu, C., Surti, J., Narain, A., Erbenova, M., & Chow, J. T. S. (2013). *Will the Volcker, Vickers, and Liikanen structural measures help?* Washington: International Monetary Fund.

Case Study 25: Southwest Airlines (2013)

The transport business is among the growing businesses that are necessary for every region and country. Every day, millions of people move from one point to another within and between countries for either employment or adventure purposes. The movement of people has led to the development of businesses, such as air travel, that seek to ensure the comfort of passengers and lower the time of moving to various destinations. A major airline in the U.S. is Southwest Airlines, which encountered a problem in 2013 and efficiently managed to communicate through social media and mainstream media to win back the trust of its customers.

On July 22, 2013, Southwest encountered a crisis when an incident resulted in the crash landing of Flight 345. The Boeing 737-7H4 (WL) had been in service for 13 years and 10 months and was traveling from Nashville International Airport in Tennessee to LaGuardia Airport in New York.[1] The airplane had five crew members and 145 passengers. There were no fatalities, but nine occupants suffered minor injuries. The pilot flying the aircraft was the first officer, while the pilot monitoring was the captain. The flight was calm all the way from departure until it was cleared for landing at the destination airport. As it approached the runway at a point just below 400 feet, the control of the airplane changed, and the captain took control to land it. However, this did not go well because the nose landing gear of the airplane hit the runway before the heavier rear landing gear. The angle at which it approached the ground was about three degrees and the nose landing gear collapsed backward and upward, into the fuselage, damaging the electronics bay.[2] The exterior of the airplane also suffered extensive damage after it slid on its nose for 2,175 feet along the runway before resting on the right side of the runway.[3]

Investigations into the incident started after the accident, with certified authorities collecting all available evidence to ascertain the reason for the accident. The National Transportation Safety Board (NTSB), which is an independent federal agency, started investigating the accident and finding clues to prevent the occurrence of a similar problem in the future. It is not recommended for a captain or co-pilot of an airplane to take control of a flight as it approaches landing and is close to the tarmac, unless there is a very serious safety issue. The captain and first officer both had extensive experience with safety procedures and had flown enough hours to know the recommendations during landing. The fact that they were experienced made it difficult to determine the reasons for their actions. The NTSB explained that the captain had been working for Southwest Airlines for over 12 years, with over 12,000 flight hours, and spent 8,000 hours on Boeing 737s. The first officer had worked for Southwest Airlines for approximately a year and a half and had flown for 5,200 hours, of which he spent 4,000 hours as the pilot in command. However, he had spent about 1,100 hours in Boeing 737s, but not as the pilot in command.[4] Therefore, their experience was enough to

Case Study 25: Southwest Airlines (2013)

know when there was a problem with the airplane and the correct security measures to take. The NTSB continued its investigation, taking into consideration all the factors, such as wind and the speed of the airplane, and gave updates as the investigation continued.

The investigations revealed that the pilot who took over to land the airplane made a mistake that violated the rules of aviation and the procedures of Southwest Airlines. The NTSB blamed the captain for attempting to recover from a bad landing by taking control from the co-pilot when the Boeing was just 27 feet from the ground. In such cases, it is always recommended for the pilots to circle the airport and try another landing attempt. The captain also failed to comply with the standard operating procedures at Southwest Airlines that require pilots to abort the landing if the aircraft is aligned improperly with the runway. The landing attempt was a violation of the operating procedures and aviation requirements, and therefore, the pilot had to take the blame for the accident that led to minor injuries and dented the reputation of the aviation industry and Southwest Airlines. Airplanes are delicate, and safety is one of the most important things that pilots need to observe. The Board explained that the incident was a major concern because 75% of investigated aviation accidents as a result of pilots attempting to land the airplane instead of aborting as required by aviation regulations.[5] A study during an International Air Safety Summit in 2011 revealed that pilots continue to land an airplane in 97% of unstoppable approaches. This is a worrying trend that warrants proper scrutiny and better training of pilots to avoid landing when they doubt the ability to make it safely. Therefore, the pilot was just a representation of most pilots who would do the same thing. The accident represented the poor training of the crews in landing airplanes and the procedures they need to take in case of doubt. The main problem emanated from the wind in the area. They approached the airport when the speed of the tailwind was slightly above 30 meters per hour, and they agreed to tilt the wing flaps to 40 degrees rather than the usual 30 degrees to slow down the airplane for a better landing. However, the first officer said he always landed with flaps at the usual 30 degrees. When the airplane was at about 500 feet, the captain realized the flaps were at 30 degrees, and she adjusted them to 40 degrees before taking control at about three seconds to touchdown. Her decision to take control at that time denied her enough time to make a safe landing.[6]

In response to the accident, Southwest Airlines dismissed the 49-year-old captain in October after an internal investigation and the completion of investigations by the NTSB. She violated Southwest Airlines' standard operating procedures, which require a plane to abort the landing if it is in the wrong configuration when it is 1,000 feet from the ground.[7] She had the chance to circle the airport and make another landing, but chose to violate the regulations and take over. The first officer had worked for the Air Force for 20 years and had enough experience with landing planes at different wind speeds. Taking over from the first officer revealed the lack of trust that the captain had in the ability of the first officer to land the plane safely. The airline company was already informing the public about the incident and the procedures via social media about 30 minutes after it happened.[8] The fast response to the public improved the company's ratings and showed its willingness to collaborate with the public and investigators to acquire the right information. Southwest also maintained open communication with the mainstream media and held various press conferences to keep people updated about the investigations and its views about the accident.

Social media is important in communication, and companies need to take advantage of its presence to build better reputations. Southwest Airlines understood this principle, and its constant updates about the investigations showed its sincere concern for the welfare of its passengers. The method of communication can help a business to thrive or collapse. The constant stream of information from Southwest Airlines ensured that customers understood their importance to the company and its dedication to their safety.

Endnotes

Case Study 25: Southwest Airlines (2013)

1 Aviation Safety Network. (2013). *Accident description*. Retrieved from http://aviation-safety.net/database/record.php?id=20130722-0

2 Aviation Safety Network. (2013). *Accident description*. Retrieved from http://aviation-safety.net/database/record.php?id=20130722-0

3 Aviation Safety Network. (2013). *Accident description*. Retrieved from http://aviation-safety.net/database/record.php?id=20130722-0

4 Dobnik, V. (2013). Southwest Airlines captain of flight 345 took command before NY accident: NTSB. *The Huffington Post*. Retrieved from http://www.huffingtonpost.com/2013/08/06/southwest-airlines-captain_n_3716700.html

5 Jansen, B. (2015, July). NTSB: Southwest nose landing at LaGuardia was captain's fault. *USA Today*. Retrieved from http://www.usatoday.com/story/news/2015/07/27/ntsb-southwest-nose-landing-laguardia/30736777/

6 Jansen, B. (2015, July). NTSB: Southwest nose landing at LaGuardia was captain's fault. *USA Today*. Retrieved from http://www.usatoday.com/story/news/2015/07/27/ntsb-southwest-nose-landing-laguardia/30736777/

7 Jansen, B. (2015, July). NTSB: Southwest nose landing at LaGuardia was captain's fault. *USA Today*. Retrieved from http://www.usatoday.com/story/news/2015/07/27/ntsb-southwest-nose-landing-laguardia/30736777/

8 Cohn, R. (2014). *How social media is elevating airline crisis communication*. Retrieved from https://www.linkedin.com/pulse/20140313141909-14626191-how-social-media-is-elevating-airline-crisis-communication

Case Study 26: Asiana Airlines Crisis (2013)

On July 6, 2013, at approximately 11:28 a.m. Pacific time, a Boeing flight bearing a Korean registration, operating as Asiana Airlines Flight 214, crashed short of reaching San Francisco International Airport. The airplane was flying from its main airport, Incheon International Airport, and everything looked good until the last minutes of the landing series. Upon trying to land, its landing gear, together with the tail, knocked out the seawall at the start of the landing strip. This caused a crash that left three people dead and several injured. While the number of fatalities was undeniably low as opposed to several other crashes, it was heartbreaking for the families of the victims. In fact, the shocking scene will always remain in the minds of the survivors. Studies have reported that the number of plane crashes has been significantly reduced since flying became safer. Nevertheless, accidents can and will continue to occur. Admittedly, airline safety is a matter that people take lightly until an accident occurs. As such, the crash of Flight 214 raised concerns about air safety, responses to emergencies, and Asiana's safety record, and also brought training practices into the limelight. This section describes how Asiana failed to respond swiftly to the crisis and how it dealt with the media. The discussion also provides suggestions for crisis management initiatives to handle future situations.

HOW DID ASIANA FAIL TO RESPOND SWIFTLY TO THE CRISIS?

It is everyone's expectation that, when accidents occur, airline owners will respond swiftly and in a timely manner by offering immediate assistance to the victims and survivors. However, Asiana Airlines responded slowly to the crisis, ultimately raising eyebrows. Asiana Airlines' approach to crisis communication one day after the incident clearly demonstrated the slow rate of their response to critical issues like crashes. Although the airline had a toll-free disaster hotline for families and passengers to get updates, the hotline was not posted on the company's website until nine hours after the crash. Several media outlets reported that it took about three days for the airline to send its chief executives, along with a team of staffers, to the site where the plane crashed. The managers were expected to apologize, hold discussions with officials from the U.S. federal government, and initiate a thorough investigation.[1] The company also declined offers to establish a large communication team in the U.S. to assist with queries from the media and families. When the hotline for the airline was congested with calls, the company had to establish additional lines to respond to the calls.

What also signified Asiana Airlines' failure to respond swiftly to the crisis was the lack of posts on its social network accounts. For instance, studies have reported that Asiana Airlines only posted a few times on Facebook, and a majority of the posts directed people to the website to get information on press conferences or the hotline number for emergencies.[2] Because of this, the airline refused to speak to any journalist who was not from Korea after the crash. In fact, there were instances when the media dogged several influential journalists and many bloggers from the U.S. Several reports have also indicated that families or victims were not happy with the manner in which the airline responded to the crisis. They totally relied on the airline after the crash and complaints began to emerge. For example, according to Haijun Xu, one of the passengers on the plane, Asiana instructed him to not give any information to the media. While accommodations were provided to the families of the victims, they were compelled to share beds because of the scarcity of the accommodations given to them.

The inability of Asiana Airlines to respond swiftly to the crisis is also evident in its communication with workers. In fact, information about staff communication regarding the accident and the actions taken by Asiana employees following the accident is very scarce. Apart from the first tweet stating that the airline's thoughts and prayers were with the crew and passengers, the affected workers were never mentioned. Nevertheless, there were many statements from the company defending the pilots' experience. The press release provided by the company only stressed that the employees of the airline would respond to the crisis, but provided no account of the support offered to the crew.

HOW DID ASIANA AIRLINES DEAL WITH THE MEDIA?

To console the families of the survivors and the deceased, Asiana Airlines used the media to distribute information regarding the course of action it was undertaking. At the same time that the White House held its press conferences, Asiana Airlines released statements on Twitter, expressing its thoughts and prayers for the crew and passengers on the flight. Seven hours later, it released another press statement on Facebook, Twitter, Google+, and its website. The release stated that the company was working to find out the exact causes of the crash and that it was cooperating with federal agencies to conduct a thorough investigation. In fact, the press statement finished with the company claiming that it could confirm nothing. However, it is worth noting that Asiana Airlines declined to respond to all the comments posted on social media and refused to respond to any media attention from outside Korea.

Asiana Airlines also dealt with the media by using it as a communication conduit for both the passengers and families. Essentially, the company designed a toll-free crisis hotline for families and passengers to get updates. Through constant updates, the company provided vital information to family members on the status of their loved ones and the company's initiatives to offer assistance to the injured. The company also used the media to deliver its apologies to the public for having taken too long to respond to the crisis.

CRISIS MANAGEMENT INITIATIVES

Studies have reported that several human factors can cause airline crashes. One such factor is inadequate knowledge or a lack of knowledge. It is instrumental that workers have sufficient training since the risk of an accident when they are not trained properly is very high.[3] Pundits have argued that complacency is another detrimental challenge in airline safety. This happens when the job is monotonous, and the members of the crew spend little time concentrating on everything they do. By becoming complacent, they might be unable to offer a safe experience for passengers. On the same note, a lack of understanding can result in airplane crashes. As a matter of fact, for pilots who are not keen, a simple issue can easily become a bigger one. Theoretically, it is questionable that the pilot of Flight 214 was comfortable since he had only flown for a few hours on that plane. Nevertheless, he may have been uninformed about the danger of the seawall or had insufficient training in that particular plane or airport. However, in the meantime, Asiana Airlines, as well as other flight operators, should re-examine their training and other requirements for crewmembers and pilots.

Another crisis management initiative included enhancements in emergency communications at Asiana Airlines. Essentially, many communication challenges happened during the crisis response, with the most significant one being the inability to respond to mutual assistance units and communicate directly with units from an airplane on one radio frequency. While some communication difficulties experienced during the response to the emergency, such as the absence of radio interoperability, have been solved, others, including the communications breakdown between the city dispatch center and the airport, need to be addressed. The next vital crisis management initiative is the consideration of cultural differences. When handling communication across cultures, it is instrumental to take into account the cultural differences in the communication platforms and strategies.[4]

In conclusion, the Asiana Airlines crisis exemplified

CRISIS MANAGEMENT:
THE ART OF SUCCESS AND FAILURE

concerns about pilot requirements and air safety. On the same note, it brought the safety records of the company into the limelight and elicited questions concerning whether the aircraft's pilot had sufficient training to fly safely. While traveling by air remains the safest mode of transport for long distances, incidences such as the one experienced by Flight 214 often elicit questions on how airlines prepare and train their crews. Since most crashes result in injuries or the deaths of many people, the aim is to lower the incidences of accidents as much as possible. As such, airplanes are becoming safer, and cases of accidents are seen less often compared to in the past. For most individuals, entering an airplane is a risk they are willing to take because of the convenience it provides. On the same note, traveling through the air will continue to become safer. Therefore, careful screenings of crews; demanding stricter requirements for pilots; and stronger, better, and more durable airplanes will improve the experience of flying and safeguard passengers from danger even in unforeseen events.

Endnotes

Case Study 26: Asiana Airlines Crisis (2013)

1 Cha, S., & Park, K. (2011). Asiana Boeing 747 freighter crashes in South Korean waters. Bloomberg. Retrieved from http://www.bloomberg.com/news/2011-07-28/asiana-boeing-747-freighter-crashes-inkorean-

2 Ranter, H. (2008). ASN aircraft accident Boeing 737-5Lp HL7229 Mokpo. *Aviation Safety Network Review*, 24(6), 12–15.

3 Washington, A. (2015). The need for cultural intelligence: An analysis of Asiana Airlines' response to the crash landing of Flight 214. *Case Study Competition*, 2(5), 3–36.

4 Washington, A. (2015). The need for cultural intelligence: An analysis of Asiana Airlines' response to the crash landing of Flight 214. *Case Study Competition*, 2(5), 3–36.

Case Study 27: Tesla Motors Crisis (2013)

Founded in July 2003, Tesla Motors deals in the design, development, manufacture, and sales of electric power train components, electric vehicles, and stationary energy storage systems. The company employs the use of manufacturing processes and energy management technologies that are specifically developed for the vehicle power train. Moreover, the company manufactures stationary energy storage products, which are used in commercial sites, homes, and utilities.

Some of the company's technologies include safety systems, cooling systems, battery engineering, charge balancing systems, environmental durability, battery engineering for vibration, customized motor design, manufacturing processes, and software and electronic management systems crucial in managing vehicle and battery performance. Some of the renowned company's products include the Tesla Roadster and Model S.

The reason behind the establishment of this company was to affirm that electric cars could be more efficacious than gasoline-powered cars. Having incredible power, instant torque, and zero emissions, Tesla Motors was expected to produce cars without any defects or compromises. Furthermore, each generation of Tesla's cars was expected to be more affordable and in line with the company's mission: to transit the world toward sustainable transport.

The company's Model S, the first premium electric sedan globally and the major subject of the crisis discussed in this section, was launched in 2012. Having been built to be 100% electric, the sedan has increasingly redefined the concept of the four-door car. With 64 cubic feet of storage and room for seven passengers, the model is renowned for providing utility and comfort while having the acceleration of a sports car, with an estimated 0-to-60-mph time of approximately five seconds.

THE TESLA MOTORS CRISIS

Launched in 2012, the Model S has since recorded remarkable profitability in the global market. The model joined the league of the blossoming market's bestsellers. Detroit[1] asserted that, since the commencement of the year, the company's sales have been tremendous, exceeding expectations. This has been evidenced by a surging of its stock by 400%, giving Tesla a market valuation of over $20 billion, a value that is considered better than those of most conventional manufacturers.[2]

Nonetheless, hours after a video surfaced on YouTube that showed a Model S sedan on fire caused by Tesla's battery, the company's share price lost more than 5%. Though it is not clear that the reverse trend of buying the car will persist, the most serious concern in respect to what happened in the video is whether the fire would scare off prospective battery-powered car buyers. Already, issues have been raised in respect to the safety of lithium-ion technology, which has increasingly become commonplace in battery manufacturing.

As opined by Detroit,[3] issues have been raised about batteries in a number of circumstances, such as in the Chevrolet Volt plug-in hybrid, which had been tested with faulty government crash-test procedures. Additionally, there have been a number of incidents with the Fisker Karma plug-ins. Even Boeing, a leading airline company, has not been spared, as it recently got unwanted headlines resulting from a plethora of battery "incidents," including, though not limited to, a lithium back-up battery in the new 787 Dreamliner passenger jet. This is a clear indication that the lithium battery has been a big problem and is thus a threat to Tesla's corporate image.

TESLA'S MODEL S

The Tesla Model S experienced a promising beginning. In May 2013, the model was recorded as the best electric car, winning several awards.[4] The testing of the car saw it score 99%, the only demerit being the recharging time when compared to time required for fueling gasoline cars. In fact, in 2013, the Model S recorded the best-ever safety rating given by the National Highway Traffic Safety Administration (NHTSA). The tests conducted by the federal government earned five-star safety ratings in all of them.[5]

October was not a good month for the company, as it began experiencing issues in respect to its Model S. The model made news headlines since three of its cars experienced fires within a six-week time frame. The car fires were reported in Mexico and the U.S. and had been caused by accidents rather than spontaneous events. The three fire incidents had a damaging effect on the company's corporate image.

CRISIS MANAGEMENT:
THE ART OF SUCCESS AND FAILURE

Tesla's 2013 crisis has mostly been blamed on their lack of an efficacious crisis communication strategy. It would have been prudent for the company to effectively address the crisis from the very day it happened to thwart the negative impact on the company's corporate image that came with the crisis. According to Coombs and Holladay,[6] crisis communication has been integral over the years when it comes to addressing topics related to a crisis, including failure, product, terrorism, natural disaster, environmental, and scandal crises. Such crises happen on a daily basis, hence, the need to put strategies and mechanisms in place to deal with crises of such nature.

No organization is immune from crises, meaning that crises in any form, including product failure, can happen to any organization. The fact that a crisis within an organization is inevitable justifies the need to institute mechanisms to deal effectively with crises. Olsson[7] posited that corporate reputation and public relations experts have dominated the literature about the sphere of an organization. Prompt communication following a crisis is crucial in the organization's ability to deal with or address crisis effectively. Tesla's failure to communicate in good time after the video emerged was a big mistake that ought not to be repeated. Such a failure presented a double tragedy because, besides denting their corporate image, it also led to a significant reduction in the Model S's product volume.

CRISIS AND ORGANIZATIONAL CORPORATE IMAGE
The role played by crisis in denting a company's corporate image cannot be refuted. Research has indicated that an organizational crisis is a major threat to an organization's

corporate image. Brønn and Berg[8] posited that crisis experts contend that, irrespective of the type, a crisis can demolish belief and trust within the organization, in addition to influencing the organization's reputation. In the most basic form, reputation refers to the assessment of an organization. The organization's corporate image is one of the precious, intangible resources critical to organizational competitiveness. In this respect, it is prudent that an organization maintains a strong corporate image if it is to remain competitive in the global market.

A positive organizational reputation is crucial in terms of attracting investors, customers, and top employee talent, in addition to generating positive media coverage.[9] Organizational reputation can, therefore, be built through organizational stakeholder relationships. Corporate organizational culture is pivotal in building stronger competitiveness, which also translates to a broader market share. According to Fombrun and Van Riel,[10] organizational reputation can be either favorable or unfavorable, based on the level of negative or positive interaction.

Considering the fact that a crisis is a big threat to an organization's image, it is imperative that Tesla builds a stronger crisis management strategy as a way of protecting its organizational reputation.[11] The success of any organization in the present tumultuous business environment is, to a large extent, dependent on the organization's corporate image. This further translates to massive market shares and, hence, higher profitability. The YouTube video displayed Tesla in a bad light, significantly denting its corporate image. Lack of communication in good time worsened the situation further. It would have been prudent for the organization to address the situation as quickly as possible to protect the organization's image.

CRISIS MANAGEMENT INITIATIVES

Crisis management initiatives are crucial in maintaining a successful transition during a crisis. Despite the lack of literature regarding the crisis management strategies employed by Tesla, the fact remains that they ought to do as much as possible to curb damage to the reputation of the organization. Among the measures that ought to be taken are conducting product vulnerability audits to ensure product safety.

Endnotes

Case Study 27: Tesla Motors Crisis (2013)

1 Detroit. (2013). *The fire this time*. Retrieved from http://www.economist.com/blogs/schumpeter/2013/10/tesla-motors.

2 Detroit. (2013). *The fire this time*. Retrieved from http://www.economist.com/blogs/schumpeter/2013/10/tesla-motors.

3 Detroit. (2013). *The fire this time*. Retrieved from http://www.economist.com/blogs/schumpeter/2013/10/tesla-motors.

4 Valdes-Dapena, P. (2013, May). Tesla: Consumer Reports' best car ever tested. CNN, [online]. . Retrieved from http://money.cnn.com/2013/05/09/autos/tesla-model-s-consumer-reports

5 Tesla. (2013a). Tesla Model S achieves best safety rating of any car ever tested. Retrieved from http://ir.teslamotors.com/releasedetail.cfm?releaseid=786136

6 Coombs, W. T., & Holladay, S. J. (2012). *The handbook of crisis communication* (1st ed.). Wiley-Blackwell, Oxford: Blackwell Publishing Ltd.

7 Olsson, E. (2014). Crisis communication in public organizations: Dimensions of crisis communication revisited. *Journal of Contingencies and Crisis Management*, 22(2), 113–125.

8 Brønn, P. S., & Berg, R. W. (2011) *Corporate communication: A strategic approach to building reputation* (2nd ed.). Oslo: Gyldendal Akademisk.

9 Brønn, P. S., & Berg, R. W. (2011) *Corporate communication: A strategic approach to building reputation* (2nd ed.). Oslo: Gyldendal Akademisk.

10 Fombrun, C. J., & Van Riel, C. B. M. (2003). *Fame and fortune: How the world's top companies develop winning reputations*. Pearson Education.

11 Coombs, W. T., & Holladay, S. J. (2012). *The handbook of crisis communication* (1st ed.). Wiley-Blackwell, Oxford: Blackwell Publishing Ltd.

Case Study 28: The Fall of Lehman Brothers

Lehman Brothers Holdings Inc. was the fourth-largest U.S. investment bank before seeking Chapter 11 protection on September 15, 2008. The event initiated the largest-ever bankruptcy proceeding in the history of the U.S. The collapse of this old firm, which had been operating for over 164 years, was indeed a formative event in the world financial crisis. Lehman Brothers successfully managed to pursue a high-leverage, high-risk business model, and this compelled it to raise billions of dollars to allow the company to fund its business operations.[1] The company started to invest heavily in real estate assets in early 2006, and within a short time, it had significant exposure to subprime mortgages and housing; these markets immediately started to sour. The company hired a team of risk experts and accountants to monitor its risks, key ratios, and balance sheet constantly. It assumed frantic, dubious actions to stay alive. However, Lehman Brothers ultimately failed because it was unable to finance its operations. This case overview offers background information on why Lehman Brothers could not survive the financial crisis of 2008 and why letting a key financial institution fall can adversely affect the world.[2]

THE CAUSES OF LEHMAN BROTHERS' FAILURE

The failure of Lehman Brothers is attributed to a multiple of reasons, including massive credit default swaps, Repo 105, financial leverage, the repeal of the Glass-Steagall Act, a liquidity crisis, excessive loss, poor management decisions alongside unethical actions, an intricate capital structure, the subprime mortgage crisis, futile bailouts, and take-overs.[3]

Revocation of the 1993 Glass-Steagall Act

The Glass-Steagall Act revocation was enacted to minimize or abolish conflicts of interest by separating investment banking from commercial banking, following the depression that occurred in 1990–1993. During this historic depression, over 9,000 banks collapsed globally.[4] The Glass-Steagall Act was later amended and replaced in 1999, enabling commercial banks to engage in investment banking activities. This new act facilitated mergers between commercial banks and investment banks. According to most financial analysts, this factor greatly contributed to the collapse of Lehman Brothers. In an effort to compete effectively with the commercial banks that had a high competitive advantage, Lehman Brothers merged with or acquired numerous investment and commercial banks. The company's merger activities were conducted in an unethical way, making it vulnerable to many risks that caused it to go bankrupt.[5]

Unethical Management Practices

In its pursuit of attaining its specific missions and expansion strategy, Lehman Brothers executives employed several unethical practices, including improper accounting practices, along with their deliberate contempt for far-sighted corporate governance practices. The company used window dressing presentations; this facilitated the manipulation of its financial statements in order to attract investors and portray a unique image of the company.[6] In addition, Lehman brothers employed Repo 105 transactions in an effort to improve its financial strength at the year's end. The managers of the firm deliberately breached the Sarbanes-Oxley Act. The act was enacted to improve internal control practices, create stronger external auditing practices and independence, restore client trust, offer timely disclosure, strengthen directors' actions and roles, and improve rigorous securities practices. Most of the executives of Lehman Brothers engaged in unethical actions, such as increasing their bonuses to about $480 million. Most of these senior managers of the firm violated various acts set to govern the operation of the business, and this largely contributed to its failure.[7]

Liquidity Crisis

Lehman Brothers lacked the capacity to sustain its short-term obligations. Even though it had high assets, the company was faced with sporadic liquidity troubles. This caused the company to lose its market confidence, thus triggering most banks to withdraw their services and credit lines to the firm. Gradually, the level of confidence of the customers and lenders waned, and this made Lehman Brothers unattractive to potential investors. The company tried to solve its liquidity problem by reducing its gross assets base of $147 billion to enhance its liquidity position of $45 billion. Unfortunately, the company proposed bailouts, a strategy that did not rescue it from its liquidity problem.[8]

Collateralized Debt Obligation and Derivatives Crisis

The company ventured into numerous risky and redundant investments. In addition, residential whole loans (RWLs) are believed to be one of the contributors to Lehman Brothers' collapse. RWLs are generally residential mortgages that are traded and pooled in a securitization process and finally transmuted into residential mortgaged-backed securities.[9] The company lacked a vigorous product control process that could account for RWLs, marred with misstatements in assets, making its condition even worse. The company engaged in the derivative market to exploit the speculative opportunities and reduce its vulnerability to credit risks.[10] Derivatives instruments allow companies to derive investment values from changes in price, as well as the net worth of other underlying assets, including commodities or stocks. Most of the company derivatives were credit default swaps. During the 2007 recession period, the prices of properties went down, causing the repossession of assets. The company is believed to have overwritten its credit swaps by approximately $2.5 billion.[11] The weakened value of collateralized debt obligations contributed significantly to the failure of the company.

Leveraging

The company developed a culture of massive borrowing in an effort to finance its assets. This climaxed into Lehman Brothers having a high leverage position. The high leverage ratio was 20 in 2004. This value increased to 44 to 1 shareholders' equity. This high leverage was next to impossible to maintain. The financial depression had a massive effect on the company's fiscal position, causing it to go bankrupt.[12]

Complex Capital Structure

Since the company had more than 3,000 legal entities to handle, it was faced with challenges to its capital structure. This was attributed to its massive growth and expansion. Such expansion and growth often leads to a very complex capital structure, and that is what Lehman Brothers faced. Some financial experts attribute Lehman Brothers Holdings' downfall to its intricate capital structure.[13]

Fruitless Bailout and Takeover Efforts

Before the liquidation of Lehman Brothers, it tried several measures to redeem its business operations. The company's massive losses in 2008 and fruitless efforts to dispose of a number of its subsidiaries contributed largely to its downfall. In the last quarter alone, Lehman Brothers had a loss of $2.8 billion. This resulted in the disposal of $6 billion of its assets because of the low-rated mortgage tranches in its subprime position. By the end of September 2008, the company had recorded $3.9 billion in losses in its effort to sell off its main shares in most of its holdings, such as Neuberger Bermen. This reduced consumers' confidence.[14]

All these problems made the issue of Lehman Brothers so complex that saving it from collapsing was next to impossible. The only rescuer was the U.S. government. Unfortunately, the Troubled Asset Relief Program (TARP) had not been passed by Congress. This implies that the Department of the Treasury had no legal right to bail out Lehman Brothers.[15]

Impact of the Failure of Lehman Brothers Holdings

The folding of Lehman Brothers Holdings disclosed hardship in the operations of most companies, not only in the U.S., but also globally. In the U.S. alone, the failure of Lehman Brothers caused depreciations in commercial real estate prices. In addition, the hedge market was adversely affected because more than 1,000 hedge funds employed Lehman Brothers as the main broker and often depended on the company for funding. The exposure of Freddie Mac, in conjunction with the single-family loan, was $400 million. The collapse of Lehman Brothers also caused a debt of $40 million owed to the Federal Agricultural Corporation (Farmer Mac) to be written off. Constellation Energy also reported a decrease of its stock on the New York Stock Exchange. The stumbled trading of Constellation Energy resulted in Mid-American Energy buying it out. Many banks reported billions in losses.[16]

The consequences of Lehman Brothers' fall were massive. Over 25,000 Lehman Brothers employees lost their jobs. Consumers lost their confidence in other banks, causing a global crisis and deep depression in many nations. The consequences of the fall of Lehman Brothers were more massive than expected. The global market felt it, and the dollar declined as most investors across the U.S. sold their assets and stored their money in the safest security available, such as government bonds.[17]

Endnotes

Case Study 28: The Fall of Lehman Brothers

1 Authers, J. (2012). *Europe's financial crisis: A short guide to how the euro fell into crisis and the consequences for the world.* FT Press.

2 Authers, J. (2012). *Europe's financial crisis: A short guide to how the euro fell into crisis and the consequences for the world.* FT Press.

3 Kirke, L. (2012). What caused the failure of Lehman Brothers? Could it have been prevented? *SSRN Electronic Journal.*

4 Kirke, L. (2012). What caused the failure of Lehman Brothers? Could it have been prevented? *SSRN Electronic Journal.*

5 Kirke, L. (2012). What caused the failure of Lehman Brothers? Could it have been prevented? *SSRN Electronic Journal.*

6 Kirke, L. (2012). What caused the failure of Lehman Brothers? Could it have been prevented? *SSRN Electronic Journal.*

7 Kirke, L. (2012). What caused the failure of Lehman Brothers? Could it have been prevented? *SSRN Electronic Journal.*

8 MacEwan, A., & Miller, J. (2011). *Economic collapse, economic change: Getting to the roots of the crisis.* Armonk, N.Y.: M.E. Sharpe.

9 MacEwan, A., & Miller, J. (2011). *Economic collapse, economic change: Getting to the roots of the crisis.* Armonk, N.Y.: M.E. Sharpe.

10 Kirke, L. (2012). What caused the failure of Lehman Brothers? Could it have been prevented? *SSRN Electronic Journal.*

11 MacEwan, A., & Miller, J. (2011). *Economic collapse, economic change: Getting to the roots of the crisis.* Armonk, N.Y.: M.E. Sharpe.

12 Schapiro, M. (2010). *Lehman Brothers examiner's report: Congressional testimony.* DIANE Publishing.

13 Schapiro, M. (2010). *Lehman Brothers examiner's report: Congressional testimony.* DIANE Publishing.

14 MacEwan, A., & Miller, J. (2011). *Economic collapse, economic change: Getting to the roots of the crisis.* Armonk, N.Y.: M.E. Sharpe.

15 Schapiro, M. (2010). *Lehman Brothers examiner's report: Congressional testimony.* DIANE Publishing.

CRISIS MANAGEMENT:
THE ART OF SUCCESS AND FAILURE

16 Blythe, N. (2010, September). How did Lehman's collapse affect the world of finance? BBC News. Retrieved February 05, 2016, from http://www.bbc.com/news/business-11310143.

17 Blythe, N. (2010, September). How did Lehman's collapse affect the world of finance? BBC News. Retrieved February 05, 2016, from http://www.bbc.com/news/business-11310143.

Case Study 29: Siemens China (2012)

In the course of doing business, companies and organizations are likely to encounter several challenges that require expertise to solve. Some of the challenges may interfere with the organization's normal daily activities, and others go to the extent of affecting consumers. The way an organization or business entity responds to challenges can help to boost its image and lead to better sales, but it can also lead to the collapse of a whole business or many departments within the business.

Siemens was established in 1847 and is known for manufacturing numerous electrical home appliances. The success of such a company depends on the trust that consumers have in their products and how well the company meets the different consumer demands for electrical appliances. In 2011, several complaints were received about the quality of Siemens home appliances. A popular Chinese Internet celebrity, Luo Yonghao, initiated the complaints by writing in his blog about the breakdown of a washing machine and refrigerator he bought from the company.[1] He was more concerned about the refrigerator door, which did not shut tightly.[2] A company that cares about consumers should be able to respond to such claims and assess the products that have similar problems. In most cases, people have similar problems but wait for an individual who is bold enough to start making complaints. The best way to tackle these issues is by filing complaints with the organization's customer care section. Luo filed various complaints with Siemens, but it refused to admit that its products had defects.[3] Social media is an important tool in society and for business. The Internet allows people from different areas with common problems or likes and visions to communicate. Luo's blog attracted attention from different customers with similar problems. Soon afterward, other bloggers also wrote about the problem.[4] The number of complainants increased, leading to the formation of an anti-Siemens group.

After a long time and much outrage from customers on the Internet, Siemens offered a customer service number that affected consumers could call to get their appliances repaired. Despite the phone number and promise to repair the affected appliances onsite, Siemens did not respond to customers' complaints. A company's refusal to acknowledge the presence of fault and to work toward ensuring a good relationship with consumers can be detrimental to the company. The consumers decided to take action and demonstrate outside the Siemens headquarters in Beijing. Luo met with some other victims, and together they went to the headquarters and smashed three refrigerators that had problems with their doors.[5] Despite their efforts, however, nobody from the headquarters came to address the problem with the demonstrators and media personalities who were filming the demonstration. This was another blow to the company and a confirmation of its inability to respond to customer complaints. Rather than address the demonstrators, Siemens called the police to disperse them.[6] The demonstrators may have caused a disturbance, which was expected, by smashing the refrigerators as a way of showing their annoyance with Siemens' customer service. However, a company that seeks to prosper in any market must listen to the needs of its customers, as it helps with their plans in marketing and the innovation of appliances, eliminating previous problems.

Siemens failed in communicating efficiently with its customers. Communication should always be open, and management should reassure customers of the company's willingness to solve problems and win back customer trust. The reaction from Siemens was hostile, and having the police disperse the demonstrators depicted its unwillingness to be associated with the faulty refrigerators. Social media has created a new force in markets all over the world. Consumers are more willing to criticize companies that provide bad services, and it is much easier to find people with similar problems. Therefore, the response and attention that a company gives to consumers who express their dissatisfaction on social media should come from someone with authority in the organization, and it should contribute to finding a solution to the problem. After dispersing the protesters, Siemens issued a statement through its official Sina Weibo account and explained that BSH Home Appliances was responsible for producing, selling, and offering after-sale services for its products.[7] Through the statement, Siemens shifted the blame onto BSH Home Appliances, and this further dented its image. Siemens was portrayed as a company that only takes credit when the appliances are successful and shifts blame in the case of problems. It was depicted as a company afraid of tackling problems that could affect its growth.

CRISIS MANAGEMENT:
THE ART OF SUCCESS AND FAILURE

Every company encounters problems at one point or another in the business cycle, and Siemens' problem was the faulty refrigerator doors. It communicated poorly with its customers, and this led to lower sales of its products. It made people believe that they would not respond to problems in their products. It was important for management to understand the need for efficient communication in business success.

Endnotes

Case Study 29: Siemens China (2012)

1 ChinaHush. (2011, November). Smashing refrigerators in China. *Business Insider*. Retrieved from http://www.businessinsider.com.au/this-chinese-internet-celebrity-smashed-siemens-fridges-to-protest-their-quality-2011-11

2 ChinaHush. (2011, November). Smashing refrigerators in China. *Business Insider*. Retrieved from http://www.businessinsider.com.au/this-chinese-internet-celebrity-smashed-siemens-fridges-to-protest-their-quality-2011-11

3 ChinaHush. (2011, November). Smashing refrigerators in China. *Business Insider*. Retrieved from http://www.businessinsider.com.au/this-chinese-internet-celebrity-smashed-siemens-fridges-to-protest-their-quality-2011-11

4 Giang, V. (2011, November). Here's why people started hammering fridges outside Siemens' Beijing headquarters. *Business Insider*. Retrieved from http://www.businessinsider.com/siemens-fridge-doors-2011-11

5 ChinaHush. (2011, November). Smashing refrigerators in China. *Business Insider*. Retrieved from http://www.businessinsider.com.au/this-chinese-internet-celebrity-smashed-siemens-fridges-to-protest-their-quality-2011-11

6 ChinaHush. (2011, November). Smashing refrigerators in China. *Business Insider*. Retrieved from http://www.businessinsider.com.au/this-chinese-internet-celebrity-smashed-siemens-fridges-to-protest-their-quality-2011-11

7 Chujian, G. (2011). *Siemens sparks refrigerator rage*. Retrieved from http://www.eeo.com.cn/ens/2011/1124/216405.shtml

Case Study 30: Toyota Recall 2010

Cars are common in every country and are among the things most young people want to own. They offer a convenient mode of transport from one point to another and are also a form of prestige for owners. One of the most popular vehicle manufacturers in the world is Toyota. It has different types of vehicles that are adaptable to various environments. Vehicles are important for transport, and it is necessary for manufacturers to ensure the safety of passengers, pedestrians, and drivers by upholding high-quality standards for their vehicles. In 2010, Toyota suffered a crisis that ruined its reputation and lowered its sales.

The problems at Toyota started in 2009, when it had to recall several vehicles to rectify problems that had occurred during assembly. In January 2009, Toyota announced that it would recall 1.3 million vehicles worldwide because they had a problem with the exhaust systems and seatbelts.[1] A problem of such a magnitude is bound to affect the sales of vehicles because people will be more concerned about their safety, and consumers cannot predict which exact vehicles will have the problem. The announcement also made people start looking for more faults in the Toyota vehicles they bought within the announced time. The main problem came after a car accident in the U.S. On August 28, 2009, an off-duty Highway Patrol officer in California, Mark Saylor, was traveling on a highway with three family members when the Toyota Lexus ES350 he was driving started accelerating uncontrollably before hitting another car and rolling into a ditch, where it caught fire and killed every occupant. The driver had called 911 before the crash to complain that the brakes were not working and the car was moving at a speed of over 100 miles per hour.[2] After the accident, in September 2009, Toyota announced the biggest recall in its history after fears that there could be about four million vehicles with a similar problem and whose accelerator pedals may get trapped under the floor mats, leading to high speeds that could cause a crash leading to serious injury or death.[3] This created fear among customers and the owners of various Toyota models.

The company had to recall more vehicles to solve the problem with the braking systems. At the start of 2010, it announced that it would recall approximately 2.3 million vehicles in the U.S. besides the four million it had announced in September 2009. Toyota suspended sales and halted the production of eight models in North America, including the best-selling vehicle in the region, the Camry. The company also advised the owners of affected vehicles to remove their floor mats to avoid the possibility of the accelerator pedal getting stuck to the floor of the vehicles.[4] The problem seemed to be getting worse over time. People have models of cars they prefer, and consumers from different parts of the world may have had similar Toyota models. Therefore, the affected models were distributed around the world, and Toyota had to recall every affected model. In January 2010, Toyota announced the expansion of the recall to include Europe and China and explained that the recalls in Europe amounted to approximately 1.8 million vehicles and included eight models.[5] Even as the company thought it had contained the problem, more complaints came from different countries, requiring it to look into the claims and ascertain if there was a cause for alarm among the car owners. Vehicle owners who had experienced slight problems with their vehicles started communicating with Toyota through their governments and the media. In February 2010, the Japanese government urged Toyota to investigate complaints from 77 car owners with problems in the braking systems of the Prius model. To ensure that all the faulty vehicles around the world were repaired, Toyota globally recalled all Toyota Prius vehicles that were manufactured before January 27, 2010; this affected 8,500 cars in the United Kingdom.[6] The total number of affected vehicles was a great blow to Toyota.

This recall had various negative impacts on Toyota and its customers. People always expect such companies to ensure high quality during manufacturing processes that will not interfere with their daily activities by causing great inconveniences. In most cases, people buy one car at a time according to their budget and priorities. The popularity of Toyota emanated from the quality and affordability of its vehicles. The recall of the vehicles was a great inconvenience to people who relied on them for transport to different places. Inasmuch as they cared about their safety, their lives were disrupted by being denied the use of a vehicle they bought from the company due to a defect that was not their fault. Life is precious, and the death of the family of four because of a defect in their vehicle was a depiction of the company's inability to consider and respect the lives of its customers. The media from different countries asked questions and posted information that led to further damage to Toyota's image. Some publications explained that there had been problems with the vehicles for a long time, but the company did not bother to verify the claims. The *Los Angeles Times* wrote that the company had previously ignored more than 1,200 similar unintended acceleration complaints within the previous eight years after the National Highway Traffic Safety Administration dismissed the cases. It explained that the cases of unintended acceleration jumped from 26 cases in 2001 to 132 cases in 2002, and it resulted in 19 deaths from 2002 until the time of the recall.[7] These claims further portrayed the company as careless in investigating claims from consumers. It depicted Toyota as a selfish company that only cares about its revenues and does not worry about the consumers who ensure its profitability. According to a survey conducted by Anne Kelly, [3] the popularity of the company diminished after the recall, for good reasons. Before the recall, 83% of American adults believed in the brand, and only 17% were negative about it. From the results of that survey, most consumers purchasing a vehicle would have opted for a Toyota model they preferred. The Consumers' confidence in the brand was a reason for the company's high revenues. After the accident that triggered the massive recall, confidence in the brand fell from 83% to 78% by the end of 2009. At first, consumers thought it was only a minor problem, but another recall lowered their confidence further. After a massive recall in January 2010 that extended to April of the same year, confidence in the brand reduced to 59%. The company had to change its motto after the recalls to portray their state at the time and their willingness to capture consumer attention. Before the recalls, its motto was "I love what you do for me, Toyota!"; it changed to "Moving forward!" after the 2009 and 2010 recalls.[3] The new motto was an indication of Toyota's willingness to make a fresh start in winning the confidence of consumers and improving its sales and the safety measures of its vehicles.

The recall also had a negative financial impact on Toyota. The accidents from the unintended acceleration lowered the trust that customers had in the brand, leading to low sales of its vehicles all over the world. The financial costs included the recall of the vehicles, the money used to repair the vehicles, the losses from the lack of sales, and the money incurred in trying to repair the company's image. Toyota admitted to financial losses as a result of the recalls. It announced that the company suffered $2 billion in extra costs because of the global recall.[8] This is a large amount of money that it could have used in developing other projects to earn revenue and increase its popularity and sales all over the world. This money was spent to improve the acceleration problem and safety measures in the recalled vehicles. Toyota also suffered financially because of low sales from the lack of confidence in their brand. It had to suspend its production, respond to complaints, and answer government questions about its safety measures. On February 19, 2010, it confirmed the suspension of production at the Toyota plant in Burnaston, Derbyshire.[9] The suspension of production resulted in a limited number of vehicles available for sale. Toyota admitted that the recall cost it $54 million daily from lack of sales.[10] It could have prevented these losses by adhering to high-quality safety measures in its production processes.

The recall was a lesson to Toyota and other manufac-

CRISIS MANAGEMENT:
THE ART OF SUCCESS AND FAILURE

turers about the need to maintain safety and ensure the high quality of goods and services in business. The CEO of Toyota North America, Jim Lentz, explained that the recall taught the company the importance of transparency and the need to listen to their customers.[4] The Internet has created a platform for people from all over the world to interact, and a slight problem can lead to massive losses for businesses. Therefore, the need for transparency and communication is greater for businesses than ever before. Toyota was seeking to expand in different countries and increase its production in plants in some countries, such as the U.S. and Japan. The high rate of growth may have led to concealing some of the information about safety and ignoring minor issues that did not gain much public attention. Toyota may have overlooked some safety requirements and not tested its vehicles efficiently enough to ensure a lack of defects before sales. Eventually, this cost the company in terms of revenue, and it had to work hard to create a better image and restore the confidence of its customers. Its fast, extensive growth created an unmanageable risk that spread in various parts of the world. However, the company is now more transparent in its safety procedures and is slowly winning the trust of consumers all over the world.

Endnotes

Case Study 30: Toyota Recall 2010

1 The Economist Intelligence Unit. (2009). *Organizational agility: How business can survive and thrive in turbulent times.* London: The Economist.

2 Grier, S. (2009, March). *5 ways to stay positive in negative situations.* Retrieved from IT Managers Inbox: http://itmanagersinbox.com/1894/5-ways-to-stay-positive-in-negative-situations/

3 The Economist Intelligence Unit. (2009). *Organizational agility: How business can survive and thrive in turbulent times.* London: The Economist.

4 The Economist Intelligence Unit. (2009). *Organizational agility: How business can survive and thrive in turbulent times.* London: The Economist.

5 The Economist Intelligence Unit. (2009). *Organizational agility: How business can survive and thrive in turbulent times.* London: The Economist.

6 The Economist Intelligence Unit. (2009). *Organizational agility: How business can survive and thrive in turbulent times.* London: The Economist.

7 Grier, S. (2009, March). *5 ways to stay positive in negative situations.* Retrieved from IT Managers Inbox: http://itmanagersinbox.com/1894/5-ways-to-stay-positive-in-negative-situations/

8 The Economist Intelligence Unit. (2009). *Organizational agility: How business can survive and thrive in turbulent times.* London: The Economist.

9 The Economist Intelligence Unit. (2009). *Organizational agility: How business can survive and thrive in turbulent times.* London: The Economist.

10 Grier, S. (2009, March). *5 ways to stay positive in negative situations.* Retrieved from IT Managers Inbox: http://itmanagersinbox.com/1894/5-ways-to-stay-positive-in-negative-situations/

Conclusion: Lessons Learned from Crisis Management

While working on this book, I have extensively discussed with my colleagues the various forms of crises that businesses and political systems may face in the course of their operations. Having noted the nature of crises, I have also managed to bring about discussions on their probable impacts on organizations, along with their corresponding measures. Therefore, it is important to also take a look at the lessons that might be learned from the crisis management strategies.

Generally, crisis management includes aspects and strategies that organizations and individuals put in place with the aim of addressing situations deemed to create discomfort and ineffective organizational operations. While looking at a number of organizational crises, different measures were put in place to address key crisis situations; a number of them have proven fruitful, while some have witnessed massive failures in their applications. During 2015, the Chinese stock market faced a crash, but a number of mitigating factors were employed to realize successful crisis management later. The government of China came up with a number of valuable steps, inclusive of limiting the sale of investment stocks on a short-term basis; such conditions were attached to threats of arrest and prosecution. The Chinese administration made good use of the media in trying to rescue their collapsing stock market; the media was the best platform for spreading the campaign, allowing citizens to buy shares from the market to save the situation.

While working on achieving success in crisis mitigation, the U.S. achieved more during its crisis preceding World War II; during that time, the continent was faced with a major economic backlash that left it empty-handed with no ability to even purchase weapons for the war. However, the crisis formed more of an opportunity for the federal government who never perceived this as a mere challenge, but rather an eye-opening opportunity for which they set up construction sites with the aim of improving their infrastructural facilities, such as roads and buildings, while also providing employment opportunities for the large number of citizens who needed to provide food and shelter for their families.

However, there have been instances whereby crisis management never bore any fruit, but rather worsened the situation. While looking at crisis management through the use of social media platforms, many organizations have failed to address actual crisis situations, as they were unable to effectively use the platform. When a social media crisis goes viral, it is important to address it with utmost soberness so that the situation does not spiral out of control.

On the one hand, since 2003, Iraq has failed terribly in managing its crisis; such a failure in crisis management has been attributed to the ineffective constitutional provisions that have not adhered to the policy of natural resource distribution and utilization, thus creating discomfort among the citizens. Major crises in Iraq have emanated from the initial policy formulations of the U.S. that were put in place to salvage the Middle East; the strategies have failed terribly and have never met their intended objectives. However, the U.S. succeeded in destroying the social, economic, and political structures that had existed in Iraq, thus making it a more worthless state than it had been before such mitigation interventions by foreigners.

LESSONS THAT CAN SERVE BUSINESS AND POLITICAL ORGANIZATIONS

Under normal circumstances, there are policy plans that seem to be concerned with technical and political feasibility. The feasibility of a concept during an organizational crisis is always determined by the need to survive politically other than the technical feasibility; this will always be favored by the existence of sufficient political actors with the aim of creating reforms that would likely be adopted. When trying to manage difficult times and survive political pressures, it is prudent to take note of a number of lessons.

There is a need to devote rigor to the management of a crisis prior to and during its occurrence to save organizations. In most cases, people view volatility as being beyond their human control, thus putting them on the edge, compromising sound decision-making, and heightening their emotions. During a crisis, organizations have always moved to overcompensate through the rigorous introduction of new measures, creating mounds of employee data analysis.[1] However, during such times, there is a need for organizations to ensure that all employees at all levels have exercised calm while remaining focused, so as to preserve the daily business environment even during the rough times;

the company is supposed to have energy at such times of stress through the placement of the right controls.

There is a need to ensure that there is no lapse in teamwork and communication; on many occasions, people have withdrawn when trouble brews within their organizations. Such withdrawals in times of crisis will lead to a collapse in the teamwork strategy of crisis management; it is, therefore, important for organizational management to swing fast and provide assurance to anxious employees with lower confidence in the company's directions. Leaders are called upon to be honest, direct, and forthright when handling their employees, while ensuring regular, frequent communications. It is necessary to engage employees in issuing ideas that would be instrumental in solving crises within organizations.

The third lesson that can assist organizations in surviving during a crisis is the idea of being aware of the organizational status quo, particularly whenever things begin to go wrong;[2] in most cases, managers do not recognize the warning signs of a failing organization until it becomes too late to rectify. It is good and ethical to probe the origin of good results, especially when dealing with increased profitability, while realizing that there is no notable change within the organizational model explaining such changes; managers will probe poor organizational results more than they probe the good results, and such a step may be quite problematic when analyzing the financial books in the future.

The survival of an organization requires impartial strategies to be applied to operations in addition to fast response to potential changes within the external and internal environments that would threaten its existence. It is necessary for organizational leaders to be constantly adapting to the ever-changing organizational landscape, shifting the focus from being a market-centered one to a more sustainable one. The organization and its leadership should not undervalue any available information that would be important in the competitive market; a sleeping organization is literally compared to the dinosaurs that had only pinned their survival on winning competitions with the amphibians, but later became extinct due to the challenges put forth by the ever-changing environments. For an organization to survive a crisis and avoid a fatal flaw, it is important that leadership focuses not only on the competitors within the market, but also on the challenges that are brought about by the ever-changing operations environment.

The key to organizational survival during a crisis is based on the challenge and response; it is significant for organizations to focus on the challenges that they face within suitable timelines. Within dynamic market situations, each and every organizational level sees the situations in which they exist as being forms of challenges, and thus the need to establish a creative change management strategy. While this begins to pick up, individuals will no longer be affected individuals who are battling to cope with the changes, but rather people working hard to recover a form of control in whatever they need to concentrate on in trying to achieve individual changes within the group.

PREPARATION BEFORE A CRISIS AND IN THE AFTERMATH

Crisis preparedness is a very crucial step in crisis management, as it reduces the chances of losses that may accrue during the occurrence of a crisis; it is advisable that a well-developed crisis preparedness plan be instituted.

CRISIS MANAGEMENT:
THE ART OF SUCCESS AND FAILURE

Linking to the 9/11 attacks in the U.S., a number of lessons on disaster preparedness have been learned and should be put into use while dealing with any form of crisis. During crisis preparedness, people should always come first; it is the responsibility of leaders to protect the people within their country from catastrophes during and even immediately following disasters. During the Ebola outbreak in Liberia, the major concerns were based on saving citizens from the pandemic that had hit the country.

For crisis preparedness to be effective, better planning procedures and drills are important; according to Fred Becker from the National Association of Federal Credit Unions, the events that followed the 9/11 terrorist attacks displayed the need to carry out proper planning and drills in relation to an imagined crisis that could affect an organization or group of individuals. It is significant to plan for crises and carry out important drills with the aim of reinforcing and putting into practice various kinds of management plans to avoid confusion in the event of a crisis. While making plans for crisis management, it is advisable that complacency be avoided; according to Christian Chuck,[3] complacency is a very dangerous attribute—moreso in the healthcare delivery sector, where there is always a great need for sharing protected patient information. When organizations are well-organized, they may enjoy the benefits accrued from expertise in data security and communication during data breach events.

In crisis preparation, it is necessary that one think about the unthinkable. This supernormal kind of thinking will enable organizations to adequately handle a crisis situation that initially appears to be beyond their capabilities. Therefore, it is important that an organization has an updated crisis plan with the ability to tackle the unthinkable nature of crises, the ability to update, and the aim of preparing the organization for potential challenges that come in due course.

THE GOLDEN RULES OF PERSONAL ATTITUDES UNDER PRESSURE SITUATIONS

Within the business and political realms, we are often faced with challenging situations that create a feeling of crisis within us and the organization as a whole; even though it might be difficult to remain positive through such challenges, it is important to remain professional when reacting to adverse situations. When handling pressurized situations and crises, it is important to have a positive approach, as any negative reaction will only worsen the case, creating disappointment and anger. This is a valuable skill to learn as a business manager, so as to uphold a professional reputation.

In crisis management, there are rules that are quite important in ensuring that crisis situations are arrested. The first rule is the control of the responses given at critical times; as noted above, it is a golden rule to always remain positive in negative situations. It is advisable that one try to stay outside of the frame of negativity being experienced. Becoming relaxed after the first wave of crisis hits is a challenging matter, but it is a must before any press conference or media interviews. If one gives a response out of emotion, this will only worsen the situation. It is prudent to apply Thumper's rule: "If you cannot say anything positive, then do not say it at all." This could serve as good advice when one finds himself or herself in a negative situation, so as to avoid the stress that comes with such situations;[4] therefore, it is important to learn how to deal with stress to avoid such negativity and pressure.

The second rule here states, "Learn from negative situations." Not only do such situations come in the form of crises and problems, but they can also appear as opportunities through which the affected individuals may be able to learn how to reenergize and handle such crises. It is advisable that we look at a negative situation in the form of an opportunity through which one is able to learn and grow. According to Albert Einstein, "In the midst of difficulty lies opportunity." Thus, is inadvisable to channel one's energy toward negative reactions, but rather into something positive that could improve the crisis situation. If one does react negatively, then it will be necessary to learn from such a reaction to check on the causal agents so that such mistakes can be avoided in the future.

Immediately after a crisis, the victims should come out stronger than they were before it happened; in most cases, a crisis should provide a situation for deriving an opportunity for success, as it will highlight the various loopholes within the organization that would make management wiser and more responsive to a new wave of challenges that might strike the organization. The results of crises in organizations have always acted as turning points for such entities to address their different weaknesses.

Conclusion: Lessons Learned from Crisis Management

Endnotes

Conclusion: Lessons Learned from Crisis Management

1 The Economist Intelligence Unit. (2009). *Organizational agility: How business can survive and thrive in turbulent times.* London : The Economist.

2 The Economist Intelligence Unit. (2009). *Organizational agility: How business can survive and thrive in turbulent times.* London : The Economist.

3 Grier, S. (2009, March 02). *5 Ways to Stay Positive in Negative Situations.* Retrieved from IT Managers Inbox: http://itmanagersinbox.com/1894/5-ways-to-stay-positive-in-negative-situations.

4 Grier, S. (2009, March 02). *5 Ways to Stay Positive in Negative Situations.* Retrieved from IT Managers Inbox: http://itmanagersinbox.com/1894/5-ways-to-stay-positive-in-negative-situations.

References

- Abaza, M. (2014). Post January revolution Cairo: Urban wars and the reshaping of public space. *Theory, Culture & Society*, 0263276414549264.

- Ackerman, R. H. & Maslin-Ostrowski, P. (2002). *The wounded leader: How real leadership emerges in times of crisis. The Jossey-Bass Education Series*. San Francisco, CA: Jossey-Bass, Inc.

- Adair, J. E. (2005). *How to grow leaders: The seven key principles of effective leadership development*. Kogan Page Publishers.

- Adams, S. (2014). Did Sony do the right thing when it pulled "the interview"? *Forbes.com*, 7. Retrieved from http://search.ebscohost.com/login.aspx?direct=true&db=buh&AN=100126504&site=ehost-live

- Aliber, R. Z., Kindleberger, C. P., & Kindleberger, C. P. (2011). *Manias, panics, and crashes: A history of financial crises*. New York: Palgrave Macmillan.

- Allen, K. (2015). Why is China's stock market falling and how might it affect the global economy? Retrieved from http://www.theguardian.com/business/2015/aug/24/china-stock-market-fall-effects-global-economy-shares-interest-rates-inflation

- Arsenault, A. (2014, October). *Liberia's Ellen Johnson Sirleaf says Ebola was like "unknown enemy."* Retrieved from http://www.cbc.ca/news/world/liberia-s-ellen-johnson-sirleaf-says-ebola-was-like-unknown-enemy-1.2785503

- Associated Press. (2012, January). *Cancer charity halts grants to Planned Parenthood*. Retrieved December 14, 2015, from http://www.foxnews.com/us/2012/01/31/cancer-charity-halts-grants-to-planned-parenthood-1227146736/

- Auer, M. R. (2011). The policy sciences of social media. *The Policy Studies Journal, 39*(4), 707–736.

- Augustine, N. R. (2000). Managing the crisis you tried to prevent. Harvard Business Review, 73(6), 147.

- Australian Politics. (n.d.). *Pressure groups and democracy*. Retrieved from: http://australianpolitics.com/democracy-and-politics/pg/pressure-groups-and-democracy

- Authers, J. (2012). *Europe's financial crisis: A short guide to how the euro fell into crisis and the consequences for the world*. FT Press.

- Avey, J. B., Palanski, M. E., & Walumbwa, F. O. (2011). When leadership goes unnoticed: The moderating role of follower self-esteem on the relationship between ethical leadership and follower behavior. *Journal of Business Ethics, 98*(4), 573–582.

- Aviation Safety Network. (2013). *Accident description.* Retrieved from http://aviation-safety.net/database/record.php?id=20130722-0

- Avolio, B. J., & Yammarino, F. J. (Eds.). (2013). *Transformational and charismatic leadership: The road ahead* (Vol. 5). Emerald Group Publishing.

- Avsar, V., & Unal, U. (2014). Trading effects of the FIFA World Cup. *Kyklos, 67*(3), 315–329.

- Ayyub, B. M. (2011). *Vulnerability, uncertainty, and risk: Analysis, modeling, and management.* Reston, VA: American Society of Civil Engineers.

- Barkey, H. J., Lasensky, S., & Marr, P. (2011). *Iraq, its neighbors, and the United States: Competition, crisis, and the reordering of power.* Washington, D.C.: United States Institute of Peace.

- Barton, M. J. (2013). *Crisis preparedness for professionals.* U.S.A.: Independent Publisher.

- BBC News. (2014). Costa Concordia: What happened. Retrieved from http://www.bbc.co.uk/news/world-europe-16563562

- BBC. (2011). *Q&A: What's the BA dispute about?* Retrieved from http://www.bbc.com/news/business-11868081

- BBC.com. (2015). *Syria: The story of the conflict.* Retrieved from http://www.bbc.com/news/world-middle-east26116868

- Bello, W. (2015). China's stock market crash is the latest crisis of global capitalism. Retrieved from http://www.commondreams.org/views/2015/10/02/chinas-stock-market-crash-latest-crisis-global-capitalism

- Bernanke, B. (2013). *The Federal Reserve and the financial crisis*. Princeton University Press.

- Bigas, H., & Institute for Water, Environment and Health. (2012). *The global water crisis: Addressing an urgent security issue*. Hamilton, Ont: United Nations University—Institute for Water, Environment and Health.

- Birgfeld, R. (2010). Focus:Why crisis management and social media must co-exist. *SmartBlog–on Social Media*.

- Blythe, B. T. (2004, July). The human side of crisis management. *Occupational Hazards*, Retrieved from www.cmiatl.com

- Blythe, N. (2010, September). How did Lehman's collapse affect the world of finance? BBC News. Retrieved February 05, 2016, from http://www.bbc.com/news/business-11310143.

- Boin, A. (2005). *The politics of crisis management: Public leadership under pressure*. Cambridge University Press.

- Borremans, P. (2010). Ready for anything: Support and enhance your crisis communication plan with social media. *Communication World*, 31–33.

References

- Boulos, M. N. K., Resch, B., Crowley, D. N., Breslin, J. G., Sohn, G., Burtner, R.... & Chuang, K. Y. S. (2011). Crowdsourcing, citizen sensing & sensor web technologies for public & environmental health surveillance and crisis management: Trends, OGC standards & application examples. *International Journal of Health Geographics, 10*(1), 67.

- Brecher, M. (2013). *Crises in world politics: Theory and reality*. Elsevier.

- Brønn, P. S., & Berg, R. W. (2011) *Corporate communication: A strategic approach to building reputation* (2nd ed.). Oslo: Gyldendal Akademisk.

- Brown, R. (2009). *Public relations and the social web: How to use social media and Web 2.0 in communications*, [e-book]. London: Kogan Page Limited.

- Calamur, K. (2015, November). The economic impact of the European refugee crisis. *The Atlantic*. Retrieved from http://www.theatlantic.com/international/archive/2015/11/economic-impact-european-refugee-crisis/414364/

- Carrion, D. (2015, September). Syrian refugees are not the security threat that they are feared to be. *Chatham House*. Retrieved December 23, 2015, from https://www.chathamhouse.org/expert/comment/syrian-refugees-are-not-security-threat-they-are-feared-be

- Carroll, A., & Buchholtz, A. (2014). *Business and society: Ethics, sustainability, and stakeholder management*. Cengage Learning.

- Cha, S., & Park, K. (2011). Asiana Boeing 747 freighter crashes in South Korean waters. Bloomberg. Retrieved from http://www.bloomberg.com/news/2011-07-28/asiana-boeing-747-freighter-crashes-inkorean-

- Chang, C. L., Jiménez-Martín, J. Á., McAleer, M., & Perez Amaral, T. (2011). Risk management of risk under the Basel Accord: Forecasting value-at-risk of VIX futures. Available at *SSRN 1765202*.

- Chen, L. C., Liu, Y. C., & Chan, K. C. (2006). Integrated community-based disaster management program in Taiwan: a case study of Shang-An village. *Natural Hazards, 37*(1-2), 209–223.

- ChinaHush. (2011, November). Smashing refrigerators in China. *Business Insider*. Retrieved from http://www.businessinsider.com.au/this-chinese-internet-celebrity-smashed-siemens-fridges-to-protest-their-quality-2011-11

- Choi, H., & Kim, H. (2011). The influence of OPR (organization-public relationships) formed by the usage of Twitter on publics' conflict resolution will. *Journal of PR Research, 15*(3), 5–40.

- Chujian, G. (2011). *Siemens sparks refrigerator rage*. Retrieved from http://www.eeo.com.cn/ens/2011/1124/216405.shtml

- Clark, J., & Harman, M. (2004, May). On crisis management and rehearsing a plan. *Risk Management, 51*(5), 40–44.

- Clifford, S. (2012, January). J.C. Penney to revise pricing methods and limit promotions. *New York Times*, B1.
- Clinton, J. R. (2012). *The making of a leader: Recognizing the lessons and stages of leadership development.* NavPress.
- Coatney, L. (2015, September). *Turning crisis into opportunity: How to make good on big change.* Retrieved from Information Services Group: http://blog.isg-one.com/turning-crisis-into-opportunity-how-to-make-good-on-big-change
- Cohn, R. (2014). *How social media is elevating airline crisis communication.* Retrieved from https://www.linkedin.com/pulse/20140313141909-14626191-how-social-media-is-elevating-airline-crisis-communication.
- Colombo, J. (2015, July). Watch these charts to better understand China's stock market crash. *Forbes*.
- Coombs, W. T. (2010). Parameters for crisis communication. *The handbook of Crisis Communication*, 17–53.
- Coombs, W. T. (2011). *Ongoing crisis communication: Planning, managing and responding.* Sage Publications.
- Coombs, W. T. (2012). *Ongoing crisis communication: Planning, managing, and responding.* Thousand Oaks, CA: Sage.
- Coombs, W. T., & Holladay, S. J. (2012). *The handbook of crisis communication* (1st ed.). Wiley-Blackwell, Oxford: Blackwell Publishing Ltd.

- Coombs, W. T., & Holladay, S. J. (2012). *The handbook of crisis communication*. Chichester, U.K: Wiley-Blackwell.

- Coombs, W. T., & Holladay, S. J. (Eds.). (2011). *The handbook of crisis communication* (Vol. 22). John Wiley & Sons.

- Cooper, H. (2014, October). *Liberia's Ebola crisis puts president in harsh light*. Retrieved from http://www.nytimes.com/2014/10/31/world/africa/liberias-ebola-crisis-puts-president-in-harsh-light.html

- Cordesman, A. H. (1991). *Weapons of mass destruction in the Middle East*. London: Brassey's (UK).

- Corkindale, G. (2010). Five leadership lessons from the BP oil spill. Retrieved from https://hbr.org/2010/06/five-lessons-in-leadership-fro

- Cornelissen, J. (2014). *Corporate communication: A guide to theory and practice*. Sage.

- Cowell, A. (2014, June). *U.K. inquiry finds "Truly Awful" sexual abuse by TV host at medical facilities*. Retrieved from http://www.nytimes.com/2014/06/27/world/europe/britain-jimmy-savile-sexual-abuse.html?_r=0

- Crothers, B. (2014). *Sony to shutter 20 stores in US, implement staff cuts*. Retrieved from http://news.cnet.com/8301-1001_3-57619601-92/sony-to-shutter-20-stores-in-us-implement-staff-cuts/

- Curtis, L., Florance, C., Lohman, W., & Phillips, J. (2014). *Pursuing a freedom agenda amidst rising global Islamism*.

- Daft, R. (2012). *Organization theory and design*. Cengage Learning.
- Daft, R. (2014). *The leadership experience*. Cengage Learning.
- Daily Mail Online. (n.d.). Costa Concordia accident: Pictures of cruise ship sinking off coast of Italy "in Titanic-like scene." Retrieved from http://www.dailymail.co.uk/news/article-2086527/Costa-Concordia-accident-Pictures-cruise-ship-sinking-coast-Italy-Titanic-like-scene.html
- De Wolf, D. (2013). Crisis communication failures: The BP case study. *International Journal of Advances in Management and Economics, 2*(2).
- Denis, J., Lamothe, L., & Langley, A. (2001). The dynamics of collective leadership and strategic change in pluralistic organizations. *Academy of Management Journal, 44*(4), 809–837.
- Deschouwer, K. (2012). *The politics of Belgium: Governing a divided society*. Palgrave Macmillan.
- Detroit. (2013). *The fire this time*. Retrieved from http://www.economist.com/blogs/schumpeter/2013/10/tesla-motors.
- Devlin, E. S. (2007). *Crisis management planning and execution*. Boca Raton, FL: Auerbach.
- Dobnik, V. (2013). Southwest Airlines captain of flight 345 took command before NY accident: NTSB. *The*

Huffington Post. Retrieved from http://www.huffingtonpost.com/2013/08/06/southwest-airlines-captain_n_3716700.html

- Doherty, G. W. (2007). *Crisis intervention training for disaster workers: An introduction*. Ann Arbor, MI: Loving Healing Press.

- Donnelly, J. (2010). Sudden impact: An analysis of five commonly held beliefs about managing crises that erupt online. *The Public Relations Strategist*, Winter 2010, 30–32.

- Dougherty, C. (2008). Stopping a financial crisis, the Swedish way. *New York Times*, 22.

- Drennan, L. T., McConnell, A., & Stark, A. (2014). *Risk and crisis management in the public sector*. Routledge.

- Drennan, L. T., McConnell, A., & Stark, A. (2014). *Risk and crisis management in the public sector*. Routledge.

- Driskell, J. E., & Salas, E. (1991). Group decision making under stress. *Journal of Applied Psychology, 76*(3), 473.

- DuBrin, A. (2015). *Leadership: Research findings, practice, and skills*. Boston, MA: Cengage Learning.

- Dubrovski, D. (2004). *Crisis management and renovation companies*. Koper: Faculty of Management.

- Dubrovski, D. (2010). Management mistakes as causes of corporate crises: Countries in transition. *Managing Global Transitions, 5*(4).

- Easterby-Smith, M., & Lyles, M. A. (Eds.). (2011). *Handbook of organizational learning and knowledge management*. John Wiley & Sons.
- Edison, T. (2014, April). *Turning crisis into opportunity: 5 ways to deal with hardship*. Retrieved from Entrepreneur: http://www.entrepreneur.com/article/232848
- Fagel, M. J. (2013). *Crisis management and emergency planning: Preparing for today's challenges*. U.S.A.: CRC Press.
- Fearn-Banks, K. (2007). *Crisis communications: A casebook approach*. 3rd edition. Mahwah, N.J.: Lawrence Erlbaum Associates.
- Ferrell, O. C., & Fraedrich, J. (2014). *Business ethics: Ethical decision making & cases*. Cengage Learning.
- Fischbacher-Smith, D., & Fischbacher-Smith, M. (2014). When good management theory hits the fan: Crisis management and the challenge to the rational-positivistic paradigm of MBA programmes.
- Fombrun, C. J., & Van Riel, C. B. M. (2003). *Fame and fortune: How the world's top companies develop winning reputations*. Pearson Education.
- Fouche, G. (2011, August). *Why Scandinavia can teach us a thing or two about surviving a recession*. Retrieved from http://www.guardian.co.uk/society/joepublic/2009/aug/05/scandinavia-recession-welfare-state

- Fratianni, M. U., & Marchionne, F. (2009). The role of banks in the subprime financial crisis. *Review of Economic Conditions in Italy, 1*.

- Frost, P. (1985). *Organizational culture.* Beverly Hills: Sage Publications.

- Galasso, V. (2014). The role of political partisanship during economic crises. *Public Choice, 158*(1/2), 143–165.

- Garcia, H. (2006). Effective leadership response to crisis. *Strategy and Leadership, 34*(1), 4–10.

- Gates, S., & Hexter, E. (2005). *From risk management to risk strategy.* New York: The Conference Board.

- Giang, V. (2011, November). Here's why people started hammering fridges outside Siemens' Beijing headquarters. *Business Insider.* Retrieved from http://www.businessinsider.com/siemens-fridge-doors-2011-11

- Glendon, A. I., Clarke, S., & McKenna, E. F. (2006). *Human safety and risk management.* Boca Raton, FL: CRC/Taylor & Francis.

- Godfrey, H. (2012). *Utoya and Oslo terrorist attacks.* New York, USA: Yale University Press.

- Goleman, D., Boyatzis, R., & McKee, A. (2013). *Primal leadership: Unleashing the power of emotional intelligence.* Harvard Business Press.

- González-Herrero, A., & Smith, S. (2008). Crisis communications management on the web: How internal-based technologies are changing the way public relations professionals handle business crises. *Journal of Contingencies and Crisis Management, 16*(3), 143–153.

- Gough, N. (2015, July). Chinese shares tumble again. *The New York Times*.

- Graham, R. (2014). *Accounting scandal made Tesco suppliers call in audit teams*: The Telegram story on Tesco shares losing half their value in 2014.

- Graham, R. (2014). Tesco crisis: Everything you need to know. *The Telegram*.

- Graham, R., & Ben, M. (2014). The investigation into Tesco's £250m profit shortfall unearths corruption of culture. *The Telegram News*.

- Green, R. L. (2012). *Practicing the art of leadership: A problem-based approach to implementing the ISLLC standards*. Pearson Higher Ed.

- Greenberg, J., & Elliott, C. (2009). A cold cut crisis: Listeriosis, Maple Leaf Foods, and the politics of apology. *Canadian Journal of Communication, 34*(2), 189–204.

- Greenglass, E., Antonides, G., Christandl, F., Foster, G., Katter, J. K., Kaufman, B. E., & Lea, S. E. (2014). The financial crisis and its effects: Perspectives from economics and psychology. *Journal of Behavioral and Experimental Economics, 50*, 10–12.

- Greenpeace. (2014). *LEGO: Everything is NOT awesome*. Retrieved from https://www.youtube.com/watch?v=qhbliUq0_r4

CRISIS MANAGEMENT:
THE ART OF SUCCESS AND FAILURE

- Greenspan, A. (2007). *The age of turbulence: Adventures in a new world.* Sydney: Allen Lane.

- Grier, S. (2009, March 02). *5 Ways to Stay Positive in Negative Situations.* Retrieved from IT Managers Inbox: http://itmanagersinbox.com/1894/5-ways-to-stay-positive-in-negative-situations.

- Gunther, R., Seitchik, M., Parayre, R., Schuurmans, F., & Schramm, J. (2005). *2015: Scenarios on the future of human resource management.* Alexandria, VA: Society for Human Resource Management.

- Hagar, C. (2012). *Crisis information management: Communication and technologies.* Oxford, UK: Chandos Pub.

- Hagman, H. C. (2013). *European crisis management and defence: The search for capabilities* (No. 353). Routledge.

- Hamilton, S., & Micklethwait, A. (2006). *Greed and corporate failure.* New York: Palgrave Macmillan.

- Hanna, J. (2008, March). *JetBlue's Valentine's Day crisis.* Harvard Business School. Retrieved from http://hbswk.hbs.edu/item/jetblues-valentines-day-crisis

- Hanna, R., Rohn, A., and Crittenden, V.L. (2011). We're all connected: The power of the social media ecosystem. *Business Horizons,* [online] 54(3), 265–273.

- Hartley, R. F. (2005). *Management mistakes and success.* New York: Wiley.

- Hayes, J. (2014). *The theory and practice of change management.* Palgrave Macmillan.

- Hendrikse, R. P., & Sidaway, J. D. (2014). Financial wizardry and the Golden City: Tracking the financial crisis through Pforzheim, Germany. *Transactions of the Institute of British Geographers, 39*(2), 195–208.

- Hensen, T., Desouza, K. C., & Kraft, G. D. (2003). Games, signal detection, and processing in the context of crisis management. *Journal of Contingencies and Crisis Management, 11*(2), 67–72.

- Herbane, B., Elliott, D., & Swartz, E. M. (2004). Business continuity management: Time for a strategic role? *Long Range Planning, 37*(5), 435–457.

- Herriot, P., & Pemberton, C. (1995). *Competitive advantage through diversity: Organizational learning from difference.* London: Sage Publications.

- Hess, P. (2015, November). *How likely is a financial crisis in China?* Retrieved from The Diplomat: http://thediplomat.com/2015/11/how-likely-is-a-financial-crisis-in-china/

- Hewitt Associates LLC. (2004, March). *Communicating with employee during times of crisis.* Retrieved September 2, 2005, from www.hewitt.com.

- Higgins, G., & Freedman, J. (2013). Improving decision making in crisis. *Journal of Business Continuity & Emergency Planning, 7*(1), 65–76.

- Hooghe, M. (2012). The political crisis in Belgium (2007–2011): A federal system without federal loyalty. *Representation, 48*(1), 131–138.

- Hughey, S. (2015). Social media, football, and crisis: An exploratory case study examining the FIFA World Cup addressing player concussions. *Journal of Media Critiques, 1*(4), 51–65.

- Huttl, P., & Leandro, A. (2015, October). How will refugees affect European economies? *Bruegel.* Retrieved December 22, 2015, from http://bruegel.org/2015/10/how-will-refugees-affect-european-economies/

- IBM. (2015). *Build a viable plan for disaster recovery and crisis management.* Retrieved from https://www-935.ibm.com/services/au/gts/pdf/disasterrecovery-crisisplanningsolution.pdf.

- ISDR, U. (2005, March). Hyogo framework for action 2005-2015: Building the resilience of nations and communities to disasters. In *Extract from the Final Report of the World Conference on Disaster Reduction (A/CONF. 206/6)*.

- Jahangiri, K., et al. (2011). A comparative study on community-based disaster management in selected countries and designing a model for Iran. *Disaster Prevention and Management, 20*(1), 82–94.

- Jalabi, R. (2015, July). *Guinea's president on global aid push: "Ebola forced us to change completely".* Retrieved from http://www.theguardian.com/world/2015/jul/12/guinea-president-alpha-conde-ebola-aid

References

- Jansen, B. (2015, July). NTSB: Southwest nose landing at LaGuardia was captain's fault. *USA Today*. Retrieved from http://www.usatoday.com/story/news/2015/07/27/ntsb-southwest-nose-landing-laguardia/30736777/

- Janssen, M. A., & Ostrom, E. (2006). Resilience, vulnerability and adaptation: A cross-cutting theme of the International Human Dimensions Programme on Global Environmental Change. *Global Environmental Change Part B: Environmental Hazards, 16*, 2.

- Jaques, T. (2012). Crisis leadership: A view from the executive suite. *Journal of Public Affairs, 12*(4), 366–372.

- Jennex, M. E. (2012). *Managing crises and disasters with emerging technologies: Advancements*. Hershey, PA: Information Science Reference.

- Jenny, A. (2014). The accounting scandal in Tesco draws scrutiny of serious fraud office in Britain. *International Business*.

- Jick, T. D. (1979). *Process and impacts of a merger: Individual and organizational perspectives* (Doctoral dissertation, ProQuest Information & Learning).

- Johansen, W., & Frandsen, F. (2007). *Krisekommunikation: Når virksomhedens image og omdømme er truet*. Samfundslitteratur.

- Johnson, C. E. (2013). *Meeting the ethical challenges of leadership: Casting light or shadow*. Sage Publications.

- Jones, E. (2009). The euro and the financial crisis. *Survival, 51*(2), 41-54.

- Jørgensen, K. E. (1997). *European approaches to crisis management*. The Hague: Kluwer Law International.

- Karanikolos, M., Mladovsky, P., Cylus, J., Thomson, S., Basu, S., Stuckler, D., & McKee, M. (2013). Financial crisis, austerity, and health in Europe. *The Lancet, 381*(9874), 1323–1331.

- Kash, T. J., & Darling, J. R. (1998). Crisis management: Prevention, diagnosis and intervention. *Leadership & Organization Development Journal, 19*(4), 179.

- Kash, T. J., & Darling, J. R. (1998). Crisis management: Prevention, diagnosis and intervention. *Leadership & Organization Development Journal, 19*(4), 179.

- Kellerman, B. (2012, December). Lax leadership. Retrieved from http://barbarakellerman.com/lax-leadership

- Kickert, W. (2012). State responses to the fiscal crisis in Britain, Germany and the Netherlands. *Public Management Review, 14*(3), 299–309.

- Kieny, M., Evans, D. B., Schmets, G., & Kadandale, S. (2014). Health-system resilience: Reflections on the Ebola crisis in western Africa. *Bulletin of the World Health Organization, 92*(12), 849–924.

- Kilmann, R., Saxton, M., & Serpa, R. (1986). Issues in understanding and changing culture. *California Management Review, 28*, 87–94.

- Kirke, L. (2012). What caused the failure of Lehman Brothers? Could it have been prevented? *SSRN Electronic Journal.*

- Kollewe, J., & Duggan, J. (2015, July). China stocks bounce back after days of panic selling among investors. *The Guardian.*

- Korosi, K., & Brown, K. (2014). Sporting events as sites of international law, society, and governance: The 2014 Brazilian World Cup. *Southwestern Journal of International Law, 21*(8), 2–28.

- Kovoor-Mısra, S., Zammuta, Raymond F., & Mitroff, Ian I. (2000). Crisis preparation in organizations: Prescription versus reality. *Technological Forecasting and Social Change, 63,* 43–62.

- Kozlowski, C. (2010, January). Crisis management. *Crisis Control Newsletter from RQA, Inc.—A Catlin Preferred Provider to Foodservice, Food Processing and Consumer Products Industries. U0110*(1).

- Kumpikaite, V., Grybauskas, A., Juodelis, M., & Strumyla, D. (2011). Companies' management during economic crisis. *Economics and Management, 16,* 789–795.

- Kuzgun, I. A. (2010). The temporary lay-off as an instrument in crisis management: Case of Turkey. *International Journal of Emerging and Transition Economies, 3*(2), 195–207.

- Lakhal, S. Y. (2014). Morsi's failure in Egypt: The impact of energy-supply chains. *Middle East Policy, 21*(3), 134–144.

- Larsson, G., Johansson, A., Jansson, T., & Grönlund, G. (2001). Leadership under severe stress: A grounded theory study. *Concepts for Air Force Leadership*, 441–447.

- Latif, M., Gulzar, H., Bukhari, S. R., & Sameen, S. N. (2014). Starbucks sustained during economic crisis. *International Journal of Accounting and Financial Reporting*, 4(1), 307.

- Lawrence, D. (2011). A digital crisis is coming your way. Are you ready? *Forbes*.

- Lawrence, E., Alexander, C., & Geoffrey, G. (2014). *Risk management and crisis response: Tesco's accounting scandal a lesson for all public companies.*

- Lee, M. (2006). *New directions? A view from multiple perspectives.* Unpublished Thesis. Queensland University of Technology.

- Lee, S., & Kim, D. (2012). The impact of using social media with political purposes on the intention of political participation of social media users. *Journal of PR Research*, 16(1), 78–111.

- Lerbinger, O. (2012). *The crisis manager*. London: Routledge.

- Lerbinger, O. (2012). *The crisis manager*. Routledge.

- Levitt, B., & March, J. (1988). Organizational learning. *Annual Review of Sociology*, 14, 319–340.

- Lewis, G. W. (2006). *Organizational crisis management: The human factor*. Boca Raton: Auerbach Publications.

- López-Marrero, T., & Tschakert, P. (2011). From theory to practice: Building more resilient communities in flood-prone areas. *Environment and Urbanization, 23*, 229–249.

- MacEwan, A., & Miller, J. (2011). *Economic collapse, economic change: Getting to the roots of the crisis*. Armonk, N.Y.: M.E. Sharpe.

- Maital, S., & Seshadri, D. V. R. (2012). *Innovation management*. Sage.

- Malloch, T. R., & Mamorsky, J. D. (2013). *The end of ethics and a way back: How to fix a fundamentally broken global financial system*. Singapore: Wiley.

- Maskrey, A. (2011). Revisiting community-based disaster risk management. *Environmental Hazards, 10*, 42–52.

- Mazeel, M. A. (2011). *Iraq oil and gas papers 2010*. Hamburg: Disserta-Verl.

- McMains, M. J., & Mullins, W. C. (2014). *Crisis negotiations: Managing critical incidents and hostage situations in law enforcement and corrections*. Routledge.

- Mei, J. S. A., Bansal, N., and Pang, A. (2010). New media: A new medium in escalating crises? *Corporate Communications*, [online] *15*(2), 143–155.

- Mejri, M., & Daniel, D. E. (2013). Crisis management: Lessons learnt from the BP Deepwater Horizon spill oil. *Business Management and Strategy, 4*(2), 67.

- Mishra, A. K. (1996). Organizational responses to crisis. *Trust in Organizations. Frontiers of Theory and Research*, 261–287.

- Mitroff, I. (2005). *Why some companies emerge stronger and better from a crisis: 7 essential lessons for surviving disaster.* New York: American Management Association.

- Mitroff, I. (2005). *Why some companies emerge stronger and better from a crisis: 7 essential lessons for surviving disaster.* New York: American Management Association.

- Mitroff, I. I. (2004). *Crisis leadership: Planning for the unthinkable.* John Wiley & Sons Inc.

- Molyneux, J. (2015). Lessons from the Egyptian Revolution. *Irish Marxist Review, 4*(13), 18–32.

- Moore, S., & Seymour, M. (2005). *Global technology and corporate crisis.* London: Routledge.

- Murad, A. (2014). *Sony, Microsoft battle hackers as gamers question their call of duty.* Retrieved from http://www.ft.com/intl/cms/s/0/b7d3d47a-8ce4-11e4-9f52-00144feabdc0.html#axzz3fE5G95G7

- Nestle, M. (2013). *Food politics: How the food industry influences nutrition and health* (Vol. 3). Univ of California Press.

- Noah, D. (2015). The series of scandals have not only tainted FIFA but undermined trust in the game as well. *Americas Quarterly*. Retrieved December 24, 2015, from http://www.americasquarterly.org/content/series-scandals-have-not-only-tainted-fifa-undermined-trust-game-well

- NY Daily News. (n.d.). 5 convicted for Costa Concordia shipwreck. Retrieved from http://www.nydailynews.com/news/crime/5-convicted-costa-concordia-shipwreck-article-1.1404333

- Ofek, E., & Avery, J. (2013). J.C. Penny's "fair and square" pricing strategy. *Harvard Business School*.

- Okunogbe, A. (2015). *What the Ebola crisis taught us about emergency preparedness in Africa*. Retrieved from http://www.rand.org/blog/2015/06/what-the-ebola-crisis-taught-us-about-emergency-preparedness.html

- Olsson, E. (2014). Crisis communication in public organizations: Dimensions of crisis communication revisited. *Journal of Contingencies and Crisis Management, 22*(2), 113–125.

- Owram, K. (2009, October). Maple Leaf Foods recovers from listeria crisis. *The Star*. Retrieved from http://www.thestar.com/business/2009/10/28/maple_leaf_foods_recovers_from_listeria_crisis.html

- Ōyama, T. (2010). *Post-crisis risk management: Bracing for the next perfect storm*. Singapore: John Wiley & Sons.

- Palen, L., & Liu, S. B. (2007). Citizen communications in crisis: Anticipating a future of ICT-supported public participation.

- Palen, L., & Liu, Sophia B. (2007). Citizen communications in crisis: Anticipating a future of ICT-supported participation. *Proceedings of the ACM Conference on Human Factors in Computing Systems*, CHI 2007, 727–736.

- Pandey, B., & Okazaki, K. (2005). Community based disaster management: Empowering communities to cope with disaster risks. *Regional Development Dialogue*, 26(2).

- Paraskevas, A. (2006), Crisis management or crisis response system? A complexity science approach to organizational crises. *Management Decision*, 44(7), 892–907.

- Parent M., Plangger, K. & Bal, A. (2011). The New WTP: Willingness to Participate. *Business Horizons*, [online] 54(3), 219–229.

- Park, H., & Reber, B. H. (2012). The organization-public relationship and crisis communication: The effect of the organization-public relationship on public's perceptions of crisis and attitudes toward the organization. *International Journal of Strategic Communication*, 5, 240–260.

- Perera, L. C. J., Lenk, H. U., de Souza Corrêa, M., Yoshikawa, A. N., Silva, A. A. G. D., & Arasaki, R. K. (2012). Effects of the 2007 financial crisis on Starbucks. *Journal of International Business Strategy*, 12(1).

References

- Pettigrew, A. M. (2014). *The politics of organizational decision-making*. Routledge.

- Pettinger, T. (2015). Impact of Chinese stock market crash. Retrieved from http://www.economicshelp.org/blog/14212/growth/impact-of-chinese-stock-market-crash/

- Pillai, R. & Meindl, J. R. (1998). Context and charisma: A "meso" level examination of the relationship of organic structure, collectivism, and crisis to charismatic leadership. *Journal of Management, 24*(5), 643–671.

- Ponder, M. (2013). *Susan G. Komen and the national women's healthcare debate: A crisis communication case study*. Atlanta, GA: National Conference on Health Communication, Marketing and Media.

- Pritchard, C. (2015). Can the ambush of Greenpeace be seen as a method of ambush marketing, and if so, what (if any) effect did it have? *Laws of the Game, 1*(1), 5.

- Qualman, E. (2009). *Socialnomics: How social media transforms the way we live and do business*. NJ: Wiley.

- Quora. (2013, February). *What are the main reasons India survived the global economic recession of 2008*. Retrieved from https://www.quora.com/What-are-the-main-reasons-India-survived-the-global-economic-recession-of-2008

- Rachman, G. (2015, November). Refugees or migrants—what's in a word? *Financial Times*. Retrieved from http://blogs.ft.com/the-world/2015/09/refugees-or-migrants-whats-in-a-word/

- Ranter, H. (2008). ASN aircraft accident Boeing 737-5Lp HL7229 Mokpo. *Aviation Safety Network Review*, 24(6), 12–15.

- Reestorff, C. M. (2015). "LEGO: Everything is not awesome!" A conversation about mediatized activism, Greenpeace, Lego, and Shell. *Conjunctions. Transdisciplinary Journal of Cultural Participation*, 2(1), 21–43.

- Regester, M., & Larkin, J. (2005). *Risk issues and crisis management: A casebook of best practice.* Sterling, VA: Kogan Page US.

- Regester, M., & Larkin, J. (2005). *Risk issues and crisis management: A casebook of best practice.* London: Kogan Page.

- Reid, J. (2000). *Crisis management planning and media relations for construction and engineering firms.* New York: Wiley.

- Reinhart, C. M., & Rogoff, K. S. (2014). *Recovery from financial crises: Evidence from 100 episodes* (No. w19823). National Bureau of Economic Research.

- Ritchie, B. W. (2009). *Crisis and disaster management for tourism.* Bristol, UK: Channel View Publications.

- Rodríguez, H., & Aguirre, B. (2005). Education, sustainable development, and disasters: An interactive and collaborative approach. *Preliminary paper #350*, University of Delaware, Disaster Research Center.

- Rosenkopf, L., & Nerkar, A. (2001). Beyond local search: Boundary spanning, exploration, and impact in the operational disk industry. *Strategic Journal Management, 22*, 19.

- Rosenthal, U., Boin, A., & Comfort, L. K. (2001). *Managing crises: Threats, dilemmas, opportunities*. Charles C Thomas Publisher.

- Roux-Dufort, C. (2003). *Gérer et décider en situation de crise*. Paris: Dunod.

- Ruse, A. (2013, June). *What really happened at the Komen Foundation*. Retrieved December 14, 2015, from http://www.crisismagazine.com/2013/what-really-happened-at-the-komen-foundation

- Russell, R. F. & Gregory Stone, A. (2002). A review of servant leadership attributes: Developing a practical model. *Leadership & Organization Development Journal, 23*(3), 145–157.

- Salman, S. (2014). For freedom or security? A critical appraisal of Egypt's unfinished revolution. *Situations: Project of the Radical Imagination, 5*(2).

- Scancomark. (2013, June). *More evidence that Sweden survived the economic crisis best*. Retrieved January 2016, from http://scancomark.com/Market/More-evidence-that-Sweden-survived-the-economic-crisis-best-105013062013

- Schafer, M., & Crichlow, S. (2013). *Groupthink versus high-quality decision making in international relations*. Columbia University Press.

- Schapiro, M. (2010). *Lehman Brothers examiner's report: Congressional testimony*. DIANE Publishing.

- Schultz, F., Utz, S., & Goritz, A. (2011). Is the medium the message? Perceptions of and reactions to crisis communication via Twitter, blogs and traditional media. *Public Relations Review, 37*, 20-27.

- Schultz, H., & Jones Yang, D. (1999). *Pour your heart into it: How Starbucks built a company one cup at a time*. Hyperion.

- Scientific research. (2010, November). Retrieved from http://www.SciRP.org/journal/me

- Seeger, M. W., & Ulmer, R.R. (2001). Virtuous responses to organizational responses to organizational crisis: Aaron Feuestein and Milt Cole. *Journal of Business Ethics, 31*, 369-376.

- Seeger, M. W., Sellnow, T. L., & Ulmer, R. R. (2012). Communication, organization, and crisis. *Communication Yearbook, 21*, 231.

- Seeger, M. W., Sellnow, T. L., & Ulmer, R. R. (2012). Communication, organization, and crisis. *Communication Yearbook, 21*, 231.

- Seeger, M., Sellnow, T., & Ulmer, R. (1998). Communication, organization, and crisis. *Communication Yearbook, 21*, 231-275.

- Senge, P. (1990). *The fifth discipline*. New York: Doubleday.

References

- Seybolt, T. B. (2008). *Humanitarian military intervention: The conditions for success and failure.* Oxford: Oxford University Press.

- Shang, L. (2007). The crisis of Starbucks "brand problem." Globrand, accessed, 1.

- Sheel, A. (2015, October). How India's central bank has survived a global crisis of confidence. Retrieved from Afrweekend: http://www.afr.com/opinion/how-indias-central-bank-has-survived-a-global-crisis-of-confidence-20151011-gk676b

- Shiller, R. J. (2012). *The subprime solution: How today's global financial crisis happened, and what to do about it.* Princeton University Press.

- Sieghart, W., Hucke, F., Pinter, M., Graziadei, I., Vogel, W., Müller, C., & Peck-Radosavljevic, M. (2013). The ART of decision making: Retreatment with transarterial chemoembolization in patients with hepatocellular carcinoma. *Hepatology, 57*(6), 2261–2273.

- Simon, D. R. (2013). *Meatonomics: How the rigged economics of meat and dairy make you consume too much–and how to eat better, live longer, and spend smarter.* Conari Press.

- Smith, B., & Villarreal, K. (2015). Hire, fire, re-hire: The case of J.C. Penney's decision to fire CEO Ron Johnson. *Journal of International Academic Research for Multimedia Disciplinary, 3*(7), 190–197.

- Smith, D., & Sipika, C. (1993). Back from the brink: Post crisis management. *Long Range Planning, 26*(1), 10.

- Smout, E. (2015, April). *Communicating in a crisis like Ebola: Facts and figures.* Retrieved from http://www.scidev.net/global/ebola/feature/communicating-crisis-ebola-facts-figures.html

- Snedaker, S., & Rima, C. (2014). *Business continuity and disaster recovery planning for IT professionals.* Waltham, MA: Syngress.

- Snowden, D. J., & Boone, M. E. (2007). A leader's framework for decision making. *Harvard Business Review, 85*(11), 68.

- Snyder, G. H., & Diesing, P. (2015). *Conflict among nations: Bargaining, decision making, and system structure in international crises.* Princeton University Press.

- Society for Human Resource Management. (2005). *Glossary of human resource terms.* Retrieved from www.shrm.org/hrresources/hrglossary_published

- Solis, B., & Breakenridge, D. (2009). *Putting the public back in public relations. How social media is reinventing the aging business of PR.* FT Press.

- Sorcha, P. (2015, May). LÉ Eithne to be dispatched in migrant search on May 8th. *Irish Times.*

- Spreitzer, G., & Quinn, R. (2001). *A company of leaders: Five disciplines for unleashing the power of your workforce.* San Francisco: Jossey-Bass.

References

- Starla, M. (2011). *Tragedy in Norway: Oslo bombing.* Cambridge, UK: Cambridge University Press.

- Stein, M. R., & Rawles, J. W. (2011). *When disaster strikes: A comprehensive guide for emergency planning and crisis survival.* U.S.A.: Chelsea Green Publishing.

- Steinmeier, F.-W., & Gabriel, S. (2015, August). How the EU can solve the migrant crisis, in ten points. *The Telegraph.* Retrieved from http://www.telegraph.co.uk/news/uknews/immigration/11822752/How-the-EU-can-solve-the-migrant-crisis-in-ten-points.html

- Storm, S., & Naastepad, C. W. M. (2015). Crisis and recovery in the German economy: The real lessons. *Structural Change and Economic Dynamics, 32,* 11–24.

- Sugden, J., & Tomlinson, A. (1998). *FIFA and the contest for world football.* Cambridge, UK: Polity Press.

- Sun, L. K. (2012, February). *Susan G. Komen foundation takes steps to rebuild trust after PR fiasco.* Retrieved December 14, 2015, from https://www.washingtonpost.com/national/health-science/2012/02/04/gIQAdljRqQ_story.html

- Svedin, L. (2009). *Organizational cooperation in crises.* Farnham, England: Ashgate Pub.

- Swenden, W. (2013). Conclusion: The future of Belgian federalism—Between reform and swansong? 2007–11: A critical juncture in the transformation of the Belgian state? *Regional & Federal Studies, 23*(3), 369–382.

- Tanase, D. (2012). Procedural and systematic crisis approach and crisis management. *Theoretical and Applied Economics, 5*(5), 177.

- Taylor, M., & Perry, D. (2005). Diffusion of traditional and new media tactics in crisis communication. *Public Relations Review, 31*(2), 209–217.

- Tesla. (2013a). Tesla Model S achieves best safety rating of any car ever tested. Retrieved from http://ir.teslamotors.com/releasedetail.cfm?releaseid=786136

- Tharoor, S. (2010, August). *How India survived the financial crisis.* Retrieved from Project syndicate: https://www.quora.com/What-are-the-main-reasons-India-survived-the-global-economic-recession-of-2008

- The Business Roundtable. (2005, February). *Committed to protecting America: CEO guide to security challenges.* Washington, D.C.: Author.

- The Economist Intelligence Unit. (2009). *Organizational agility: How business can survive and thrive in turbulent times.* London: The Economist.

- The Economist Intelligence Unit. (2009). *Organizational agility: How business can survive and thrive in turbulent times.* London : The Economist.

- Trueman, C. (2015, May). *What are pressure groups.* Retrieved from The History Learning Site: http://www.historylearningsite.co.uk/british-politics/pressure-groups/what-are-pressure-groups/

- Turner, J. R. (2014). *The handbook of project-based management* (Vol. 92). McGraw-Hill.

- Tziarras, Z. (2014, July). The Iraq crisis and its geopolitical implications. *E-International Relations*.

- United Nations. (2011). Revealing risk, redefining development. *Global Assessment Report on Disaster Risk Reduction* (GAR). Retrieved from www.preventionweb.net/english/hyogo/gar/2011/en/home/

- Valdes-Dapena, P. (2013, May). Tesla: Consumer Reports' best car ever tested. CNN, [online].. Retrieved from http://money.cnn.com/2013/05/09/autos/tesla-model-s-consumer-reports

- Van de Walle, S., Thijs, N., & Bouckaert, G. (2005). A tale of two charters: Political crisis, political realignment and administrative reform in Belgium. *Public Management Review*, 7(3), 367–390.

- Various. (2014). *Open letter to Michael Lynton, Sony Pictures Entertainment Chairman and CEO re: The interview*. Retrieved from http://www.pen.org/blog/open-letter-michael-lynton-sony-pictures-entertainment-chairman-and-ceo-re-interview

- Veil, S. R., Buehner, T., & Palenchar, M. J. (2011). A work-in-process literature review: Incorporating social media in risk and crisis communication. *Journal of Contingencies and Crisis Management*, 19(2), 110–122.

- Venette, S. J. (2003). *Risk communication in a high reliability organization* (Doctoral dissertation, North Dakota State University).

- Victoria, L. (2002) Community based approaches to disaster mitigation. *The Asian Disaster Preparedness Center (ADPC)*.

- Vinãls, J., Pazarbasioglu, C., Surti, J., Narain, A., Erbenova, M., & Chow, J. T. S. (2013). *Will the Volcker, Vickers, and Liikanen structural measures help?* Washington: International Monetary Fund.

- Viswanathan, B. (2013, February). *What are the main reasons India survived the global economic recession of 2008*. Retrieved from http://www.project-syndicate.org/commentary/how-india-survived-the-financial-crisis

- Wallis, D. (2012, November). *Komen Foundation struggles to regain wide support*. Retrieved December 14, 2015, from http://www.nytimes.com/2012/11/09/giving/komen-foundation-works-to-regain-support-after-planned-parenthood-controversy.html?_r=0

- Walsh, J. (1995). Managerial and organizational cognition: Notes from a trip down memory lane. *Organization Science, 6*(3), 280–321.

- Wang, W., & Belardo, S. (2005). Strategic integration: A knowledge management approach to crisis management. *Proceedings of the 38th Hawaii International Conference on System Sciences* (pp. 252–260). Big Island, Hawaii: IEEE Computer Society.

- Washington, A. (2015). The need for cultural intelligence: An analysis of Asiana Airlines' response to the crash landing of Flight 214. *Case Study Competition, 2*(5), 3–36.

- Waters, R. (2014). *Public relations in the nonprofit sector: Theory and practice.* New York, NY: Routledge.

- Watt, S. (2012). A postfeminist apologia: Susan G. Komen for the Cure's evolving response to the Planned Parenthood controversy. *Journal of Contemporary Rhetoric, 2(3),* 65–79.

- Weatherly, L. (2005). HR outsourcing: Reaping strategic value for your organization. *SHRM Research Quarterly, 3,* 29.

- Weaver, C. (2015, July). *Using brave ideas to turn crisis into an opportunity.* Retrieved from APCO Worldwide: http://www.apcoworldwide.com/blog/detail/apcoforum/2015/07/10/using-brave-ideas-to-turn-a-crisis-into-an-opportunity

- Webb, T. (2010). BP's clumsy response to oil spill threatens to make a bad situation worse. Retrieved from http://www.theguardian.com/business/2010/jun/01/bp-response-oil-spill-tony-hayward

- Webb, T. (2011). *Japan's economy heads into freefall after earthquake and tsunami.* Retrieved from http://www.theguardian.com/world/2011/mar/13/japan-economy-recession-earthquake-tsunami

- Werema, G., Banafe, A., Luter, S., Beltran, J., Franscioni, Hagedorn, M., Pak, J., & Press, E. (2013). JC Penney, INC: The impact of rebranding on internal and external communication. *Center for Management Communication.*

- White, K. (1999). *Organizational culture.* Hove, East Sussex, UK: Psychology Press.

- Wiarda, H. J., & Skelley, E. M. (2006). *The crisis of American foreign policy: The effects of a divided America*. New York: Rowman & Littlefield.

- Wigley, S., & Zhang, W. (2011), A study of PR practitioners' use of social media in crisis planning. *Public Relations Journal, 5*(3), 1–16.

- Willett, W. (2013). *Nutritional epidemiology*. Oxford: Oxford University Press.

- Wilson, J. (2014). *Why stamping out corruption in FIFA will not be easy. The conversation*. Retrieved December 24, 2015, from http://theconversation.com/why-stamping-out-corruption-in-fifa-wont-be-easy-34264

- Witzel, M. (2013, April). Maple Leaf Food's response to a crisis. *Financial Times*. Retrieved from http://www.ft.com/intl/cms/s/0/8c8d3668-adb5-11e2-82b8-00144feabdc0.html#axzz3u8RDU1Xh

- Wong, C. (2013). *Oslo bombing: Victims story*. New York: Associated Press.

- Wooten, L. P., & James, E. H. (2004). When firms fail to learn: The perpetuation of discrimination in the workplace. *Journal of Management Inquiry, 13*(1), 23–33.

- Yukl, G. A. (2002). Leadership in organizations. *National College for School Leadership*.

- Zaremba, A. J. (2014). *Crisis Communication: Theory and Practice*. Hoboken: Taylor and Francis.

- Zee Media Corporation. (2015, June). *Sierra Leone*

References

launches new operation to eradicate Ebola. Retrieved from http://zeenews.india.com/news/health/health-news/sierra-leone-launches-new-operation-to-eradicate-ebola_1615242.html

- Zhiwu, Chen. (2013). Capital freedom in China as viewed from the evolution of the stock market. *CATO Journal, 33*(3), 587–601.

- Zuzak, R. (2001). Corporate culture as a source of crisis in companies. *Agricultural Economics-UZPI (Czech Republic)*.

www.ingramcontent.com/pod-product-compliance
Lightning Source LLC
LaVergne TN
LVHW091033150525
811259LV00008B/37